Confronting Cancer

How to Care for Today and Tomorrow

Confronting Cancer

How to Care for Today and Tomorrow

Michael M. Sherry, M. D.

Foreword by
Geoffrey Kurland, M. D.

 **INSIGHT BOOKS**

Plenum Press • New York and London

Library of Congress Cataloging in Publication Data

Sherry, Michael M.
  Confronting cancer: how to care for today and tomorrow / Michael M. Sherry;
foreword by Geoffrey Kurland.
     p.   cm.
  Includes bibliographical references and index.
  ISBN 0-306-44643-X (hardbound). —ISBN 0-306-44644-8 (pbk.)
  1. Cancer—Popular works. I. Title.
  [DNLM: 1. Neoplasms. QZ 200 S553c 1994]
RC263.S457 1994
616.99′4—dc20
DNLM/DLC   94-2301
for Library of Congress   CIP

The treatments outlined in this volume are intended to serve only as examples. You
should consult your personal physician before beginning any
medical treatment regimen.

ISBN 0-306-44643-X (Hardbound)
ISBN 0-306-44644-8 (Paperback)

© 1994 Michael M. Sherry
Insight Books is a Division of Plenum Publishing Corporation
233 Spring Street, New York, N.Y. 10013-1578

An Insight Book

To the living memory of
Thomas F. Sherry, Sr.
Marjorie D. McKeating
and
Philip J. McKeating, M. D.

Foreword

In 1926 Dr. Charles H. Mayo of the Mayo Clinic wrote, "While there are several chronic diseases more destructive to life than cancer, none is more feared." Perhaps today, nearly 70 years later, acquired immunodeficiency syndrome (AIDS) has replaced cancer as the illness most feared by our population; and the history of our century is filled with advances in the diagnosis, treatment, and cure of cancer. Yet cancer, in all its forms, claims more lives than AIDS and remains a foe whose name still conjures up images that color all our lives.

The first confrontation with the diagnosis of cancer leaves the patient paralyzed with the fear of the unknown and an often terrifying feeling of despair and impending loss, as if the very word cancer—pervasive, mysterious to the point of seeming occult—renders him unable to appreciate the advances of modern medicine in the treatment of the disease. The patient and family see only pain and death, which the older traditions of medicine and the lay literature tell us will inexorably follow the diagnosis.

When I was first told of my diagnosis of leukemia, in the same Mayo Clinic in which Dr. Charles Mayo had worked, I felt nothing and then everything. I sat disbelieving, frozen with the name of this disease, my internal enemy seeking to rip off my mortal coil, yanking it out by its roots, leaving me to die. I felt I had no weapons with which to fight back against my attacker. I felt I had no knowledge of leukemia, no understanding of the therapy I might receive, its side effects, its chances of success. Yet I am a physician (even if I am a pediatrician); as an intern and resident, I had treated numerous children with leukemia and other forms of cancer. But as I sat there in my own physician's office, I felt totally unarmed in what was to be the fight of (and for) my life.

How, then, must it be for the nonphysician, hurled into that terrible reality without so much as a clue of the truth about cancer, its meaning, its treatment, its potential cure? Surely there should be something to help these people face their illness, something written that will give them the facts they need to know without overwhelming them with minutiae that will unnecessarily clutter their minds and obscure their thinking. All too often, the "facts" about cancer are held locked in medical and scientific journals, difficult sometimes even for physicians to decipher. And, like many sciences, medicine is evolving: new knowledge about cancer and new medications for its treatment are constantly being discovered.

In the midst of this ever-changing tableau, the patient needs to know certain things: What is cancer? How will my physician treat it? What are the side effects of the treatment? What are my alternatives? How can I continue to live my life? How do I prepare for the future? Most physicians probably know the answers to these questions, but the answers are rarely conveyed. Physicians' schedules are too hectic. The "science" of medicine all too often replaces the "art" of medicine. And, of great importance, most patients are afraid to ask the questions and are unable to hear those answers while they sit in the doctor's office. As a result, the necessary questions go unasked and, if asked, they are not always answered in ways that will truly help the patient cope with cancer.

In this book, Dr. Sherry seeks to answer those questions most patients ask about cancer. Here, the patient can seek the truth and learn it in his or her own time, at his or her own pace. Much of what is in this book may seem hard to read, not because it is technical but because it is true; for the truth, especially when we are dealing with life-threatening diseases such as cancer, may not offer us exactly what we want to hear. Telling patients the truth in medicine is often the hardest thing to do, yet it is the most important for the patient and the physician. This book is a giant step toward filling a crying need felt by all patients and families touched by cancer: the need for the truth about the disease, its many forms, and their treatment and outcome. Anyone facing cancer can now be armed to deal with that foe, and such patients can work with the entire medical team to more effectively fight the illness.

GEOFFREY KURLAND, M.D.
Associate Professor of Pediatrics
University of Pittsburgh, and
Division of Pulmonology
Department of Pediatrics
Children's Hospital of Pittsburgh
Pittsburgh, Pennsylvania

Preface

I resolved to write this book after Hodgkin's disease was diagnosed in my brother-in-law, Jack, in 1989. In attempting to answer questions and allay the fears of the extended family—large even by Irish standards—I found that no single-volume reference explained Jack's disease and treatment options adequately. My family's confusion mirrored that of my patients, who were consistently overwhelmed by the complexities of cancer. Why couldn't needed cancer information be presented in clear, concise terms for persons struggling to cope with this disease? I believed that it could. This book represents my sincere attempt to provide such a reference—a comprehensive, medically accurate, and easily understood handbook for laypersons attempting to deal head-on with the disease.

I have written *Confronting Cancer* from the heart, patterning the book on my day-to-day experience in treating patients. I approach the reader as one of these patients. As an oncologist, my first meeting with a patient usually involves explaining the details of the diagnosed cancer and differentiating it from other types of cancer. To parallel this initial meeting, Part I of *Confronting Cancer* describes the 11 most common cancers, with individual chapters defining a cancer's unique behavior and the rationale for its treatment.

Once the type of cancer is defined and understood, the patient can begin to consider a viable treatment plan. Consequently, Part

II of this book discusses both orthodox and unorthodox cancer therapies available today.

In the belief that more similarities than differences exist in the "cancer experience," I designed Part III to target those problems and situations frequently encountered by the cancer patient. Topics such as Getting a Second Opinion, Cancer and the Elderly, and Getting Your Affairs in Order receive scant attention in the lay press and yet prove to be of monumental concern to many cancer patients, families, and caregivers.

I wrote the chapter on pain control with Edward F. Seserko, Sr., in mind. My best man's father, Mr. Seserko died painfully of cancer in 1976, before I entered medical school. I wish that the advances in pain medication, as well as patient information concerning its use, had been available to him then; his suffering might have been alleviated altogether.

The 54 case studies interspersed throughout the text are derived from actual patients whom I have encountered in my practice. The Index of Case Studies lists the topics discussed in each case study. For example, the case study of D.K. in Chapter 6 refers to skin cancer, biological therapy, and investigational therapy.

Confronting Cancer is organized to accommodate the cancer patient during all stages of the disease, providing pertinent information in each of the sections as the condition of the patient changes. However, this book is not intended to substitute for competent medical care. Any medical questions raised in the mind of the patient by this text should be thoroughly discussed with the attending physician.

I firmly believe that the informed, prepared patient is best able to cope with the often formidable problems induced by cancer. In the memory of Mr. Seserko and my many patients who have fought the good fight, I offer this book as an aid to those who are now confronting and combating cancer. May victory be theirs!

MICHAEL M. SHERRY
Sewickley, Pennsylvania

Acknowledgments

I extend heartfelt thanks to the many persons who helped me on this project. My wife, Patty, and my kids—Kate, Mike, Andrew, and Nora—allowed "the book" to cut into precious family time for nearly 4 years. Ann Hathaway edited the text with a keen eye for keeping things simple so that the layperson could easily understand oftentimes confusing medical points. Robert Fusco, M.D., set up my computer and got me off to a running start. My literary agent, Gerry B. Wallertstein, believed in this book even when I had my doubts.

This book could not have been completed without the assistance of collaborating authors who contributed their expertise. The perspective of John Schlicth, Pharm.D., as a pharmacist was invaluable to the chapter on Cancer Quackery. My brother, Richard M. Sherry, M.D., drew on his experience at the National Cancer Institute for Investigational Therapy and Biological Therapy. John McKeating, M.D., an oncological surgeon, helped me to capture the surgeon's viewpoint in Surgical Therapy. Attorney Edward Kabala's understanding of estate planning and the law laid the foundation for Getting Your Affairs in Order. Sandra Labuda, A.C.S.W., L.S.W., used her social work background to enhance Survivorship. The unique experience of Marmee Maylone, R.N., M.S.N., O.C.N., as both a Hodgkin's survivor and a nurse manager of an oncology unit added immeasurably to Survivorship and Day-to-Day Problems. My partner, Alfred P. Doyle, M.D., deserves special thanks for his contribution to Chemotherapy and Hormonal Therapy, as well as for providing ongoing encouragement.

The information contained in this book is, to the best of my knowledge, accurate. It is primarily based on my experiences and those of the contributing authors. Where controversy exists, we have tried to take a "middle-of-the-road" approach.

Throughout this book, I have kept footnotes to a minimum in an attempt to make the book easy to read. My definitive reference for medical information was the National Cancer Institute's Physician Data Query FAX. This medical data base is provided and updated monthly by the National Cancer Institute. It is a public domain service that is available to both patients and physicians. It provided me with the exact statistics found throughout the book on topics like survival and incidence. The National Cancer Institute should be commended for developing such an outstanding resource. The phone number of the Cancer Information Service of the National Cancer Institute is 1-800-422-6237.

Barbara Osella did a great job as proofreader. Eileen McKeating-Esterle's anatomic illustrations are both clear and accurate. Joseph Bikowski, M.D., George Cheponis, M.D., Robert Dobler, M.D., Jacqueline Lermire, John Moraca, M.D., John Moyer, M.D., Carol Sicatella, D.O., and Johan Zabkar, M.D., all contributed editorial suggestions.

Finally, I thank the cancer patients of the Ohio River Valley in western Pennsylvania who inspired this book. Caring for them has been an honor and a joy.

Contents

II. Cancer Treatments

13. *Radiation Therapy*

14. *Chemotherapy and Hormonal Therapy*

15. *Bone Marrow Transplantation*

III. Common Problems Encountered
   by the Cancer Patient

20. Getting a Second Opinion

21. *Day-to-Day Symptoms*

22. *Cancer and the Elderly*

23. *Control of Cancer Pain*

24. *Getting One's Affairs in Order*

I

The Kinds of Cancer

1

Breast Cancer

Breast cancer receives more coverage in the popular press than any other single cancer. Women's and family magazines regularly feature informative articles on prevention, early detection, and surgery. During the last decade, breast cancer has quite rightfully become a "woman's issue."

Today, when a woman's breast cancer is diagnosed, her physician is likely to emphasize three important points. First, the treatment of breast cancer has changed dramatically over the last 20 years. Treatment received by a friend or relative 20 years ago is probably inappropriate today. Second, the treatment of any given breast cancer is completely individualized. Third, all of her first-degree relatives (i.e., mother, sister) need to be screened for breast cancer, because early detection remains the best treatment for this disease.

Incidence and Risk Factors

The American Cancer Society estimates that nearly 182,000 women in the United States are diagnosed with breast cancer each year. Tragically, as many as 40% of these women will eventually die of the disease. Among women 40–50 years of age, breast cancer is the leading cause of death. Only lung cancer surpasses breast cancer as the primary cause of cancer death in the general female population. Clearly, breast cancer is a public health problem of epidemic proportions.

Several factors are associated with an increased risk of developing breast cancer. A key risk factor is family history. Women whose first-degree relatives have had breast cancer are twice as likely to develop it themselves. The risk becomes greater still if the relative developed breast cancer before the age of 50. Conversely, women whose first-degree relatives are breast cancer free run a slightly reduced risk of developing it.

Two characteristics are especially critical in assessing the risk of breast cancer: sex and age. Breast cancer is undeniably a female disease, in that 99% of all cases develop in women. Age also disposes a woman to risk, because 66% of all breast cancers are discovered in women who have experienced menopause. The incidence of breast cancer begins to rise in women older than 40 years and steadily increases until they reach their early 80s. (See Chapter 22, Cancer and the Elderly.)

Although the major risk factors for breast cancer are family history, sex, and age, other factors have been associated with increased risk. Both a high-fat diet and obesity appear to increase risk. Although women in North America have a higher incidence of breast cancer than do Asian or African women, most experts now attribute this difference to diet rather than race.

A number of poorly understood hormonal factors also escalate the risk of breast cancer. The incidence of breast cancer is higher in women who have never given birth and among those who give birth for the first time after the age of 30. Moreover, menstrual history is significant. Early menopause, whether occurring naturally or surgically, serves to decrease risk. Although the relation of oral contraceptives to breast cancer has been extensively studied, conclusions are contradictory. Similarly, the link between breast cancer and estrogen therapy remains unproven. Nonetheless, the Food and Drug Administration requires a warning about the possible risk of breast cancer for women using either oral contraceptives or estrogen preparations.

Unfortunately, aside from avoiding dietary fats and controlling weight, modifications in life-style do not *significantly* lessen the risk of breast cancer. How is it possible, then, for a woman to combat the threat of breast cancer? A woman's primary defense lies in the early detection and treatment of the disease.

Early Detection: Screening

As with so many public health problems, *education* is perhaps the most effective means of prevention. Women need to be aware of screening guidelines for the early detection of breast cancer, and they need to follow the guidelines as part of their health-maintenance routine.

The American Cancer Society recommends the following steps for the early detection of breast cancer:

1. A woman should have an initial breast examination by a physician at the age of 20 and another every 3 years until the age of 40. Thereafter, she should have an examination yearly.
2. Every adult woman should perform a breast self-examination each month.
3. A woman should have a baseline mammogram between the ages of 35 and 40. Between the ages of 40 and 50, she should have a mammogram every 2 years. After the age of 50, she should have a mammogram annually.

These steps are complementary, in that a mammogram can detect abnormalities missed by a physical examination, and a physical examination can detect abnormalities missed by a mammogram.

Breast self-examination (BSE) should be done each month so that a woman becomes familiar with the normal appearance and texture of her breasts. The best time for a menstruating woman to perform BSE is 2 or 3 days after her period; the best time for a postmenopausal woman to perform this examination is the same day of each month.

One suggested way to perform BSE is to follow these steps.

Step 1. Stand before a mirror. Watching the breasts closely, clasp hands behind the head and then press hands firmly on the hips. Visually inspect both breasts for any change such as puckering of the skin, nipple discharge, or asymmetry of the breasts.

Step 2. Raise the left arm. With the right hand, examine the left breast by moving clockwise from the outer area, including the underarm, toward the nipple. Now gently squeeze the nipple and look for a discharge. In like manner, examine the right breast. Some women prefer to perform this step in the shower.

Step 3. Step 2 should now be repeated while lying down. The breast flattens in this position and is easier to examine.

Obviously, BSE is simple to perform and requires only minutes each month. Moreover, BSE costs nothing! Unfortunately, it is estimated that only 20% of American women regularly perform BSE.

Another screening procedure for breast cancer is mammography, the x-raying of the breast. Mammography is the only routine test that can discover breast cancer in its earliest stages. Identifying a breast cancer too small as yet to be found by physical examination can greatly increase a woman's chance of survival. Should a questionable area appear on the mammogram, a biopsy may be necessary.

The value of mammography screening has been clearly established in several studies, including the Breast Cancer Detection Demonstration Project. When breast cancer mortality was compared in women who had received screening mammograms with that of those who had not, the mammogram group's mortality was 25–50% lower than that of the other group. Furthermore, the survival benefit of mammograms has been shown to be greatest in women older than 50 years.

Understandably, some women fear that the radiation exposure of the mammogram may, itself, cause breast cancer. This concern is shared by physicians. However, modern mammographic equipment exposes the breast to far less radiation than that in the past. Today, the risk of mammography-induced breast cancer is extremely remote.

Symptoms of Breast Cancer

A woman's breasts change throughout her life. These changes are natural and can be due to pregnancy, the menstrual cycle, or menopause. Through the regular practice of BSE, a woman can determine the normal texture of her breasts and readily notice any changes associated with breast cancer.

Breast cancer can cause a number of symptoms. The warning signs publicized by the National Institutes of Health are

1. Discharge from the nipple;
2. A lump in the breast or armpit;
3. A change in the skin color or texture of the breast (dimpling or puckering); or
4. A change in the size or shape of the breast.

Diagnosis of Breast Cancer

Whenever a suspicious lump in the breast is discovered, it should be investigated. If the lump appears to be a fluid-filled cyst, the first step is a needle aspiration. In this procedure, the physician inserts a thin needle into the lump and attempts to drain the fluid. If the lump is indeed fluid filled, aspiration may be all that is necessary.

However, when the suspicious lump is solid or the aspirated fluid contains cancer cells, all or part of the lump must be removed for definitive diagnosis. This procedure is called a biopsy. Examining questionable tissue under a microscope is the only sure way to determine whether the tissue is cancerous. Frequently, screening mammograms detect abnormalities that cannot be felt. When no lump exists, the surgeon excises the entire abnormal area that is isolated on the mammogram.

Factors Influencing Prognosis

Well into the 1960s, all breast cancers were considered similar. Physicians believed that the more extensive the surgery, the higher the chance of cure. Breast cancers also were thought to spread predictably from the breast to underarm and then on to distant sites. If a patient relapsed, surgery was judged to have been too little, too late.

Today, the type and extent of surgery no longer determine the patient's chance of cure. Physicians now understand that all breast cancers are unique and, at the time of diagnosis, breast cancer may be a generalized disease whose tumor cells are blood borne. For these reasons, physicians carefully consider specific characteristics of the cancer, called *prognostic factors,* to assess and predict a patient's chance of cure. Prognostic factors identify patients who have a high risk of recurrence. These patients then can be given preventive treatment.

Three factors are widely used in determining the prognosis and treatment plan of a breast cancer patient. They are (1) the stage of the cancer, (2) the *estrogen receptor* measurement of the cancer, and (3) the woman's age.

Stage of the Cancer

Physicians use a set of guidelines known as a *staging system* to classify cancers and gauge prognosis. To determine the stage of a breast cancer, both tumor size and the status of the lymph nodes in the underarm must be known.

Lymph nodes are pea-like structures found throughout the body. Their job is to fight infection. During breast cancer surgery, lymph nodes of the underarm are removed for staging purposes.

After laboratory examination, they are termed *positive* if cancerous and *negative* if they are cancer free.

In general, breast cancer survival rates correlate closely with the extent of disease. *The single most important factor determining the prognosis of a breast cancer patient is the status of the lymph nodes (positive or negative). A woman with negative nodes usually has a higher chance of cure than a woman with positive nodes.*

The size of the cancer is also a significant factor; large cancers generally indicate a poorer prognosis than do small cancers. Breast cancers are classified into the following four stages:

- Stage I. The cancer is no larger than 2 centimeters (cm), and lymph nodes are negative.
- Stage II. The cancer is 2 to 5 cm, or lymph nodes are positive.
- Stage III. The cancer is larger than 5 cm, or lymph nodes are both positive and markedly enlarged, or the cancer has spread to the lymph nodes above the collarbone.
- Stage IV. The cancer has spread to a site outside the breast area (e.g., bone, lung, or liver.)

Stages I and II are considered early stages because of their favorable prognosis. At the time of diagnosis, 80% of breast cancer patients are in these early stages. Expectedly, the larger the cancer and the higher the stage, the less favorable the prognosis. Table 1-1 lists the approximate survival rates after 5 years by stage. Today, with widespread breast cancer screening, nearly twice as many women are diagnosed in stage I than were diagnosed in the 1970s.

The Estrogen Receptor

For more than a century, doctors have known that breast cancer can be sustained by female hormones. In 1885, a young woman with a large breast cancer developed severe vaginal bleeding that required a hysterectomy. During the course of the surgery, her ovaries were removed. Surprisingly, the breast cancer disappeared!

Table 1-1
Stage of Breast Cancer and Survival

Stage at diagnosis	5-Year survival (%)	Newly diagnosed patients during 2 decades (%)	
		1970s	1990s
Stage I	85	20	42
Stage II	66	53	38
Stage III	41	25	15
Stage IV	10	2	5
All stages	63	100	100

Survival rates are approximate. The percentage of newly diagnosed patients in the 1970s is based on information found in Rubin P (ed). *Clinical Oncology*, 6th ed. American Cancer Society, 1987. The percentage of newly diagnosed patients in the 1990s represents statistics provided by Sewickley Valley Hospital, Sewickley, PA. The increase in early-stage breast cancer is due to the widespread use of breast cancer screening.

Her doctors concluded that breast cancer can be dependent on female hormones.

Following that celebrated observation, hormones were used to treat breast cancers. Physicians soon learned, however, that not all breast cancers respond to hormone therapy. Only 33% of menstruating women responded to hormone therapy compared with 66% of women past the age of menopause. A woman's menstrual status presumably affected her breast cancer, but the process remained poorly understood for years.

In the 1960s, certain tissues were found to possess *receptors* for estrogen, the female hormone produced by the ovaries. Estrogen receptors are structures in tissue that adhere to estrogen. This attachment is analogous to the fit of a lock and key. An estrogen receptor is the lock that accepts only the key of estrogen. By locking with estrogen receptors, estrogen controls sexual maturation.

Estrogen receptors are present in all normal breast tissue and in 50% of breast cancers. In the laboratory, the receptors present in breast cancer tissue can be counted, with their number varying from 0 to more than 400. Breast cancers are then classified according to their number of estrogen receptors. Cancers with fewer than 10 are considered estrogen receptor negative (ER negative), and cancers with more than 10 are termed estrogen receptor positive (ER positive.)

Patients with ER-positive cancers are likely to respond to hormone therapy. The greater the receptor value, the better the chance of response. Only 33% of menstruating women, in fact, have ER-positive breast cancers, which explains the time-honored statistic that 33% of menstruating women respond to hormone therapy.

The ER status of a breast tumor significantly affects prognosis as well as therapy. Patients with ER-positive breast cancers experience a higher rate of survival than do ER-negative patients. This prognostic significance is completely independent of stage. For example, stage I ER-positive patients have a better prognosis than do stage I ER-negative patients.

Menstrual Status (Age of Patient)

It has long been known that breast cancer is markedly aggressive in younger women. This phenomenon is a function of the female menstrual cycle. Doctors classify patients according to the presence or absence of the menstrual cycle. Women are considered *premenopausal* when they menstruate or, if they have undergone a hysterectomy, are aged 50 years or younger. Women are *postmenopausal* if they no longer menstruate or are older than 50 years.

Menstrual status is not considered an independent prognostic factor; rather, it is linked with ER status. For example, premenopausal women have a higher percentage of ER-negative cancers than do postmenopausal women, with the primary prognostic factor being unfavorable ER status, not menstrual status.

In some instances, however, menstrual status can become an important prognostic factor. When the sample of cancerous tissue is too small to analyze, ER information is unobtainable. In such a case, the physician must rely solely on menstrual status for prognosis. Menstrual status can also determine recommendations for treatment. For example, all premenopausal women with positive lymph nodes benefit from chemotherapy after surgery. (See Adjuvant Therapy in this chapter.)

In summary, the three characteristics of breast cancer that influence prognosis are stage, ER status, and menstrual status. Because a patient can have any combination of these factors, prognosis is quite individualized. Viewed in this way, breast cancer is never a single disease but rather a disease of subsets. To draw an analogy, breast cancers are like snowflakes; no two are exactly alike.

The analysis of chromosomes, the genetic material of breast cancer, is a promising and active area of current research. The actual growth rate of a breast cancer can be measured by the *S-phase fraction,* a test that measures the number of chromosomes actively dividing. As expected, a rising percentage of S-phase cancer cells causes the breast cancer to be increasingly aggressive. The prognostic importance of oncogenes in breast cancer is an intense area of breast cancer research. Oncogenes are chromosomes that control the growth and development of breast cancer. An oncogene known as *Her Neu* is currently being tested as a prognostic feature in breast cancer. By the end of the 1990s, both S-phase fraction and oncogenes are expected to be commonly used, thus enabling doctors to further characterize prognosis.

Treatment Options

Twenty years ago, a woman with breast cancer had little choice but to undergo the standard therapy of the time, radical mastectomy. Today, a woman has choices in both surgical procedures and follow-up therapy. As treatment options multiply, these decisions become increasingly difficult to make. Two essential questions must be answered after the diagnosis of breast cancer has been made: First, based on prognostic factors and her general health, what treatment options are realistically available to the patient? Second, what treatment does the patient choose?

It may be helpful to divide the topic of treatment into two categories: (1) local therapy—any surgical treatment of the breast, and (2) *adjuvant* or systemic therapy—the administration of drugs to destroy cancer cells outside the breast area. Adjuvant therapy is a form of preventive therapy administered after surgery.

Local Therapy

To fully appreciate the current state of breast cancer surgery, it is perhaps wise to examine the past. In the 1960s, radical mastectomy was the standard surgical treatment for breast cancer. This extensive surgery entailed the removal of the breast, chest muscles, and underarm lymph nodes. The assumption was that the more extensive the surgery, the higher the chance of cure.

Medical researchers later challenged this assumption. Most notably, Dr. Bernard Fisher of the National Surgical Adjuvant Breast Project (NSABP) compared the efficacy of radical mastectomy with a less extensive surgery, *total mastectomy*. Total mastectomy entails the removal of the breast and underarm lymph nodes, leaving intact the chest muscles. In 1971, 1600 women were randomly assigned one of three treatments: radical mastectomy, total mastectomy, or total mastectomy plus radiation therapy. When patient-survival rates were later compared, they proved to be the same for all three groups! As a direct result of this research, the number of radical mastectomies declined nationwide.

Dr. Fisher then posed the next logical question: If less surgery does not alter survival, is it necessary to remove the breast at all? The NSABP proceeded to study the effects of a less extensive surgery known as *lumpectomy*. Lumpectomy involves the removal of the tumor, lymph nodes (for staging purposes), and a margin of normal tissue. In this study, more than 1800 women with breast cancers measuring fewer than 4 cm were randomly assigned one of three treatments: total mastectomy, lumpectomy, and lumpectomy plus radiation therapy. Eight years after surgery, mastectomy showed no survival advantage over lumpectomy. However, patients who received lumpectomy without radiation often developed a recurrent breast cancer in the treated breast.

Doctors have interpreted the results of this research in the following way: *Lumpectomy without radiation does not constitute enough treatment. Lumpectomy plus radiation is as effective as total mastectomy. Radiation therapy is a necessary part of conservative surgical therapy.*

Unfortunately, not all patients are candidates for conservative therapy. Prognostic factors determine and can sometimes limit treatment options. Stage III breast cancers are generally best treated by mastectomy, as are breast cancers attached to the chest wall. *The advantage of conservative therapy is purely cosmetic.* When the breast is small or the cancer is centrally located, the cosmetic prospect may indeed be poor, and the patient is encouraged to undergo mastectomy. It should be noted that all breast cancer patients need to have their underarm lymph nodes removed for staging purposes.

Surprising as it may seem, it is not at all unusual for surgeons to hold lumpectomies in low esteem. Many physicians are simply slow to change established practices. In a recent national survey of surgeons, fully 31% cited modified mastectomy as the treatment of choice for breast cancer patients. Moreover, geographic variations in American surgical practices are apparent. For example, nearly 50% of women with operable breast cancer receive lumpectomies in the Greater Boston area, but this figure dwindles to less than 20% in some areas of the Midwest and South.

Approximately 75% of breast cancer patients qualify as candidates for conservative therapy. For these patients, deciding between mastectomy and conservative therapy is strictly a matter of personal choice. Admittedly, this choice can be a difficult one and should be the result of thoughtful rather than panicked decision making. The proposed breast surgery may raise fundamental feelings about sexuality and femininity. It is best to openly discuss such feelings with close friends and family members. Some women feel a need to discuss these choices with more than one doctor. If the patient has any doubts, she should seek a second opinion. (See Chapter 20, Getting a Second Opinion.) It is crucial that the patient feels comfortable with her choice of treatment.

Adjuvant Therapy (Systemic or Preventive Therapy)

After surgical treatment, the vast majority of patients have no detectable evidence of breast cancer. Unfortunately, 40% of breast cancer patients experience recurrences; that is, the treated cancer becomes active again. Regardless of where this cancer recurs in the body, the original breast cancer is its source. Should cancer appear in the skin following breast cancer treatment, this "new" cancer is not skin cancer but breast cancer that has spread to the skin. It is believed that, at diagnosis, a few undetectably small cancer cells already exist outside the breast, becoming detectable only after an average span of 3 years.

The aim of adjuvant therapy is to destroy stray cancer cells remaining in the body after surgery. Adjuvant drugs that act throughout the body to kill malignant cells are the same drugs used in the treatment of widespread breast cancer. However, the purpose of this adjuvant therapy is entirely preventive.

There are two categories of adjuvant therapy, hormonal therapy and chemotherapy. Both categories of drugs will be more thoroughly discussed in Part II. Tamoxifen (*Nolvadex*) is an estrogen-blocking hormone that inhibits the growth of breast cancer cells. Adjuvant tamoxifen is given in pill form twice a day for at least 2 to 5 years. Chemotherapy refers to powerful anticancer drugs typically given by injection. As adjuvant treatment, chemotherapy is usually given once a month for 6 consecutive months. *These drugs are proven to increase disease-free survival in most types of breast cancer.*

The type of adjuvant therapy recommended to a woman depends on her individual breast cancer. First, the prognostic factors of the breast cancer are used to estimate risk of recurrence, and then a treatment plan is formulated. Generally, patients at high risk require more intense adjuvant therapy.

After completion of adjuvant therapy, the patient's follow-up care includes a physical examination and blood test every 3 months, and a chest x ray and mammogram yearly. Because liver and bone scans are not considered to be useful in symptom-free patients, these tests are not performed routinely. If the patient remains well for 3 years, her routine visits are scheduled at 6-month intervals.

Guidelines for Adjuvant Therapy of Breast Cancer

With many adjuvant therapies available, it is easy for a woman to become confused about her treatment options. As stressed throughout this chapter, no single treatment is applicable to all women and, when doubt exists, a second opinion is advisable.

Physicians face a similar confusion because both cancer research and treatment are constantly changing. Often, the "experts" disagree! In 1985 and 1990, the National Institutes of Health sponsored two Consensus Conferences with the purpose of establishing recommendations for adjuvant therapy. Most physicians employ these guidelines, which are applicable to many, but not all, breast cancers. The recommendations are grouped according to stage, menstrual status, and ER status.

- Stage I. As late as the mid-1980s, stage I breast cancer was not treated with adjuvant therapy. In recent studies, however, tamoxifen improved disease-free survival in postmenopausal ER-positive patients, and chemotherapy improved disease-free survival in ER-negative patients. Until further research is completed, doctors can only carefully consider adjuvant therapy for every stage I patient and individualize recommendations.
- Stage II. The patient's menstrual status determines the recommended therapy for stage 2 breast cancer. *Adjuvant chemotherapy is recommended for all premenopausal women, regardless of ER status.* Postmenopausal women who are ER positive should receive adjuvant tamoxifen.

Although adjuvant tamoxifen is often prescribed for ER-positive premenopausal patients, its use must be better defined. Some authorities now believe that tamoxifen, when given simultaneously with chemotherapy, reduces the benefit of chemotherapy.

Adjuvant therapy for ER-negative postmenopausal patients is also debatable. The Consensus Conference recommended that chemotherapy be considered for this group of patients, although many experts advocate such treatment for women younger than 65 years. Because of this uncertainty, each patient should be individually considered.

- Stage III. Patients with locally advanced breast cancer usually receive adjuvant chemotherapy as well as radiation. If the cancer is ER positive, most doctors add adjuvant tamoxifen. Menstrual status does not influence recommendations.
- Stage IV. The cancer, by definition, has spread to an area outside the breast. Because therapy is clearly not preventive, these patients are not candidates for adjuvant therapy.

Carcinoma in Situ: The Earliest Breast Cancer

All breast cancers originate in the milk-forming ducts of the breast. At inception, the cancer remains wholly inside the duct and is known as *carcinoma in situ*. Unfortunately, at the time of detection, most breast cancers have already become invasive, meaning that malignant cells have spilled outside the duct.

In the past, carcinoma in situ was uncommon, accounting for less than 3% of breast cancers. However, the use of screening mammography has resulted in a striking rise in awareness of the incidence of this cancer. Carcinoma in situ now accounts for 15% of all cancers detected by screening mammograms.

Traditionally, the treatment for carcinoma in situ was the standard treatment for all breast cancers, mastectomy. The cure rate with this method is near 100%. However, now that breast-conserving surgery has become an accepted treatment for invasive

Table 1-2
Adjuvant Therapy of Breast Cancer by Stage

Stage	Adjuvant recommendation
Carcinoma in situ	No adjuvant therapy is recommended.
Stage I	The best adjuvant therapy is undecided. Recently, tamoxifen and chemotherapy have both been shown to increase disease-free survival.
Stage II	
Premenopausal ER (+)	Chemotherapy is given to all premenopausal stage II women.
Premenopausal ER (−)	Tamoxifen is sometimes given to ER (+) patients.
Postmenopausal ER (+)	Tamoxifen is usually given.
Postmenopausal ER (−)	Chemotherapy is a consideration.
Stage III	Chemotherapy and radiation are usually given. Tamoxifen is given to ER (+) patients. Menstrual status does not influence therapy.

SOURCE: Adapted from National Institutes of Health Consensus Conference: Breast Cancer, 1990.

breast cancer, it seems only reasonable that carcinoma in situ can be similarly treated. A recent study reports a high cure rate with conservative surgery. A woman with carcinoma in situ can be assured that her chance of survival is excellent, whether she chooses mastectomy or conservative treatment. In fact, her prognosis is so favorable that she is not even a candidate for adjuvant therapy.

Table 1-2 is a summary of adjuvant therapy recommendations for breast cancer.

Case Studies

Perhaps case studies can best give the sense of how each woman requires an individualized treatment plan. Following are two examples of women with stage I breast cancers.

S.S. is a 38-year-old woman who noted a lump in her left breast. After her gynecologist ordered a mammogram that confirmed the lump's suspicious nature, she was referred to a surgeon for an excisional biopsy. The biopsy revealed that the lump was malignant. Although S.S. was a candidate for lumpectomy, she decided to have a modified mastectomy, stating that she would "feel better with the mastectomy."

Her estrogen receptors were negative, and her lymph nodes were cancer free. S.S. was classified as having a stage I, premenopausal, ER-negative breast cancer. When adjuvant therapy became a consideration, the oncologist informed her that current medical research supported adjuvant chemotherapy for her type of breast cancer. She also was advised of the controversy surrounding this recommendation. S.S. stated, "I want to do all that I can to keep it from coming back." After a lengthy discussion, she agreed to receive adjuvant chemotherapy while participating in a National Surgical Adjuvant Breast Project trial. Recently married, S.S. continues to do very well and receives follow-up examinations every 3 months.

K.M. is a 68-year-old widow who had a screening mammogram as part of her routine health care. After the mammogram revealed a suspicious abnormality, her family doctor referred K.M. to a surgeon, who performed a biopsy. This procedure confirmed a malignancy. After discussing the various surgical options, K.M. decided to have a lumpectomy, stating, "I want to still feel good about my appearance."

Because her tumor was ER positive and the lymph nodes were negative for cancer cells, she was classified as having a stage I, ER-positive postmenopausal breast cancer. Meeting with a medical oncologist, K.M. was advised that her breast should be radiated. In view of her menopausal status and the ER positivity, she was also advised to take adjuvant tamoxifen. Two years after surgery, she continues to do well.

These two cases are quite instructive. Although both women had stage I breast cancers, the younger woman, S.S., opted for extensive surgery, and the older woman, K.M., chose the conservative approach. In 1994, this choice has become highly personal. Although both women were free to choose a local therapy, the menopausal status and the ER status of their cancers determined the adjuvant therapy recommended by their oncologists. These two cases illustrate that breast cancer surgery can be a matter of personal choice, whereas adjuvant therapy is essentially defined by key prognostic factors.

Therapy for Advanced Breast Cancer

Despite adjuvant therapy, some patients develop a recurrence of breast cancer. A recurrence can develop any time after treatment, and when it does, treatment must be resumed. Therapy for advanced breast cancer is the same that is given adjuvantly: chemotherapy, hormonal therapy, and radiation therapy. (These therapies are discussed extensively in Part II.) The doctor recommends the best treatment for the patient by utilizing the prognostic factors discussed earlier.

Estrogen receptor status: A patient whose original breast cancer was classified as ER positive is a good candidate for hormonal therapy. A patient whose original tumor was classified as ER negative is usually treated with chemotherapy.

Menstrual status: The older a woman, the more likely she is to be a candidate for hormonal therapy. Premenopausal women are typically treated with chemotherapy.

The specific *site of recurrence* is also an important factor in determining treatment. Whereas liver recurrences are generally treated with chemotherapy, bone or lymph node recurrences are frequently treated with hormonal therapy. Radiation is used to treat recurrences in the brain as well as localized, painful bone sites.

The *disease-free interval* is the span of time from the original diagnosis to documentation of recurrence. The longer this period, the more favorable the prognosis. Patients whose disease-free interval is more than 2 years have a better chance of responding to hormonal therapy than do patients whose interval is less than 2 years.

The potential *side effects* of treatment must always be weighed against the potential benefits of treatment. Because chemotherapy causes more side effects than does hormonal therapy, patients who are not physically able to tolerate chemotherapy are given hormonal therapy.

Radiation can be used to treat most breast cancers, depending on the site of disease. At times, the choice between chemotherapy and hormonal therapy is a difficult one. Ultimately, the physician makes a judgment about what is best for the patient. The better the rapport between doctor and patient, the easier this decision is to make. *Individualized therapy is always the best therapy.*

The case of S.H. illustrates how a patient with advanced breast cancer benefits from individualized therapy.

S.H. is a 77-year-old woman who had a mastectomy of the right breast at the age of 67. After experiencing pain in the right shoulder blade, she consulted her family doctor. A bone scan and x rays indicated the possibility of recurrent cancer. Subsequently, a biopsy revealed that the breast cancer had spread to the bones.

At this point, S.H. was examined by an oncologist, who found her in good general health; in fact, her only complaint was the nagging pain in her right shoulder. Further testing indicated that the cancer was confined exclusively to the bones. S.H. began to receive pain medication, tamoxifen, and a series of radiation treatments to the painful shoulder area. After several weeks, the radiation successfully eliminated the pain, and the pain medication was discontinued. Presently, S.H. continues to do well and takes only tamoxifen.

Multiple factors influenced the formulation of S.H.'s treatment plan. Because of S.H.'s postmenopausal status, the disease-free interval of 10 years, and the limited site of recurrence, the recommendation of hormonal therapy was made. (Because S.H.'s estrogen receptors were unknown, they did not influence the decision.) Because painful bone areas are best treated with radiation, the recommendation of radiation was added. Should the initial plan of treatment fail at any time, chemotherapy can be introduced.

It should be emphasized that advanced breast cancer is extremely treatable and that patients can expect therapy to help them. Numerous patients with advanced breast cancer continue to respond well to therapy for many years!

An Exciting Area of Research: Preventive Therapy

During the 1980s, tamoxifen was experimentally given to women with established breast cancers. Unexpectedly, such tamoxifen therapy was found to reduce a woman's risk of developing breast cancer in the unaffected breast. As a result, researchers currently theorize that tamoxifen may be able to prevent breast cancer altogether in high-risk women.

Consequently, the National Cancer Institute and the NSABP are presently conducting a nationwide study of tamoxifen among 16,000 women whose breast cancer risk is high. To be eligible, a woman must have one or more of the following risk factors: be older than 60 years, have a mother or sister with breast cancer, have had a prior benign breast biopsy, and either be childless or have had the first child after the age of 30.

Each participant will randomly receive either tamoxifen or a placebo, that is, an inactive substitute for the hormone. Regarded as a historic attempt to develop a medication that can actually prevent the onset of cancer, this particular trial raises exciting possibilities for the future of cancer treatment.

2

Lung Cancer

Lung cancer was considered an extremely rare disease in the early 1900s and continued to be regarded as such until the 1940s. During the latter decade, however, the incidence of lung cancer began to rise dramatically. Currently in the United States, it is the leading cause of cancer-related deaths among both men and women. In 1994, it is expected that 171,000 Americans will be stricken with this disease.

Fortunately, medical understanding of lung cancer has also markedly increased since the 1950s. Cigarette smoking is now regarded as the chief risk factor associated with this type of cancer. Consequently, in 1964, the Surgeon General required a warning to be placed on all packs of cigarettes, cautioning users that smoking may be harmful to their health. Additionally, it is now known that lung cancers vary widely and that treatment must be determined by the specific subtype of the cancer.

Anatomy and Function of the Lungs

Like other body parts, such as the arms, ears, eyes and legs, human lungs exist in pairs. The right and left lungs fill most of the chest cavity and are separated from one another by the *mediasti-*

num, a region containing such vital structures as the heart, trachea, and lymph nodes.

The lungs function as the body's organ of breathing. As a person inhales, air enters the mouth or nose, travels past the larynx (voice box) and then proceeds down the trachea (windpipe). Branching from the trachea into the right and left lungs are tubes known as *bronchi* that disperse the air into ever smaller tubes throughout the lungs. Eventually, the air reaches tiny sacs embedded in the lung lining where the critical exchange of gases occurs: oxygen is extracted from the air and replaced with the gaseous waste, carbon dioxide. Figure 2-1 is an illustration of the lungs and surrounding structures in the chest.

Incidence of and Risk Factors for Lung Cancer

Lung cancer is most frequently diagnosed in patients 55 to 65 years of age. Recently, however, the incidence of lung cancer has increased threefold in the 40–45 age group and 10-fold in the 60–65 age group. Whereas lung cancer was primarily a male disease prior to 1960, it has become a common female disease as growing numbers of women claim the smoking habit. In the late 1980s, deaths due to lung cancer surpassed those due to breast cancer in American women. By 1993, it is expected that fully 28% of newly diagnosed lung cancer patients will be women. Figure 2-2 illustrates the tragic rise in the death rate from lung cancer for both sexes since 1920. While the incidence among men has seemingly leveled off, the incidence among women has increased an alarming 400% since 1960 and shows no evidence of stabilizing.

The incontestably chief risk factor for lung cancer is tobacco smoking. Smoking is associated with more than 85% of lung cancer cases. Although the type and degree of smoking determine a person's risk of developing lung cancer, the "typical" cigarette smoker is 9 times more likely to contract lung cancer than is the person who has never smoked. Cigar smokers run a lung cancer risk that is 1.8 times greater than that of nonsmokers; the risk of pipe smok-

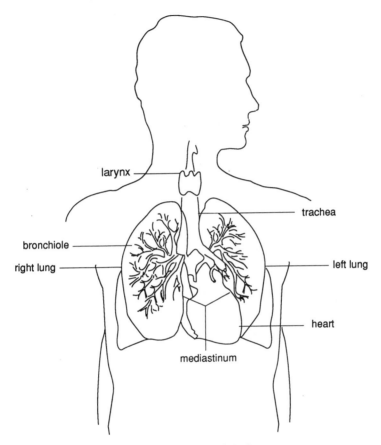

Figure 2-1. Anatomy of the lungs.

ers is 2.2 times that of nonsmokers. The lung cancer risk for cigarette smokers increases with the frequency of the habit.

Another risk factor for lung cancer that has recently been studied is passive exposure to smoke. One study concludes that a non-
smoker who lives with a smoker runs a lung cancer risk that is 1.5
times greater than that of a person who is not consistently exposed

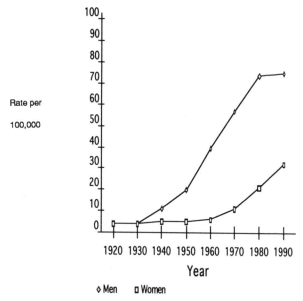

Figure 2-2. Yearly U.S. death rate from lung cancer by sex. From Boring CC, Squires TS, Tong T. Cancer statistics, 1993. *CA Cancer Journal for Clinicians* 43 (1):7–26, 1993, with permission.

to passive smoke. Findings such as this have prompted a general health movement that seeks to establish a "smoke-free" environment in public places.

Still another risk factor for lung cancer is an industrial exposure to certain substances. For example, workers who are exposed to uranium, nickle chromates, and vinyl chloride run an increased risk of developing lung cancer. Likewise, smokers who are exposed to asbestos have an especially high risk of developing this disease. Although diet, heredity, and geographic location have not been found to contribute significantly to this disease, some studies do indicate a slightly elevated incidence of lung cancer in areas of extreme pollution.

Admittedly, the development of lung cancer is a complex process currently defying any single explanation; however, the cessation of smoking is one critical solution to the problem. A smoker's risk of lung cancer decreases steadily for 15 years following cessation, at which point the risk of the former smoker begins to approach that of a person who has never smoked.

Symptoms of Lung Cancer

The initial symptoms of lung cancer, which are experienced by nearly 80% of patients with this disease, result from the growth of tumors in the chest cavity. One such common and serious symptom is the coughing up of blood-tinged phlegm, a condition usually caused by the bleeding of the cancer into the bronchus or trachea. Other initial symptoms include shortness of breath and a persistent cough, conditions that are likewise symptomatic of smokers in general. A pneumonia that never resolves may also indicate an underlying lung cancer. It should be noted that nearly 15% of lung cancer patients never do experience symptoms; rather, their cancers are detected on chest x rays ordered for other reasons. With the exception of the coughing of blood, the initial symptoms of lung cancer are nonspecific, meaning that any number of benign conditions can induce such symptoms. Unfortunately, mass screening programs utilizing chest x rays to detect early lung cancer have thus far failed to improve patient survival rates. As a result, the detection of lung cancer in its early stages can be quite difficult.

Diagnosis of Lung Cancer

The definitive diagnosis of any cancer requires an examination of tissue under the microscope. Generally, only a small amount of tissue is required for such an examination. The following are common techniques used in the diagnosis of lung cancer.

The simplest diagnostic method involves the examination of a patient's sputum. After slides are prepared from a specimen of sputum, which the patient collects in a small container and sends to the laboratory, the pathologist evaluates the status of the individual cells on the slides. Unfortunately, such sputum analysis yields an accurate diagnosis in only about 15% of lung cancer patients.

One of the most common diagnostic tests for lung cancer is bronchoscopy. During this procedure, the patient is sedated as the doctor inserts a flexible, lighted, narrow tube known as a bronchoscope into the nose and down into the trachea. With the use of this instrument, the doctor is able to inspect the patient's bronchial tubes thoroughly and to perform a biopsy of suspicious areas as needed. Should the bronchial tubes appear normal, the doctor can even pass the bronchoscope into the lung and perform a biopsy of any mass previously revealed by chest x ray. With sophisticated fiberoptic instruments in the hands of highly trained specialists, bronchoscopy has become an extremely safe procedure; fewer than 2% of bronchoscopy patients experience complications. Moreover, bronchoscopy leads to a definitive diagnosis in approximately 70% of lung cancer patients.

Another reliable diagnostic test for lung cancer is a needle biopsy of the suspicious mass. This procedure is typically employed when the tumor is located in the periphery of the lung. During this type of biopsy, x rays are used to delineate the patient's lungs, thus enabling the doctor to insert a needle directly into the mass in order to sample the tissue. The major complication of needle biopsy is *pneumothorax*, the leakage of air into the lung, resulting in its collapse. Pneumothorax occurs in 5 to 10% of patients who undergo this procedure. Needle aspiration yields a definitive diagnosis in about 70% of lung cancer patients.

For a small number of patients in whom lung cancer is suspected, all diagnostic testing proves inconclusive. For such patients, diagnostic surgery is indicated. The common surgical procedures used in the diagnosis of lung cancer are *mediastinoscopy* and *thoracotomy*.

Mediastinoscopy is the surgical exploration of the mediastinum, a procedure usually employed when the lymph nodes of the mediastinum appear to be involved. Using general anesthesia, the surgeon passes a scope through a small incision in the patient's neck and down into the middle of the chest area. This flexible scope enables the surgeon to examine the mediastinum and, if necessary, to excise samples of suspicious tissue. The patient is typically discharged within a day or two of this quite safe procedure.

The second type of diagnostic surgery for lung cancer is thoracotomy, the surgical exploration of the chest. Although thoracotomy is virtually always diagnostic, this procedure entails all the risks of major surgery. Once the nature of the mass is established, the surgeon decides whether the removal of the cancer is feasible. Such a patient can be expected to remain in the hospital for 7 days following the thoracotomy.

Although all lung masses are approached in the same diagnostic fashion, not all lung masses are lung cancer. Once a definitive diagnosis is reached, appropriate treatment can be undertaken, as illustrated by the case of G.K.

G.K. was a 55-year-old man who was admitted to the hospital from the emergency room after complaining of chest pain. Initially, he was believed to have had a heart attack. G.K. had no significant medical history and, most important, he had never smoked. An x ray of the chest revealed a mass on the left lung between the heart and trachea. After ruling out the possibility of any heart problem, G.K.'s doctor ordered a computed tomography (CT) scan to evaluate the lung abnormality. The CT scan revealed what appeared to be a group of enlarged lymph nodes in the mediastinum and left lung. All other blood tests and scans were normal.

On the recommendation of a lung specialist, G.K. underwent a bronchoscopy; the results of this exam were entirely normal. A needle biopsy was then performed. Although this test confirmed the presence of malignant cells, the type of cancer could not be established.

At this point, an oncologist was consulted. The oncologist recommended that more tissue be examined in order to establish the cancer's specific type. Because of the tumor's proximity to the heart, the consulting surgeon advised against a mediastinoscopy and recommended, instead, a modified thoracotomy. In this procedure, an ample number of lymph nodes were removed and then pathologically analyzed. The final diagnosis was Hodgkin's disease, for which G.K. was successfully treated.

G.K.'s case represents the typical diagnostic approach used to evaluate a lung abnormality. Because G.K. was not a smoker, his doctors initially considered the possibility of noncancerous disease. Also quite typically, testing proceeded from simple to increasingly complex procedures. When a needle biopsy proved inconclusive, G.K. required a thoracotomy. This case also illustrates a fundamental diagnostic principle: the type of the cancer must be identified as precisely as possible in order to determine appropriate treatment.

Types of Lung Cancers

All lung cancers have a distinct appearance when viewed under the microscope by a pathologist. They are classifiable into two general categories: non–small-cell and small-cell. As does their appearance, the behavior of these two types of lung cancers also differs. As a class, small-cell lung cancers are rapidly growing, quite responsive to chemotherapy, and rarely treatable by surgery. In contrast, non–small-cell lung cancers are slow growing, less responsive to chemotherapy, and often surgically treatable. At the time of initial diagnosis, the majority of patients with non–small-cell lung cancer have disease that is confined to the chest area, whereas 66% of patients with small-cell lung cancer already have evidence of distant spread. Consequently, these two types of lung cancers are regarded as two distinct diseases.

Non–Small-Cell Lung Cancer

Staging and Prognosis

Non–small-cell cancer constitutes 75% of all lung cancers. This type of cancer is further classified into three categories: squamous cell, adenocarcinoma, and large-cell. Typically, squamous cell lung cancer arises in the middle of the chest, remaining there for prolonged periods before spreading to other organs. This particular type of cancer accounts for fully one third of all lung cancers. Adenocarcinoma tends to develop in the periphery of the lung. This type of cancer, which accounts for 25% of all lung cancers, develops rather inexplicably in nonsmokers as well as smokers. Large-cell lung cancer accounts for 16% of lung cancers. As the three types of non–small-cell lung cancers are quite similar in both behavior and treatment, they will simply be considered collectively as non–small-cell lung cancer.

To classify a cancer and determine treatment, physicians employ a set of guidelines known as a *staging system*. A lung cancer's stage is an estimate of the disease's extent and is the single most important prognostic factor. Routine staging tests for non–small-cell lung cancer include a physical examination, blood tests, and CT scans of the chest, abdomen, and, frequently, the head. Based on the results of these tests, the cancer is classified into one of four stages:

- Stage I. The cancer is confined exclusively to the lung tissue.
- Stage II. The cancer has spread from the lung tissue to adjacent lymph nodes; however, the cancer has not penetrated the mediastinum or any other area.
- Stage III. The cancer has spread to the lymph nodes of the mediastinum, neck, or other side of the involved lung. Any cancer that penetrates the outer boundary of the lung, extending to such areas as the chest wall or ribs, is likewise classified in this stage.
- Stage IV. The cancer has spread beyond the chest area to other sites in the body.

Patients whose non–small-cell lung cancer is diagnosed in the early stages are typically given a more favorable prognosis than those diagnosed in advanced stages. Whereas 50% of stage I patients with this disease survive 5 years after diagnosis, fewer than 10% of patients in stages 3 and 4 do.

However, another important and sometimes mitigating factor affecting prognosis is the patient's overall physical condition. Regardless of the cancer's stage, patients who do not experience such cancer-induced symptoms as loss of appetite and weakness generally fare much better than do patients who are chronically plagued by these problems.

Treatment

Because chemotherapy is not particularly effective in the treatment of non–small-cell lung cancer, such drugs are not routinely administered. As more than 85% of these patients have cancers that are exclusively confined to the chest area, however, the localized therapies of radiation and surgery are ideal treatments for this disease.

Surgical removal of the cancer, which requires a thoracotomy, results in the longest survival for patients with non–small-cell lung cancer. Nevertheless, because of coexisting medical conditions, surgery is not an appropriate option for all patients. Conditions that may disqualify the patient from surgery include general weakness, emphysema, or advanced age. Determining the best therapy for the patient often becomes a matter of judgment on the part of the physician.

Treatment recommendations on a stage-by-stage basis are as follows.

- Stage I. Surgical removal of the cancer is the preferred treatment whenever the patient's medical condition can tolerate this option. Such surgery results in cure in greater than 60% of patients. In lieu of surgery, radiation can be given, though the cure rate is somewhat lower.
- Stage II. Surgical removal of the cancer is the preferred treatment, resulting in a 5-year survival rate of 35–40%.

When the patient's medical condition makes surgery inappropriate, radiation is given. Frequently, however, the exact stage of an early lung cancer cannot be established until the time of surgical exploration. The case of J.J. provides such an example:

J.J. is a 65-year-old man who began to cough up blood while on a fishing trip in Canada. On returning home, he consulted his family physician, who ordered a chest x ray. This test showed a mass on the right side of the chest, while a CT scan further revealed several enlarged lymph nodes in the lung, raising the possibility of involved lymph nodes in the mediastinum. All other tests—physical examination, blood work, and scans—were normal.

The family doctor referred J.J. to a lung specialist, who recommended bronchoscopy. This exam revealed a non–small-cell lung cancer that appeared to originate in the upper right lung. As J.J.'s physical condition was good, he was considered a likely candidate for surgery.

The surgeon whom J.J. consulted for a possible thoracotomy believed that the lymph nodes of the mediastinum were suspicious for cancer. Consequently, he performed a mediastinoscopy but obtained negative results. At this juncture, J.J.'s team of doctors—family doctor, lung specialist, and surgeon—conferred. Although the stage of the lung cancer had not been established definitively as either stage II or III, the doctors recommended that J.J. undergo a thoracotomy. It was decided, however, that the surgeon would first perform another biopsy of the lymph nodes of the mediastinum before removing lung tissue. In the event that these lymph nodes proved cancerous, lung surgery would not be performed.

Fortunately, surgical exploration showed that the lymph nodes of the mediastinum were normal; therefore, J.J. underwent an uneventful removal of the lung cancer. After a steady recovery, he was discharged 6 days after surgery. Three years later, J.J. shows no evidence of lung cancer.

Despite the sophisticated testing presently available, including mediastinoscopy, J.J.'s case illustrates the common need for staging lung cancers by surgical exploration. Whenever the feasibility of surgically removing a non–small-cell lung cancer remains questionable, most physicians are inclined to recommend an exploration of the chest in order to stage the cancer and, if at all possible, to remove it.

- Stage III. Radiation therapy is typically used, often in conjunction with surgery or chemotherapy. In early stage III patients, that is, those without extensive involvement of the mediastinum, surgery is frequently performed. Actually, what occurs in such cases is that the surgeon performs chest exploration for a probable stage II cancer, only to discover that a stage III exists. Should the staging tests reveal extensive mediastinal cancer, however, surgery is not considered a treatment option; instead, the patient is treated with radiation. The role of chemotherapy is presently being defined in this stage and is considered on a patient-by-patient basis. Unfortunately, patients with stage III non–small-cell lung cancers face a serious prognosis, with only 15% surviving longer than 5 years after diagnosis.

- Stage IV. The disease has spread from the lung area to other parts of the body. As surgical removal of the lung cancer is of little benefit to the patient, surgery is not recommended. Nevertheless, radiation is often used to control specific problems, such as pain, that are caused by the cancer's spread. Because chemotherapy is palliative in approximately 33% of these patients, it is generally recommended for those who can physically tolerate the side effects of therapy. For patients in poor physical condition, however, the risks of chemotherapy may outweigh its benefits. For this reason, chemotherapy must be considered on a patient-by-patient basis.

Small-Cell Lung Cancer

Staging and Prognosis

The distinct behavior of small-cell lung cancers determines their treatment. Categorically, they are aggressive and rapidly growing malignancies, so much so that at the time of diagnosis, only 10% of patients are found to be in stage I, whereas more than 66% are found to be in stage IV (having evidence of spread outside the chest area.) As a result, surgery is generally not used to treat small-cell lung cancer, though it may be employed to establish the type of cancer. Fortunately, small-cell lung cancer is quite responsive to both chemotherapy and radiation therapy.

The peculiar behavior of this disease is accommodated by a special staging system that recognizes, instead of the traditional four stages, only two stages: limited and extensive. Limited-stage small-cell lung cancer is confined to one half of the chest area. In this type of cancer, the exact status of the mediastinal lymph nodes need not be known in order to plan treatment, because surgical removal of the cancer is not routinely performed. Extensive-stage small-cell lung cancer has spread outside the chest to other organs of the body.

The prognosis of patients with small-cell lung cancer has improved dramatically over the past 20 years. Whereas *limited stage* patients survived only 11 weeks after diagnosis in the 1960s, such patients today survive an average of 15 months after diagnosis. Patients with extensive-stage cancers, which are similarly responsive to modern therapies, now survive an average of 9 months after diagnosis. Of course, the overall physical condition of the patient with this type of cancer is prognostically important in that the patient who is in good physical condition can better tolerate the rigors of treatment.

Treatment

Nearly all patients with small-cell lung cancer receive some form of chemotherapy with positive results. A discernible shrinkage of the cancer occurs in approximately 80% of all small-cell lung cancer patients. Moreover, total disappearance of the cancer occurs in 66% of patients with limited stage disease. Although the optimal combination of chemotherapeutic drugs has yet to be established, patients generally do receive at least two of the following drugs: cyclophosphamide, doxorubicin, vincristine, VP-16, and cisplatin.

Radiation therapy is also often used successfully in the treatment of small-cell lung cancers. In addition to chemotherapy, patients with limited stage disease typically receive radiation in the chest area. Frequently, radiation is used to control specific cancer-induced problems such as bone pain. Although patients with small-cell lung cancer routinely received brain irradiation in the past to reduce their risk of developing brain tumors, such treatment is currently under investigation.

Stage-by-stage recommendations for treatment of small-cell lung cancers are as follows.

- Limited-stage small-cell lung cancer. The patient is treated with chemotherapy. In the event that the tumor completely disap-

Table 2-1
Comparison of Non–Small-Cell and Small-Cell Lung Cancers

Characteristic	Type of lung cancer	
	Non–small-cell	Small-cell
Smoking a risk factor	Yes	Yes
Staging system	Stages I to IV	Limited or extensive
Growth rate of cancer	Slow to moderate	Rapid
Response rate to chemotherapy	Low (30%)	High (80%)
Surgery as a treatment option	Preferred in appropriate patients	Used in fewer than 10% of patients
Radiation as a treatment option	Frequently used	Frequently used
Favorable prognosis	Stages I and II	Limited stage
	Good physical condition	Good physical condition

pears, the original site of the cancer is subsequently irradiated. If the tumor shrinks but does not disappear, the patient generally receives a second course of chemotherapy. When treatment is completed, the patient receives follow-up examinations and x rays of the chest every 4 to 6 weeks.

- Extensive-stage small-cell lung cancer. The patient is treated with chemotherapy. In about 33% of patients, the cancer disappears completely. Although radiation is used to treat specific problems such as bone pain, the original site of the cancer is not routinely irradiated in patients with this particular type of cancer.

Practically speaking, lung cancer can be viewed as two distinct diseases, non–small-cell and small-cell cancers. These two types of lung cancer do share a few similarities, but they actually behave as separate entities, claiming quite distinct behaviors, staging systems, and methods of treatment. Table 2-1 summarizes the similarities and differences between these two types of lung cancer.

3

Colon and Rectal Cancer

Cancer of the colon and rectum, or colorectal cancer, ranks as the third most common lethal cancer with 152,000 cases expected to be diagnosed next year in the United States. This form of cancer strikes men and women at equally high rates. However, it is hoped that recent advances in screening, surgery, and chemotherapy will result in an improved mortality rate for this disease in the 1990s.

Anatomy of the Colon and Rectum

To complete the process of digestion, swallowed food passes from the stomach into the small intestine, a narrow organ measuring 25 feet in length. Undigested food then enters the large intestine or colon, an organ measuring 6 feet in length, where excess water is removed. The remaining waste (stool) is then stored in the lowest 12 inches of colon, which is known as the rectum.

The colon and rectum compose the lower portion of the digestive tract. Anatomically, the colon begins in the right lower abdomen at the point where the small intestine joins it. The colon ascends to the level of the ninth or 10th rib, crosses the abdomen, and then descends to the rectum and anus. Figure 3-1 offers a schematic diagram of the colon and rectum.

Incidence and Risk Factors

It is estimated that 6% of the American population will eventually develop colorectal cancer. This form of cancer strikes the sexes equally; however, its incidence continues to escalate gradually in persons older than 40 years. In addition to advancing age, other risk factors exist for colorectal cancer. For example, patients who have ulcerative colitis are at increased risk, with the degree of risk determined by the severity and duration of the inflammatory condition. Moreover, patients who have a first-degree relative (sibling or parent) with colorectal cancer run a double risk of developing the disease. Similarly, patients with a history of any malignancy, including an earlier colorectal cancer, are at increased risk.

Another risk factor associated with colon cancer is diet, particularly the low-fiber, high-protein, high-fat diet relied on by industrialized societies. Conversely, high-fiber diets have been shown to decrease the risk of colorectal cancer.

Heredity, too, is a risk factor for colorectal cancer. The tendency to develop multiple colon polyps can actually be inherited as a genetic trait known as familial polyposis syndrome. Although this syndrome is rare, affecting only 1 in 7000 persons in the United States, it does account for approximately 1% of colon cancers.

Polyps and Colon Cancer

Although the walls of the colon and rectum are normally smooth, the surface of the intestinal walls sometimes develops small mushroom-shaped growths known as *polyps*. Typically measuring between one quarter and 1 inch in diameter, these polyps can occur anywhere in the colon. Although the cause of polyps remains unknown, most experts now believe that tiny polyps sig-

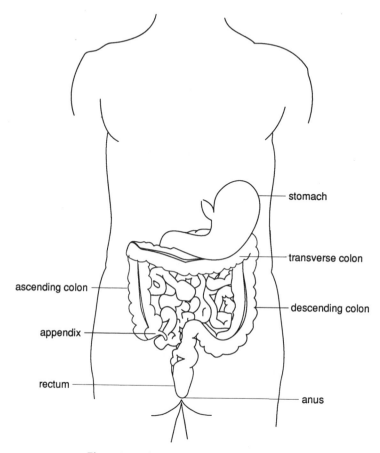

Figure 3-1. Anatomy of colon and rectum.

nal precancerous changes in the lining of the colon. Clearly, the risk of benign polyps becoming cancerous increases as polyps grow. Whereas only 1% of polyps measuring less than one third of an inch in diameter prove to be cancerous, fully 45% of polyps measuring more than 1 inch are cancerous. Fortunately, as polyps tend to grow quite slowly, a number of years may elapse before malignancy occurs.

Symptoms and Screening

As both polyps and colon cancers can develop without evidencing symptoms, these growths are best detected by screening methods during routine health check-ups. Tragically, obvious symptoms often appear only in the advanced stages of colon cancer. Because of delayed diagnosis, only 50% of colorectal cancers are currently cured. Yet, if all persons older than 50 years practiced simple screening methods on a regular basis, it is estimated that fully 90% of such cancers could be cured.

The actual symptoms indicative of colorectal cancer are varied. The most common symptom involves a change in normal bowel habits; whereas diarrhea is typical of rectal cancer, constipation is characteristic of colon cancer. A related symptom warranting investigation is a narrowing in the width of the stool. Moreover, abdominal pain or recurring gas pains are often associated with colon and rectal cancers, as are rectal bleeding and blackish stools.

It needs to be emphasized that the symptoms associated with colon and rectal cancer are often extremely vague. Interestingly enough, among healthy individuals recounting their recent medical histories, 11% note abdominal pain, and 12% report a change in bowel habits. Another potentially false symptom is bright red rectal bleeding, a condition more likely to result from hemorrhoids than from rectal cancers.

In order to detect polyps and colorectal cancers early, three specific screening tests are recommended for individuals older than 40. The first, a stool test, involves the examination of a fecal sample for traces of "hidden" blood. Because polyps and colon cancers tend to bleed in small amounts that are not visually detectible in the stool, the fecal sample, which is simply placed by the examinee on a special, sealable card, must be analyzed for blood traces with a chemical in the laboratory. In asymptomatic individuals who are tested, 1 to 5% will show evidence of blood. However, because many polyps and cancers do not shed blood during the collection period, only 33% of polyps and 66% of cancers produce a positive test for hidden blood. Consequently, other screening tests are necessary.

The second screening test involves a rectal examination in order to check for abnormal masses or growths. This test is performed by the physician, who inserts a gloved, lubricated finger into the patient's rectum. Actually, 10% of colorectal cancers are within reach of the examining finger.

In the third type of screening test, the physician employs a thin, flexible, lighted tube called an endoscope to inspect the intestinal walls. Inserted through the rectum, the endoscope enables the physician to detect irregularities in the colon as well as remove small polyps and perform a biopsy on suspicious areas.

When the lower portion of the colon, including the rectum, is examined with this type of instrument, the procedure is referred to as a *sigmoidoscopy*, a widely used screening test for colon cancer. When the entire colon is examined, the procedure is known as a *colonoscopy*. This test is commonly used in patients with a history of polyps or colon cancer. Still another test employed in examining the entire colon is the barium enema. In this procedure, barium is inserted into the rectum, and the entire colon is examined by x ray.

The American Cancer Society endorses the following screening procedures for colorectal cancer.

1. A person 50 years of age or older who has no risk factors should have a stool examination yearly and a sigmoidoscopic examination every 3 to 5 years.
2. Any person with a history of either polyps or colon cancer should have a complete examination of the colon, be it colonoscopy or barium enema x ray.

Diagnosis and Surgical Treatment

Any abnormality detected by endoscopic or x-ray procedures must be fully evaluated. If an excised polyp proves benign during laboratory analysis, no further surgery is required. However, if a polyp is malignant or if a polyp is not removable with an endo-scope, surgery is usually required. (See Chapter 12, Surgery, in-cluding case study M.W.)

The standard therapy for colorectal cancers is removal of the cancer and adjacent lymph nodes. (Lymph nodes are pea-like structures found throughout the body that fight infection.) The pa-tient generally undergoes a surgical exploration of the abdomen or *laparotomy*. After removing the cancer along with a narrow border of healthy tissue, the surgeon reattaches the segments of colon.

When such a connection is impossible, the surgeon performs a *colostomy*, a surgical opening in the colon wall that allows for the elimination of stool into a disposable bag outside the abdomen. Because of recent improvements in surgical techniques, only one colorectal cancer patient in five now actually requires a permanent colostomy. Typically, this procedure is limited to patients whose colon cancers cause obstructions/perforations or whose colon in-fections/inflammations prevent the immediate reattachment of sections. In many instances, temporary colostomies are possible.

Patients tend to fear colostomy even more than the original diagnosis of cancer, so the prevailing misconceptions regarding co-lostomy must be dispelled. Whereas this procedure did constitute the standard treatment of rectal cancers in the past, the vast major-ity of patients do not require a permanent colostomy today. Per-haps if the general public comes to appreciate the altered status of this procedure, more individuals will submit to routine screening methods and reap the benefit of early detection: cure.

Staging of Colorectal Cancer

Physicians use a set of guidelines known as a *staging system* to classify cancers, gauge prognosis, and determine therapy. In order to establish the stage of a colorectal cancer, two key factors must be known: the depth of the cancer's penetration into the intestinal wall and the status of nearby lymph nodes. The five stages of colon and rectal cancer are the following.

- Stage 0. Often found in polyps, this early cancer appears only in the innermost lining of the intestine.
- Stage A. The cancer is limited to the intestinal wall; the lymph nodes are free of malignant cells.
- Stage B. The cancer occurs outside the intestinal wall; the lymph nodes are free of malignant cells.
- Stage C. The cancer has spread beyond the intestinal wall to adjacent lymph nodes.
- Stage D. The cancer has spread to a distant site.

Adjuvant Therapy

After surgical treatment of colorectal cancer, 95% of patients show no detectable sign of cancer. Unfortunately, almost 50% of such patients do develop *recurrences,* meaning that the treated cancer becomes active again, frequently in unrelated areas such as the bone or lung. Regardless of the site of recurrence, the original colorectal cancer is its source, otherwise known as the *primary cancer.* It is believed that, at diagnosis, a few stray cancer cells already exist outside the colon or rectum, becoming detectable only after an average span of 3 years.

The aim of adjuvant therapy is preventive, that is, to destroy stray cancer cells remaining in the body after surgery. For colorectal cancers, adjuvant therapy consists of either chemotherapy or radiation therapy. (See Chapter 14, Chemotherapy and Hormonal Therapy, and Chapter 13, Radiation Therapy.)

Colon and rectal cancers are quite similar in that they both originate in the intestine. Moreover, both cancers are staged identically and treated initially with surgery. However, these cancers are also considered distinct types, particularly because of rectal cancer's unique pattern of recurrence. Whereas one half of rectal cancer recurrences arise in the tail bone, colon cancer recurrences rarely do. In that any discussion of adjuvant therapy is further complicated by the factor of stage, colon and rectal cancers will be considered separately.

Adjuvant Therapy of Colon Cancer

Until the late 1980s, no proven adjuvant therapy existed for colon cancer. After surgery, patients were simply advised to have periodic examinations and yearly colonoscopies. Then, Dr. C. Mortel at the Mayo Clinic found that two chemotherapy drugs, fluorouracil (5-FU) and levamizole, effectively reduced the recurrence rate of stage C colon cancer when administered following surgery. As a result, adjuvant chemotherapy is now considered for many colon cancer patients following surgery. To date, radiation therapy has not proven beneficial in the treatment of this cancer.

In April of 1990, the National Cancer Institute sponsored a Consensus Conference aimed at providing guidelines for the use of adjuvant therapy in the treatment of cancer. The following recommendations were made for the various stages of colon cancer.

- Stages 0 and A. Standard treatment consists of the surgical removal of the cancer. Given this treatment, stage 0 patients exhibit a cure rate of more than 95%, and stage A patients demonstrate a cure rate of more than 75%. Adjuvant therapy has not been shown to improve these cure rates.
- Stage B. Because no firm recommendations were issued, the role of adjuvant chemotherapy remains controversial. Although 55 to 75% of patients are cured with surgery, patients with poor prognostic features such as intestinal blockage or evidence of spread in nearby tissues may benefit from adjuvant chemotherapy. Recommendations are best made on an individual basis, as illustrated by the case of B.L.

B.L. is a 65-year-old woman who, in the course of her yearly medical examination, was found to have blood in the stool. As colon cancer figured strongly in her family history, her primary physician ordered a colonoscopy, the results of which revealed a cancerous growth on the right side of the colon.

Surgery was recommended. During the procedure, the cancerous section of colon was removed, and the intestines were reattached, making a colostomy unnecessary. The pathology report revealed that the cancer had invaded one half of the colon wall but had not involved adjacent lymph nodes.

At this juncture, an oncologist was consulted, who advised B.L. that she had an early stage B colon cancer. As the prognostic findings appeared good, the oncologist recommended periodic follow-up examinations in lieu of adjuvant chemotherapy. Three years after diagnosis, B.L. continues to undergo a physical examination and blood tests every 4 months with no sign of recurrence to date.

- Stage C. As 35 to 50% of patients are cured with surgery, the recommendation is that all patients be offered adjuvant chemotherapy (5-FU and levamizole) in an attempt to improve the possibility of survival.
- Stage D. Because the cancer has already spread to a distant area, adjuvant therapy in this stage is no longer preventive. Treatment options are discussed in this chapter's section, Advanced Cancer.

Adjuvant Therapy of Rectal Cancer

The traditional adjuvant treatment for rectal cancer is radiation therapy to the tail bone and pelvis, but research has recently established the benefit of chemotherapy. Following are the stage-by-stage guidelines for rectal cancer as developed by the National Cancer Institute's latest Consensus Conference.

- Stages 0 and A. Standard therapy for the earliest stages is surgical removal of the cancer. Such treatment results in cure for more than 95% of stage 0 patients and more than 75% of stage A patients. To date, adjuvant therapy has not been shown to improve these cure rates.
- Stage B. After surgery, both radiation therapy and chemotherapy should be administered. Directed at the tail bone and pelvis, radiation therapy is given daily for 5 to 6 weeks. Although the specific choice of chemotherapy drugs remains controversial, many authorities advocate that the drug 5-FU be given weekly for 9 to 12 months.
- Stage C. Treatment recommendations are identical to those for stage B.
- Stage D. Because the cancer has already spread to a distant area,

Table 3-1
Adjuvant Therapy of Colon and Rectal Cancer by Stage

	Adjuvant therapy by type of cancer	
Stage	Colon cancer	Rectal cancer
0 & A	No adjuvant therapy is recommended	No adjuvant therapy is recommended
B	No adjuvant therapy is routinely recommended. Adjuvant chemotherapy is a consideration for high-risk patients	Chemotherapy and radiation to the tail bone and pelvis
C	5-FU and levamizole or another combination of chemotherapy is usually given	Chemotherapy and radiation to the tail bone and pelvis

SOURCE: Adapted from the *National Institutes of Health Consensus Conference: Adjuvant Therapy for Patients with Colon and Rectal Cancer,* 1990.

adjuvant therapy in this stage is no longer preventive. Treatment options are discussed in this chapter's section, Advanced Cancer.

Table 3-1 summarizes the adjuvant treatment of colon and rectal cancers according to stage.

Follow-up Care

After the removal of a colorectal cancer, the patient is asked to participate in a regimen of follow-up care that includes a physical examination and blood tests every 3 months, as well as a yearly chest x ray and colonoscopy.

A blood test widely used during both the treatment and follow-up of colorectal cancers is carcinoembryonic antigen (CEA). This antigen, a natural substance produced by human fetuses during development, is often also generated by cancer cells. Early recurrences of the cancer can frequently be detected by monitoring the antigen's level in the blood, with any marked elevation usually requiring further investigation.

Advanced Colon and Rectal Cancer

Advanced colorectal cancer, that is, a disease originating in the colon or rectum that has spread to a distant site, is found at the time of original diagnosis in about 5% of all patients. When developing some months later, this advanced cancer is known as a recurrence. A serious condition requiring additional therapy, advanced colorectal cancer is treated with chemotherapy, radiation therapy, and sometimes, further surgery.

Prior to the mid-1980s, chemotherapy proved effective in only 20% of patients with advanced colorectal cancer. The standard chemotherapy program then consisted of weekly injections of the drug 5-FU. However, when this drug was later combined with a vitamin, folinic acid, the rate of effectiveness climbed to 50%. This particular combination is now widely used in treating colorectal cancer, but other approaches include continual infusions of 5-FU and standard chemotherapy drugs combined with the new drug, interferon. (Interferon is discussed in Chapter 16, Biological Therapy of Cancer.) Should one type of chemotherapy fail to control the cancer, substitute drugs are tried.

Radiation therapy is commonly used to alleviate symptoms that are caused by recurrent colon and rectal cancers. Especially effective in controlling localized bone pain, radiation therapy is also widely used in containing tumors that have spread to the brain. In many patients, radiation therapy and chemotherapy are administered simultaneously.

If the area of spread appears to be limited to one specific site, surgery may be considered a treatment option. For example, when an isolated tumor appears in the liver, an organ commonly affected by colon and rectal cancers, the growth may sometimes be removed surgically. As this procedure is rather extensive, involving the removal of an entire portion of the liver, the patient must be in strong physical condition at the outset. Should an involved liver contain multiple sites, a surgical procedure may be employed to implant a pump in the liver through which high-dose chemotherapy drugs may be directly infused.

Surgery eventually became a consideration in the case of M.S.

M.S. is a 52-year-old woman who, on developing blackish stools, consulted her family doctor. Suspecting a form of intestinal bleeding, the physician ordered a barium enema, the results of which revealed a suspicious-looking mass on the left side of the colon.

M.S. was referred to a surgeon, who advised that the mass be immediately removed. The procedure revealed that M.S. had a stage C colon cancer. As adjuvant chemotherapy was yet unproven in 1984, the year of her surgery, this type of treatment was not recommended.

For 4 years after the surgery, M.S. received follow-up care every 3 months. However, during a routine visit, the blood CEA was slightly elevated. When the CEA test was repeated 6 weeks later, the level continued to increase, an indication that further testing was necessary although no other symptoms were evident.

Although the chest x ray and bone scan proved normal, the CT scan of the abdomen revealed a tiny, single tumor in the left lobe of the liver. After lengthy discussions with the family doctor, surgeon, and oncologist, it was decided to have the isolated cancer removed, a procedure that cures approximately 25% of patients.

Immediately after the uneventful surgery, the CEA returned to the normal range. Two years later, M.S. continues to show no evidence of recurrence.

Whereas adjuvant chemotherapy remained unproven as a treatment for stage C colon cancer as recently as the mid-1980s, it is most likely that such therapy would be strongly recommended for M.S. today after the initial surgery. M.S.'s experience further serves to underscore the importance of follow-up care in the successful treatment of colon cancer. Through the close monitoring of the CEA factor in periodic blood tests, M.S.'s liver recurrence was detected in the earliest possible stage. Moreover, the experience of M.S. illustrates that surgery can be effectively used to control colorectal cancer in the event of distant spread.

In summary, colorectal cancer is highly treatable when detected in the early stages. Likewise, advances in treatment, particularly in the area of adjuvant therapies, offer hope to patients in the later stages. What remains certain is that all segments of the over-40 population, survivors as well as the cancer free, may benefit from periodic colorectal screening.

4

Prostate Cancer

Prior to 1900, prostate cancer was a rare disease. However, as the life expectancy of the population continues to rise, so does the incidence of prostate cancer. Today, prostate cancer ranks as the second most common cancer among American men and is unquestionably a disease of the elderly.

Since 1960, the medical understanding of prostate cancer has grown appreciably. At present, prostate cancer is a highly treatable disease; furthermore, it is potentially curable in the earlier stages. Even when prostate cancer spreads to other areas of the body, the disease can be treated and controlled for long periods.

What Is the Prostate?

The prostate is a male sex gland located beneath the bladder and next to the rectum. The urethra, a canal that empties urine from the bladder, enters the bladder through the prostate gland. Figure 4-1 depicts the male anatomy, including the prostate gland.

The prostate gland performs two major functions. First, the gland acts as a valve to ensure that both urine and sperm flow in the proper direction. Second, the prostate makes the white ejacu-

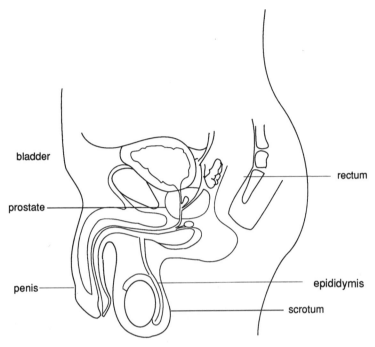

Figure 4-1. Male anatomy: prostate, testicle, bladder, and rectum.

latory fluid of the male. The prostate is dependent on the male hormone, testosterone, to function normally.

Incidence of and Risk Factors for Prostate Cancer

It is estimated that 165,000 cases of prostate cancer will be diagnosed in the United States in 1994. At the time of diagnosis, the average age of prostate cancer patients is 73 with only 2% of patients younger than 50. After the age of 50, prostate cancer rises with age more rapidly than does any other cancer. Furthermore, black males possess a higher incidence of prostate cancer than do white males.

A geographic influence also evidences itself in this cancer. Although prostate cancer is extremely common in Northern Europe, the United States, and Canada, it is quite rare in Asia. However, Japanese men who have immigrated to the United States experience a substantially higher frequency of prostate cancer than do native Japanese. The role of diet in prostate cancer has been studied extensively. A correlation does appear to exist between a high consumption of dietary fat and prostate cancer. This information appears to implicate environmental and dietary factors in the origin of prostate cancer.

Although the primary cause of prostate cancer remains unknown, many researchers believe that hormonal factors play a pivotal role. A number of studies specifically implicate testosterone, the male hormone that stimulates the growth of the normal prostate gland. For example, when high levels of testosterone are sustained in laboratory mice, the mice frequently develop prostate cancer. Moreover, prostate cancer virtually never develops in men who have been castrated. Research indicates that testosterone stimulates growth in 80% of human prostate cancers, whereas the removal of testosterone retards such growth. These observations implicate, but do not prove, a causal role for testosterone in prostate cancer.

Symptoms and Screening

Because of its location beneath the bladder, the prostate gland can affect the nature of the urine stream. Not surprisingly, the most common symptoms noted by prostate cancer patients involve changes in urinary habits. Symptoms include an inability to urinate, difficulty in either beginning or maintaining the urine stream, and pain during urination. It should be emphasized that these general symptoms can be caused by both benign and malignant conditions. Constant back pain, a common symptom in patients with advanced prostate cancer, occurs frequently in benign conditions as well. Unfortunately, most men with early prostate cancer experience no symptoms at all.

The easiest method of detecting prostate cancer in its early stages is through routine rectal examination. Because of its location, the prostate gland can be examined only by internal palpation through the anus. By inserting a finger approximately 3 inches into the rectum and pointing in the direction of the patient's navel, the doctor is able to locate the walnut-sized prostate gland. Medical students are taught that the normal prostate feels soft, like the tip of the nose, whereas a cancerous prostate feels hard, like the top of the forehead. The rectal examination is a simple but important test in evaluating the condition of the prostate.

Recently, two other tests have been developed. A laboratory test known as *prostatic specific antigen* (PSA) detects elevated levels of a certain protein antigen in patients with prostate cancer. Because this blood test can be abnormal in benign conditions of the prostate as well, the PSA cannot definitely confirm the presence of cancer. A second screening technique currently under evaluation is *transrectal sonography*. In this test, a probe utilizing high-frequency sound waves is inserted into the rectum, much like a rectal thermometer, with the purpose of projecting an image of the prostate gland. Some researchers believe that this ultrasound method offers twice the accuracy of a rectal examination in detecting prostate cancer.

However, utilizing these new tests as routine screening procedures for prostate cancer remains controversial. After reviewing all pertinent information in 1989, a United States Public Health Task Force concluded that neither the PSA nor transrectal sonography is an advisable screening test for patients without symptoms. The study cites two reasons for this conclusion: first, both screening tests are frequently abnormal in benign conditions; and second, there is no absolute proof that the early detection of prostate cancer reduces mortality due to prostate cancer. In direct contradiction of this study, the American Cancer Society studied PSA and recommended in November of 1992 that the PSA be used as a screening test for prostate cancer in all men older than 50.

At present, it is most accurate to say that the role of these screening tests is being defined. The standard screening procedure for the early detection of prostate cancer remains rectal examination by a physician, although the PSA appears to be a quite promising screening test as well.

Diagnosis of Prostate Cancer

Any area of the prostate gland appearing nodular or hard on rectal examination must be investigated. Fortunately, not all detected abnormalities are cancerous; in fact, studies indicate that only 50% of the nodules or growths detected by physicians prove cancerous.

The noncancerous condition that mimics prostate cancer and accounts for one half of all prostate nodules is *benign prostatic hypertrophy* (BPH). Associated with aging, BPH occurs when the prostate gland irregularly enlarges, giving rise to isolated nodules. BPH occurs in 50% of men older than 50 and in 75% of men older than 80. As BPH never occurs in eunuchs, testosterone is believed to stimulate the condition.

Prostate nodules can be caused by either BPH or prostate cancer, so biopsies should be performed on all suspicious nodules. The biopsy is performed by a urologist, a doctor who specializes in the urinary system. By inserting a hollow needle into the prostate, the urologist obtains a core of tissue for microscopic examination. Only by inspecting the nodule in this manner can a certain diagnosis be made.

Prognosis: Stage and Grade

If the tissue is cancerous, both the stage and grade of the cancer must be determined. Stage is a measurement of the amount of cancer; grade is an estimate of the cancer's rate of growth. The cancer's stage and grade are the factors used in formulating the patient's prognosis and treatment recommendations.

To stage a prostate cancer accurately, tests are performed to ascertain whether the cancer has spread beyond the prostate. Unlike many other types of cancer, prostate cancer tends to spread in a predictable manner to the pelvic lymph nodes and the bones. This *pattern of spread* holds true for 80% of prostate cancers. So rarely does a patient with prostate cancer develop cancer in a site such as the brain or liver that, when he does, the doctor typically suspects a second, unrelated cancer.

Staging procedures for patients with prostate cancer include bone scans and x rays. Routinely, two blood tests, PSA and prostatic acid phosphatase, are performed. Markedly elevated levels in these blood tests often indicate that the cancer has spread beyond the prostate gland.

Not uncommonly, all staging tests of the prostate cancer patient are normal. However, the possibility of cancer in the pelvic lymph nodes remains, so urologists frequently remove these nodes in a procedure known as a *pelvic lymphadenectomy*. Performed before any extensive surgery on the prostate, this procedure is necessary to confirm the presence of cancer and its stage.

Based on the collective results of rectal examination, blood tests, bone scan, and biopsies, a prostate cancer is classified into one of four stages.

- Stage A. The cancer is not detectable on rectal examination. The doctor initially suspects BPH; however, a subsequent biopsy confirms the presence of cancer.
- Stage B. The cancer is a single nodule on the prostate that appears to be confined to the gland itself.
- Stage C. The cancer has spread beyond the prostate gland but has not involved the lymph nodes or other organs.
- Stage D. The cancer has spread beyond the prostate gland to such sites as the pelvic lymph nodes or bones.

The stage of the cancer is an important prognostic indicator because the more advanced the stage, the less favorable the prognosis.

Another key prognostic indicator is the *grade* of the prostate cancer. Grade refers to the appearance of cancerous tissue under microscopic examination. Cancers are rated on a scale from 1 to 4, with the lowest grade assigned to cancers most closely resembling normal prostate tissue. Prostate cancers with grades of 1 and 2 have favorable prognoses; those with grades of 3 and 4 are decidedly more difficult to treat and cure.

Unique Characteristics of Prostate Cancer

It should be emphasized that there are two distinct types of prostate cancer. Of greatest concern to men is the active type that can spread to other organs. Because this type of prostate cancer can be life threatening, it requires aggressive treatment.

In contrast, the second type of prostate cancer, which almost never threatens the patient, is early stage and low grade. This latent type was discovered some years ago through autopsy studies of men who showed no evidence of prostate cancer while alive. Startling as it may seem, these autopsy statistics revealed that 25% of men older than 50 and 50% of men older than 70 had prostate cancer! Such disturbing information can be interpreted in this way: A substantial percentage of men older than 50 have stage A prostate cancer, an innocuous type of cancer. When examined under the microscope, stage A prostate cancers are invariably low grade. Moreover, the stage A prostate gland appears benign on rectal examination. Indeed, so inherently harmless is this type of cancer that patients die *with* the disease rather than *of* it.

Treatment of Prostate Cancer

As prostate cancer is largely a disease of elderly men, many patients have serious medical problems that must be considered when formulating programs of treatment. Patients must also be strong enough to tolerate the rigors of surgery or radiation. Frequently, doctors tailor treatment recommendations to suit the patient's overall medical condition.

Most important, the treatment of prostate cancer depends on the cancer's stage. Early-stage prostate cancers, those confined exclusively to the prostate gland, can be cured by either surgery or radiation. However, when the cancer has spread to distant sites, treatments are effective only in arresting rather than curing it. The treatment of prostate cancer is perhaps best discussed on a stage-by-stage basis with the use of case studies.

- Stage A. Patients with stage A prostate cancer typically seek medical help for problems related to urinating. On rectal examination, the stage A prostate is frequently enlarged and free of suspicious nodules. However, in order to alleviate the obstruction to the urine flow, a section of the gland is surgically removed and examined. Should this section contain low-grade cancerous tissue measuring less than 2 cm^3, the cancer is classified as stage A. One accepted treatment for stage A cancer is frequently *no therapy*. Such patients are periodically given rectal examinations and blood tests, as illustrated by the case of J.D.

  J.D. is a 77-year-old man who had experienced difficulty in voiding for 3 months before seeing a doctor. When examined by a urologist, J.D.'s prostate gland was enlarged but without any discrete nodules. Believing that J.D. had a benign enlargement, the urologist recommended removing the enlarged portion of the prostate. Laboratory analyses, however, showed that the prostate tissue contained a localized area of low-grade cancer. Further staging identified the cancer as stage A. When his doctor recommended only periodic check-ups, J.D. was greatly relieved. At present, J.D. receives a rectal examination and blood tests every 3 months.

  J.D.'s experience is quite typical of patients with stage A prostate cancer. He is elderly, and his prostate, on examination, showed no distinct nodules. Moreover, his cancer is low grade with no evidence of spread. Unfortunately, not all stage A prostate cancers are as easily diagnosed as J.D.'s. Whenever the diagnosis is doubtful, another prostate biopsy should be performed.

- Stage B. The prostate cancer involves a cancerous nodule that is wholly confined to the gland itself. The best treatment for stage B prostate cancer remains controversial, but this disease is successfully cured by either surgically removing the gland or radiating it. Most urologists advise the surgical option, recommending radiation only for patients not medically suited for surgery. Of course, treatment recommendations must be individualized after the doctor confers with the patient and family.

Before surgical removal of the prostate, a pelvic lymphadenectomy is usually performed to confirm the definitive stage of the cancer. If the lymph nodes are cancerous, the prostate gland is not removed.

- Stage C. The prostate cancer extends beyond the prostate gland without involving the pelvic lymph nodes or bones. Although surgery can occasionally cure this stage of cancer, the best form of therapy remains controversial. A staging lymphadenectomy is performed whenever the lymph nodes do not appear to be diseased. Unfortunately, patients presumed to have stage C prostate cancer who undergo this procedure are frequently found to have involvement of the pelvic lymph nodes with prostate cancer. For this reason, most urologists tend to be conservative in recommending removal of the prostate for stage C disease; instead, they generally recommend radiation.

As in all prostate cancers, both the grade of the cancer and the overall medical condition of the patient also influence treatment recommendations. The case of W.H. illustrates how multiple factors are considered in formulating a treatment plan.

W.H. is a 68-year-old man who came to the emergency room complaining of a high fever and an inability to urinate over an 18-hour period. His medical history included a massive heart attack 2 years previously.

On admission, he was found to have infections in both urine and blood. A rectal examination showed a rock-hard nodule extending beyond the prostate gland. This nodule had blocked the urine stream, causing infection. Staging studies, which included a PSA, prostatic acid phosphatase, and bone scan, revealed no evidence of distant spread. After treatment for the urine infection, a biopsy confirmed a low-grade prostate cancer.

As W.H. was believed to have a stage C prostate cancer, a pelvic lymphade-nectomy was considered in order to stage the lymph nodes. At this point, the urologist and family doctor conferred. In view of W.H.'s heart condition, they concluded that he was not a candidate for surgery and recommended radiation.

Two key facts influenced the treatment recommendation of radiation for W.H. First, there is no consensus as to the best therapy for stage C prostate cancer. Second, W.H.'s overall medical condition placed him at risk for prostate surgery. Clearly, radiation therapy was in W.H.'s best interest.

- Stage D. The cancer extends beyond the prostate, typically to the lymph nodes or bones. The aim of treatment is to control the cancer wherever it is. With therapy, stage D prostate patients frequently achieve remissions longer than 15 months. When the remission ends, therapy must be resumed.

Because prostate cancer is stimulated by the male hormone, testosterone, removing the hormone significantly retards the cancer's rate of growth. The treatment of choice for stage D prostate cancer, therefore, is a dramatic reduction in the body's level of testosterone. Three methods are commonly used to achieve such a reduction, all of which usually result in impotence. Although current research indicates that these treatments are equally effective in controlling prostate cancer, physicians often differ in their preference of treatment options.

Orchiectomy is the surgical removal of the testicles in order to rid the body of testosterone. It is a simple surgical procedure that is frequently performed on an outpatient basis. Some patients prefer such surgery because it minimizes the need for continued treatment, but others cannot accept the reality of castration.

The second method of treating stage D prostate cancer relies on *estrogen*, the female hormone, to reduce testosterone's effect. The most commonly used hormone is diethylstilbestrol (DES), which patients take in tablet form three times daily. DES should be used cautiously, however, as patients with heart conditions can develop such serious side effects as clotting in the veins and fluid retention.

The third method of treating stage D prostate cancer involves the use of a synthetic compound, *leuprolide acetate*, to suppress the body's production of testosterone. Given as a monthly injection, leuprolide acetate causes few side effects.

Despite these interventions, a small amount of testosterone can continue to be produced by the adrenal gland. A drug frequently used to block these remaining traces of testosterone is *flutamide*. Given as a tablet three times daily, flutamide often is used in conjunction with either orchiectomy or leuprolide acetate.

These methods of testosterone reduction are effective in fully 85% of stage D prostate cancer patients. Nevertheless, when the positive effects of hormonal reduction wane, the reserve treatment of chemotherapy can be considered. In contrast to the high success rate of hormonal reduction, however, chemotherapy is effective in only 15% of stage D patients. In view of chemotherapy's low response rate, many patients who are frail or elderly never do receive it. Of course, the use of chemotherapy is best considered on a patient-by-patient basis.

Because of prostate cancer's typical pattern of spread, stage D patients encounter two frequent complications. The first is bone pain resulting from prostate cancer that has invaded the bones. Patients experiencing such bone cancer pain are given radiation to shrink these cancers as well as medications to control pain. In rare instances, prostate cancer that has spread to the spinal column presses on the spinal cord, causing pain and paralysis. Because spinal cord compression constitutes a medical emergency, the patient must seek prompt medical attention. (See Chapter 23, Pain Control, and Chapter 13, Radiation Therapy.)

The second complication often experienced by stage D prostate patients is obstruction of the urine stream. Because of the prostate gland's proximity to the bladder, enlargement of the prostate can cause a blockage in the flow of urine. Frequently, the surgical removal of prostate tissue is required to relieve an obstruction. Cancerous lymph nodes in the pelvic area can also obstruct the flow of urine from the kidney to the bladder. For these patients, a tube must be inserted into the kidneys to relieve the obstruction.

Unfortunately, a high percentage of patients with stage D prostate cancer do develop either bone pain or urinary obstruction during the course of illness. Table 4-1 summarizes the treatment of prostate cancer according to stage.

Some patients who are initially diagnosed with early-stage prostate cancers (A, B, or C) ultimately develop symptoms of dis-

Table 4-1
Treatment of Prostate Cancer by Stage

Stage	Therapy recommendation	Comment
Stage A	Observation	The patient should be examined periodically. This cancer is regarded as an "incidental finding"
Stage B	Surgical removal of prostate or radiation therapy	Survival rates for both methods are equal. Although medical research remains inconclusive, most urologists believe surgery is the best treatment. Staging of pelvic lymph nodes is often required. Recommendations are made on a patient-by-patient basis
Stage C	Surgical removal of prostate or radiation therapy	The best therapy is controversial. Radiation therapy is usually favored, especially with high-grade cancers. Overall condition of the patient is crucial in determining treatment
Stage D	Testosterone reductions: orchiectomy, estrogens, or leuprolide acetate	All methods of testosterone reduction are equally effective. Bone pain and urinary obstructions are common problems
	Radiation therapy or chemotherapy	Radiation therapy is standard treatment for bone pain. Chemotherapy can be considered when testosterone reduction fails

SOURCE: *Prostate Cancer, Information for Physicians.* National Cancer Institute's PDQ System Cancer Fax, 1993.

tant spread. When this occurs, the patient immediately receives treatment for stage D prostate cancer. W.H., the patient who was previously discussed as having stage C cancer, later developed symptoms of progressive prostate cancer.

After W.H. completed the prescribed course of radiation therapy, he was symptom free for 18 months. W.H. then developed pain in the left hip. Blood tests, the prostatic acid phosphatase, and PSA showed elevations, and a bone scan further revealed abnormalities in the left hip, all of which indicated progressive prostate cancer.

W.H. now required testosterone reduction to check the stage D cancer's spread. Because of his heart condition, estrogen was not an option. With the choice of treatments narrowed to either orchiectomy or leuprolide injections, W.H. was advised that both options would prove equally effective.

After a discussion with his family and urologist, W.H. chose orchiectomy. A few days after surgery, his bone pain subsided and his blood work improved. He continued to look and feel well for 9 months, at which time he suffered a massive heart attack and died.

The prompt relief in bone pain that W.H. experienced following the orchiectomy illustrates how effective testosterone reduction can be in controlling pain. Moreover, prostate patients can expect this pain relief to continue for many months. As in the case of W.H., however, patients are frequently plagued as much by other medical conditions as by the prostate cancer itself.

5

Gynecologic Cancers

Gynecologic cancers refer to cancers that develop in the female reproductive organs, that is, the uterus, cervix, and ovaries. With more than 75,000 gynecologic cancers diagnosed each year in the United States, one in every 20 American women is expected to develop this type of cancer during her lifetime.

Although the incidence of gynecologic cancer is relatively high, this rate has declined sharply over the last 40 years. For example, since 1940, the number of deaths caused by uterine cancer has decreased more than 70%. Presently, almost all cervical cancers that are detected in the early stages are curable. Such success is primarily attributable to the routine use of screening procedures in female medical care: pelvic or internal examinations and Pap smears. Unfortunately, these screening practices are not particularly useful in either preventing or detecting ovarian cancer. A notoriously silent and elusive disease, ovarian cancer is generally diagnosed in advanced stages.

Anatomy of the Gynecologic Organs

The female reproductive organs are located in the pelvis. The vagina or birth canal, which is situated between the bladder and rectum, leads into the uterus or womb, the hollow pear-shaped organ capable of sustaining a new human life. At the base of the uterus is the cervix, which links the vagina to the uterus. The uterus is positioned above the bladder. Situated to the left and right of the uterus are the egg-producing ovaries; eggs travel from the ovaries to the uterus via the fallopian tubes. Figure 5-1 illustrates the location of the female reproductive organs.

Symptoms and Screening

In the earliest and most curable stages, gynecologic cancers produce few symptoms. The symptom most commonly evidenced by cervical and uterine cancers, however, is vaginal bleeding. In contrast to normal menstrual bleeding, cancer-induced bleeding is unpredictable in terms both of frequency and duration. In advanced stages, these cancers can also trigger pelvic pain. Although early-stage ovarian cancers cause virtually no symptoms, late-stage cancers can produce abdominal discomfort or bloating.

Because pure symptoms cannot be relied on to establish early diagnoses in this class of cancers, the routine pelvic examination becomes the essential method of prevention and detection. The gynecologic organs, especially the cervix and uterus, are quite easily and effectively screened for cancer during this procedure.

During a pelvic examination, the physician inserts a smooth tong-like instrument known as a speculum into the vagina in order to push back the vaginal walls so that the cervix can be viewed. The surface of the cervix is then gently touched with a swab in order to obtain a specimen or *Pap smear* for later analysis under the microscope. The physician then performs a manual examination or *palpation* of the uterus and ovaries.

The routine pelvic examination is an excellent screening method for uterine and cervical cancer. It is estimated that fully 90% of cervical cancers and approximately 50% of uterine cancers can be detected by this procedure.

The American Cancer Society currently recommends that all

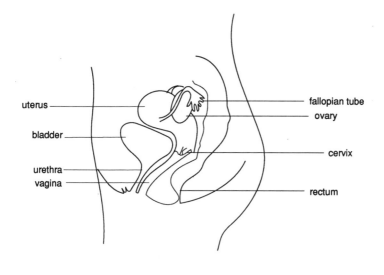

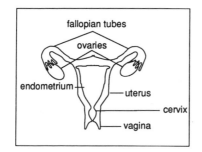

Figure 5-1. Anatomy of female gynecologic organs.

women in their early 20s initially receive pelvic examinations and Pap smears for 2 consecutive years followed by routine examinations every 3 years thereafter. Even though the widespread institution of these screening methods has effected a marked decrease in the mortality rate due to cervical and uterine cancers, 33% of American women do not regularly participate in these examinations.

At present, there is no simple and accurate screening test for ovarian cancer. As pap smears detect fewer than 5% of these cancers, and vaginal bleeding exists as a symptom in only 25% of women with this disease, ovarian cancers are generally diagnosed in the later stages. Nevertheless, a blood test known as CA-125 is usually elevated in women with this cancer. Consequently, the test is currently under evaluation as a possible screening procedure.

Common Surgeries Used to Treat Gynecologic Cancers

The most frequently used treatment for gynecologic cancer is the surgical removal of the diseased organ. A *hysterectomy* is the surgical procedure consisting of the removal of the uterus and cervix, whereas a *radical hysterectomy* involves the removal of the upper vagina, cervix, uterus, and surrounding lymph nodes. A *bilateral salpingo-oophorectomy* entails the removal of the fallopian tubes and both ovaries.

As the treatment of gynecologic cancers has become quite complex, physicians known as *gynecologic oncologists* now specialize in the treatment of these cancers. A procedure commonly performed by gynecologic oncologists, especially for the treatment of ovarian cancers, is *tumor debulking*. In addition to the complete removal of the female reproductive organs, tumor debulking involves a thorough exploration of the entire abdominal area. During this procedure, the surgeon attempts to remove all visible evidence of cancer as well as obtain tissue samples from multiple sites in the abdomen. In cases of severe spread, the surgeon may even deem it necessary to remove the bladder, lower colon, and rectum. Whenever the possibility of such extensive surgery exists, many general gynecologists opt to refer their patients to gynecologic oncologists. (See Chapter 12, Surgery.)

Although gynecologic cancers share many features, each of these cancers behaves distinctly and requires a particular mode of treatment. Therefore, each type of gynecologic cancer will be considered individually.

Cervical Cancer

Cervical cancer constitutes a success story of medical research in that the cure rate for this particular cancer is currently 90%. Not only have the risk factors for this disease been determined but a reliable screening test in the form of a Pap smear has also been established. Moreover, the slow and predictable behavior pattern of this disease is now thoroughly understood.

Research concludes that the two primary risk factors for cervical cancer are a highly active sexual life and low socioeconomic status. If a woman engages in sexual activity before the age of 20 and has multiple sexual partners, her risk of cervical cancer rises considerably. For example, the risk of prostitutes incurring cervical cancer is 4 times greater than that of celibate women. In addition, women of low socioeconomic status have 5 times the risk of developing cervical cancer as do those of higher status.

In fact, cervical cancer is now considered a sexually transmitted disease. Many authorities believe that a sexually transmitted virus, the human papillomavirus (HPV), is the probable agent of transmission because this virus is found in more than 90% of cervical cancers. The object of intensive medical research, this virus is now known to infect 20% of sexually active women, only 1% of whom eventually develop cervical cancer.

In the vast majority of patients, cervical cancer originates at the border between the cervix and uterus. As cervical cells undergo a characteristically slow progression of precancerous changes, the pap smear is able to reveal the early phases of such change.

When the Pap smear is examined under the microscope by the pathologist, the earliest change that can been detected is known as *carcinoma in situ* (CIS). This cellular change is graded on a scale of 1 to 3, with stages 1 and 2 described as *dysplastic,* meaning the cervical cells are benign but abnormal in that they have lost their normal pattern of organization. CIS 3, however, defines the earliest stage of cervical cancer, because malignant cells are present in the first layer of cells lining the cervix.

Whenever malignant or abnormal cells are detected, additional testing is necessary. Unlike the Pap smear, the supplemental procedures of biopsy and *conization* entail the excision of cervical tissue. The biopsy can usually be performed in the physician's office, but conization, which involves the more extensive removal of a cone-shaped piece of tissue from the cervix, is typically performed in a hospital operating room under general anesthesia. These tests provide adequate tissue samples for the purpose of staging the cancer. If malignant cells have not penetrated into the cervix, the cancer is classified as CIS 3. However, if malignant cells have penetrated below the first layer of the cervix, the cancer is considered invasive.

Stages of Cervical Cancer

If the cancer is considered invasive, further testing is necessary to determine the degree of spread. Initially, a procedure known as a *colposcopy* is performed. In this procedure, the cervix is coated with a solution that whitens abnormal areas on contact, thus enabling the physician to examine the suspicious site with a magnifying instrument or colposcope and to perform a more precise biopsy.

In addition to routine blood tests, computed tomography (CT) scans, and chest x ray, the patient may also be given a thorough pelvic examination under anesthesia as well as a *cystoscopy* (examination of the bladder with a lighted flexible tube) and *sigmoidoscopy* (examination of the rectum with a lighted flexible tube). Based on the results of these tests, the physician employs a set of guidelines known as a staging system to classify the cancer. The stages of cervical cancer are as follows.

- Carcinoma in situ (Stage 0). This is the earliest cancerous phase denoting cellular changes in the outermost layer of the cervix. Because of the effectiveness of the Pap screening test, fully 66% of cervical cancer patients are diagnosed in this early stage. The 5-year survival rate for these patients is 100%.
- Stage I. The cancer is confined exclusively to tissues of the cervix.

Depending on the amount of cervical involvement, the 5-year survival rate ranges from 65% to 90%.

- Stage II. The cancer has spread beyond the cervix to the border of the uterus or upper vagina. Depending on the amount of involvement, the 5-year survival rate ranges from 50 to 80%.
- Stage III. The cancer has spread throughout the pelvic area, possibly involving the lower vagina and pelvic bones. The 5-year survival rate is as high as 60%.
- Stage IV. The cancer has spread beyond the organs of the pelvis. The 5-year survival rate is less than 15%.

Treatment of Cervical Cancer

The treatment of cervical cancer is dependent on the stage of the cancer and the overall medical condition of the patient, as well as the patient's wishes concerning her reproductive capacity. The following is a synopsis of treatments by stage.

- Carcinoma in situ (Stage 0). Localized surgery, aimed at eradicating the focus of the cancer, is extremely curative for this stage. Such surgery includes the previously mentioned conization as well as *cryosurgery* and *laser surgery*. Cryosurgery employs a freezing technique to destroy cancer cells, whereas laser surgery utilizes a powerful narrow beam of light. In order to ensure that the cancer does not recur, such patients must have Pap smears every 4 to 6 months after surgery. Although the benefit of all conservative surgery is that fertility is preserved, women with CIS who no longer desire to maintain their fertility may elect hysterectomy.
- Stage I. Either hysterectomy or local radiation therapy (RT) is curative for the earliest phases of this stage. (Radiation therapy, the treatment of cancer with powerful x rays, is discussed in Chapter 13.) However, if the cancer penetrates more than 3 mm of cervical tissue, the patient must be treated with either a radical hysterectomy or RT of the cervix and pelvic lymph nodes.
- Stage II. Although this stage is treated with either RT or radical

hysterectomy, the lymph nodes of the pelvis are always routinely treated with RT. Generally, RT is used as the primary treatment in more extensive cancers.

- Stage III. This stage is treated with RT. Surgery is performed for diagnostic purposes. The role of chemotherapy is presently being evaluated.
- Stage IV. This stage can be treated with RT, surgery, or chemotherapy, with the choice of therapy depending on the extent of disease.

Fortunately, cervical cancer is diagnosed in the majority of patients in the early stages. As a result, their prognosis is excellent, as typified by the case of E.S.

E.S. is a 38-year-old woman who had not had a gynecologic exam since the birth of her only child 11 years earlier. After scheduling a routine exam with her gynecologist, she was informed that her Pap smear indicated cervical changes, a CIS 3. A repeat Pap smear yielded identical results.

She was referred to a gynecologic oncologist, who performed a colposcopy. During this magnifying procedure, the cervix was found to have a small tumorous area. When a subsequent biopsy showed no invasion of underlying tissue, and other staging tests revealed no evidence of spread, E.S. was determined to have a stage 0 cervical cancer.

A discussion of treatment options ensued with her gynecologic oncologist, centering on E.S.'s choice regarding future fertility. If E.S. desired to have children, the treatment recommendation was conization with close follow-up care, and if E.S. opted not to have children, the treatment recommendation was hysterectomy. E.S. elected the latter, and 3 years later she remains free of cancer.

As a young woman with no noticeable symptoms whose Pap smear is found to be abnormal, E.S.'s experience is quite typical of patients with cervical cancer.

Uterine Cancer

Cancer of the uterus is the most common gynecologic cancer; it is expected to affect 35,000 women in 1994. As 75% of cases occur in women older than 50 years, uterine cancer is primarily a disease of elderly women. This type of cancer is also highly curable.

The risk factors of uterine cancer are well defined. In contrast to cervical cancer, uterine cancer tends to be a disease associated with higher socioeconomic class. Heredity, too, appears to play a role, because 15 to 25% of patients claim a family history of uterine cancer. Yet another factor indicating increased risk is obesity; women who are 50 pounds overweight run a ninefold risk of developing uterine cancer. In addition, women with a history of menstrual irregularities, often caused by an imbalance of the female hormones estrogen and progesterone, are also at increased risk of contracting a specific type of uterine disease, cancer of the mucous membranes or *endometria*. Prolonged estrogen supplementation, which is usually prescribed to relieve the symptoms of menopause, has also been found to increase the risk of uterine cancer.

The first symptom of uterine cancer in 90% of patients is vaginal bleeding. Because uterine cancer develops inside the uterus, the Pap smear detects fewer than 50% of uterine cancers. Consequently, in order to diagnose this cancer, the inner lining of the uterus must usually be biopsied in a procedure known as a *dilatation and curettage* (D&C). The D&C involves the vaginal insertion of an instrument through the opening of the cervix for the purpose of scraping and removing any growths adhering to the inner uterine wall. The tissue samples obtained in this procedure are then sent to a pathologist for laboratory analysis.

Once the diagnosis of uterine cancer is established, further tests are performed to determine whether the cancer has spread to other parts of the body. Such tests generally include a chest x ray, physical examination, and blood tests. For a patient suspected of having a late-stage cancer, a CT scan and examination under general anesthesia are often performed. The stages of uterine cancer are as follows.

- Stage 0. The uterine cells are either in a precancerous condition called *hyperplasia* or in the earliest stage of true cancer, known as CIS. The rate of survival in this stage is nearly 100%.

- Stage I. The cancer is confined to the uterus with no involvement of the cervix. A crucial factor of this stage that determines prognosis is the cancer's depth of penetration into the uterine wall. Depending on the depth of penetration, the 5-year survival rate ranges between 75 and 95%.
- Stage II. The cancer involves both the uterus and cervix. The 5-year survival rate is 60%.
- Stage III. The cancer has spread beyond the uterus to the pelvic area. The 5-year survival rate is approximately 30%.
- Stage IV. The cancer has spread beyond the pelvic area to distant sites in the body. The 5-year survival rate is approximately 5%.

The stage-by-stage treatment of uterine cancer is as follows.

- Stage 0. Either hormonal therapy followed by a D&C or hysterectomy is the acceptable treatment. Increasing evidence indicates that hyperplasia can be reversed by the administration of the female hormone, progesterone. To ascertain whether abnormal cellular changes have been reversed, however, the patient must undergo a follow-up D&C.
- Stage I. Either a hysterectomy that includes the removal of the ovaries or a radical hysterectomy is the treatment of choice. So that the extent of the cancer may be definitively established, the majority of patients receive a radical hysterectomy. Depending on the surgical findings, the presence of cancerous lymph nodes or a depth of invasion greater than 50%, the patient may also receive postoperative RT.
- Stage II. The recommended therapy is a combination of radical hysterectomy and RT, the latter of which can be given either before or after the surgery because survival rates of both approaches are comparable.
- Stage III. Radical hysterectomy followed by RT is a common treatment; however, RT is the sole therapy for patients whose cancers are inoperable. Hormonal therapy in the form of progesterone is also used in selected patients. Currently, the role of chemotherapy is being investigated.
- Stage IV. Treatment is individualized. Given the distant spread

of this stage cancer, radical surgery is not generally performed. RT is often employed in an effort to control the cancer and reduce such symptoms as pain or bleeding. Progesterone and chemotherapy are also used.

Ovarian Cancer

Ovarian cancer is the third most common gynecologic cancer with 18,000 patients diagnosed yearly. As this type of cancer seldom causes symptoms before reaching an advanced stage, ovarian cancer is undoubtedly the most difficult gynecologic cancer to cure. Consequently, it causes more deaths each year than do the cervical and uterine cancers combined.

The primary risk factor for ovarian cancer is family history. A woman who has a mother or sister with ovarian cancer runs a 20-fold greater risk of developing ovarian cancer herself. Women with a history of breast or colon cancer are also known to be at increased risk. Length of menstruation is yet another risk factor; women who have menstruated longer than 40 years or who have experienced a late menopause likewise share an elevated risk. For unknown reasons, the incidence of ovarian cancer is decidedly higher in Western industrialized countries.

Unfortunately, no accepted screening test exists yet for ovarian cancer. Compounding the difficulty of diagnosis is the fact that most complaints symptomatic of this cancer are nonspecific and ascribable to various intestinal problems. As most symptoms of ovarian cancer are caused by tumor involvement of the intestinal organs, common symptoms include bloating, nausea, vomiting, abdominal discomfort, and swelling of the abdomen.

Consequently, initial diagnostic tests are often aimed at evaluating the intestinal tract and yield inconclusive results. When these symptoms persist, further testing of the pelvis is needed. During a pelvic examination, the physician carefully palpates the organs of the pelvis to check for abnormalities. In a sonogram, sound waves visually define organs to allow a more thorough examination. Blood tests are also ordered in an attempt to determine the source of the patient's symptoms.

Whenever an ovarian cancer is suspected, a biopsy must be performed to establish the diagnosis. This procedure, known as a *diagnostic laparotomy,* is a surgical exploration of the entire abdomen. Before surgery, however, other staging tests are typically performed, including kidney x rays (intravenous pyelogram), barium enema, and a sigmoidoscopy.

The diagnostic laparotomy provides information that is essential to the accurate staging of an ovarian cancer. Not only is the entire abdominal cavity closely examined, but excess fluid, known as *ascites,* is also removed and analyzed for tumor cells. Additionally, as much cancer as possible is removed in the procedure known as *tumor debulking.*

The stages of ovarian cancer are as follows.

- Stage I. The cancer exists in either one or both ovaries. The presence of malignant ascites or the rupture of the cancerous ovary are features that worsen prognosis. The 5-year survival rate is approximately 80%.
- Stage II. The cancer exists in either one or both ovaries and has spread to other pelvic organs such as the uterus or fallopian tubes. As is true of stage I, the presence of malignant ascites or the rupture of the cancerous ovary worsen prognosis. The 5-year survival rate is 60%.
- Stage III. The cancer of the ovary has spread to either the lymph nodes or to the surfaces of such abdominal organs as the liver or intestine. The 5-year survival rate is approximately 20%.
- Stage IV. The cancer has spread outside the abdomen or into the liver. The 5-year survival rate is approximately 10%.

In addition to stage, the microscopic appearance or *grade* of the ovarian cancer is prognostically important. Ovarian cancers are rated on a scale from 1 to 3 with the lowest grade assigned to cancer cells most closely resembling normal ovarian cells. Expectedly, grade 3 ovarian cancers are more difficult to treat and cure than are grade 1 and 2 cancers.

The stage-by-stage treatment of ovarian cancer is as follows.

- Stage I. Surgery is the mainstay of therapy, typically involving radical hysterectomy with the sampling of lymph nodes and other abdominal tissue.

  Features that may necessitate additional therapy in the form of chemotherapy or RT include a grade 3 cancer, malignant ascites, or the rupture of a cancerous ovary. Chemotherapy generally consists of six cycles of cisplatin and cytoxan given monthly. RT is administered by direct x-ray beam or by the injection of radioactive material into the abdomen. Both of these therapies are given on an adjuvant basis in an effort to destroy any stray cancer cells remaining in the body. (See Chapters 13, Radiation Therapy, and 14, Chemotherapy and Hormonal Therapy.)
- Stage II. The treatment is a radical hysterectomy with sampling of lymph nodes and other tissues of the abdomen. After surgery, either chemotherapy or RT is administered.
- Stage III. The treatment is *tumor-debulking* surgery. Afterward, patients routinely receive chemotherapy; some patients in the early phases of this stage may receive RT.
- Stage IV. Treatment is usually chemotherapy, with RT being used to treat localized problems such as pain.

On completion of all therapy, many gynecologic oncologists recommend a type of exploratory surgery known as a *second-look laparotomy*. This surgery involves abdominal exploration with tissue sampling of former cancerous areas. If no cancer is found, then no further treatment is planned; however, if residual cancer is detected, continued therapy is required.

Representative of many women with ovarian cancer is J.J., a patient whose experience included a second-look laparotomy:

> J.J. is a 45-year-old woman who consulted her family doctor after experiencing a sense of fullness for 3 or 4 months. Postulating that her problem was intestinal in nature, her doctor ordered an upper and lower gastrointestinal series. When these test results proved normal, her doctor then ordered a sonogram of the abdomen. This test revealed a cyst in the area of the left ovary as well as ascites.

J.J. was referred to a gynecologist who ordered a CA-125. When this test was markedly elevated, ovarian cancer was considered a likely diagnosis. At this juncture, J.J. was referred to a gynecologic oncologist.

The physician performed a battery of tests that included x rays, scans, a cystoscopy, and a sigmoidoscopy. When only an enlarged left ovary and ascites were again evidenced, a laparotomy was performed.

In the course of surgery, tiny tumors were noted on the intestines, and the ascites contained malignant cells. These findings indicated a stage III ovarian cancer. Of course, the surgeon removed all visible signs of tumor as a part of the debulking surgery.

J.J. was advised to have 6 months of chemotherapy consisting of cisplatin and cytoxan. On completion of this treatment, J.J.'s CA-125 proved normal. The surgeon then recommended a second-look laparotomy. Fortunately, this procedure evidenced no detectable cancer.

J.J's follow-up care consisted of a physical examination and blood work, including a CA-125, every 3 months. Three years later, she continues to be cancer free.

Quite typical of women with ovarian cancer, J.J. had symptoms that were gradual, nonspecific, and initially indicative of an intestinal problem. At the time of surgery, however, a cancer was found to have spread sporadically through the abdomen. In reality, 65% of women with ovarian cancer are diagnosed in stages III and IV. On completion of the recommended schedule of chemotherapy, J.J. also underwent a second-look laparotomy in order to confirm that the cancer had disappeared.

Sex after Gynecologic Surgery

After completing therapy for gynecologic cancer, the vast majority of women eventually resume their normal sexual patterns. In fact, research confirms that women regain both sexual desire and the capacity for orgasm postoperatively. In their efforts to resume normal sexual function, patients frequently benefit from professional counseling both before and after surgery. This process of sexual readjustment is a formidable problem that many cancer survivors must face after the completion of therapy. (See Chapter 25, The Next Step: Being a Survivor.)

Regardless of age, marital status, or sexual habits, the patient with gynecologic cancer must know that the cancer can be arrested and that a healthy and relaxed sex life can be resumed. Because both the patient and her partner should understand the nature of the disease and the physical as well as the emotional ramifications of therapy, the concerned parties may find a conference with the physician extremely helpful. Certainly, patients require accurate information, most of which can be fundamentally reassuring.

After surgery for gynecologic cancer, the patient is routinely cautioned to avoid intercourse until the physician determines that sufficient healing has occurred. On resuming intercourse, the patient and her partner are advised to proceed gently in a trial-and-error manner. Some couples find that lubricating jelly facilitates penetration, but other couples simply experiment with a variety of positions to achieve mutual satisfaction. In some patients, reconstructive surgery of the vagina may be necessary in order to remove excessive scar tissue.

Should intercourse continue to be painful or unsatisfactory for an extended period, the couple might profit from the counseling of a sex therapist who can instruct them in alternative methods of attaining sexual gratification. Of course, the pivotal factor in a couple's efforts to resume preoperative sexual activity is their openness and willingness to work at the process of sexual rehabilitation.

6

Skin Cancer: Melanoma and Nonmelanoma

Although not commonly viewed as such, the skin is actually a highly specialized organ of the body like the heart, lung, and brain. In addition to being the protective barrier between the body and its environment, the skin performs the vital functions of registering sensation and regulating temperature. Like other body organs, the skin can also give rise to primary cancers.

The most common of all human cancers is skin cancer. In 1993, more than 700,000 cases of skin cancer will be diagnosed in the United States. Because of the public's obsession with tanning, the incidence of skin cancer, and particularly melanoma, continues to climb at an alarming rate. Fortunately, most skin cancers can be cured when detected early.

By increasing public awareness about the methods of preventing and detecting skin cancer, perhaps the current epidemic can be stemmed. Surely, the public needs to become familiar with the techniques of self-examination described in this chapter. Recent research indicates that a skin examination by a dermatologist is as effective a screening test for melanoma as is the Pap smear for cervical cancer and the mammogram for breast cancer.

Risk Factors and Screening

Prolonged exposure to sunlight is an important risk factor for skin cancer. Skin cancer develops most often in areas of the body that are directly exposed to the sun's rays. Individuals with occupations or avocations demanding prolonged exposure to sunlight, such as sailors, farmers, ranchers, and golfers, have a higher incidence of skin cancer than do individuals with indoor occupations. One study involving British men reveals that those who live in sunny areas of the world tend to develop skin cancer more frequently than do those who live in less sunny areas.

The complexion of the individual is another important risk factor for skin cancer. At highest risk are fair-skinned people who burn rather than tan during exposure to sunlight. Traits such as blond or red hair and blue eyes have also been associated with the increased risk of skin cancer. Skin cancer rarely strikes blacks, who appear to be protected from sun damage by increased melanin, a skin pigment that filters out most of the sun's harmful rays.

Moreover, any patient with a prior skin cancer runs an increased risk of developing a second skin cancer. In addition to being periodically examined by a physician, such a patient is instructed to perform regular self-examinations of the skin. This self-examination of the skin can be performed in the following way.

1. In a well-lit room, stand before a full-length mirror and hold a small mirror in your hand. Examine the front of your trunk and, with the aid of the hand-held mirror, examine your back. Raise your arms and closely inspect the right and left sides of your body.
2. Examine your arms. Pay close attention to the palms and forearms. Bend your arms and examine the elbows, upper arms, and underarms.
3. Inspect the front and back of your legs, including the area of the genitals and buttocks, with the aid of the hand-held mirror. Be sure to examine the toes and soles of the feet.
4. Examine your neck and face. Using a comb and blow dryer, carefully inspect your scalp.

For all skin cancers, early detection is the most effective form of treatment. The American Cancer Society cites six changes in the skin that require a doctor's attention.

1. Any sore or wound of the skin that does not heal in 6 weeks.
2. Any area of the skin that bleeds persistently.
3. Any lump or growth that enlarges.
4. Any growth that changes in appearance, size, shape, or color.
5. Any mole that becomes itchy or tender.
6. Any mole that is not uniform in color, or that has irregular edges like a maple leaf.

Once discovered, a skin abnormality needs to be promptly examined by a physician. On the basis of the abnormality's appearance, an experienced family physician or dermatologist can usually make the tentative diagnosis of skin cancer. To confirm such a diagnosis, however, a skin biopsy is necessary. Most skin biopsies are simple procedures performed at the time of the office visit. Typically, the doctor injects the site with a local anesthetic and removes a portion or all of the growth. If the abnormality is large or if malignant melanoma is suspected, the patient may be referred to a surgeon for a complete surgical excision.

Nearly all skin cancers can be classified into three cell types: basal cell, squamous cell, and melanoma. As these skin cancers are quite distinct in appearance, behavior, and treatment, it is best to consider them separately.

Basal Cell Skin Cancer

Basal cell cancer is the most common form of skin cancer, constituting 65% of the 700,000 nonmelanoma skin cancers diagnosed each year in the United States. Basal cell cancer usually develops in patients older than 40 years. It occurs predominantly in men, a fact most probably attributable to the large number of men employed in outdoor occupations. Moreover, this type of skin cancer rarely occurs in members of the black race. Unless neglected for years, basal cell tumors are generally quite small and oval shaped. Occasionally pink or red in color, these tumors are typically wax-like and hard.

With early detection and treatment, basal cell cancers are cured in greater than 95% of patients. The standard therapy for these cancers is surgical removal. In most cases, only minor surgery is required. In advanced cases, however, extensive surgery may be needed, and possibly radiation therapy. As basal cell cancers rarely spread, chemotherapy is virtually never used to treat these cancers.

Squamous Cell Cancer

Squamous cell cancer is the second most common skin cancer and affects the same patient population as do basal cell cancers. More variable in appearance than basal cell cancers, squamous cell cancers often appear rough or reddened, yet also may form crusts with open sores. Unlike basal cell cancers, squamous cell cancers can grow rapidly, developing into burnlike scars and possibly penetrating into the deeper tissues. In fact, such penetration occurs in 2% of patients.

Once a biopsy confirms the diagnosis of squamous cell cancer, the tumor is surgically removed, along with an adequate margin of tissue. In some cases, radiation is given after surgery. Approximately 90% of patients with squamous cell cancer of the skin are cured with treatment. For advanced cases in which simple surgical excision is not feasible, a consultation involving a dermatologist, surgeon, and radiation oncologist is often necessary to determine the best course of treatment for the patient. When squamous cell cancer spreads to other organs, chemotherapy is usually given to control the disease.

Melanoma

Melanoma arises in skin cells that contain pigment. Whereas the other types of skin cancer predominantly affect older patients,

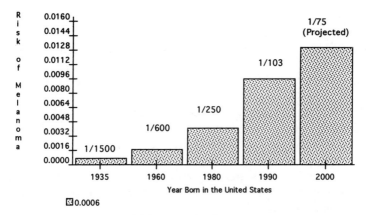

Figure 6-1. Birth year and lifetime risk of developing melanoma in the United States. Adapted from Figure 44-1 in DiVita VT (ed). *Cancer: Principles and Practice of Oncology,* 3rd ed. Philadelphia: Lippincott, 1989.

melanoma occurs frequently in younger patients. At diagnosis, the median age for patients with melanoma is the early 40s. Men and women are equally affected by this type of cancer, though it is decidedly rare in the black and Asian populations. A predisposing factor to melanoma appears to be a history of it in one's immediate family.

According to recent cancer statistics, melanoma may reach epidemic proportions within 15 years. Today, an American's risk of developing melanoma is 12 times as great as it was in the 1930s. As Figure 6-1 illustrates, one in 75 Americans born in the year 2000 is expected to develop melanoma.

It is not known exactly why the incidence of melanoma has risen so rapidly in recent years. Most authorities believe that the dominant cause may be the marked increase in sun exposure that began in the 1950s and 1960s. One recognized authority, Dr. Darrell Rigel of New York University, has found that the duration and intensity of sun exposure during the adolescent years is a major determinant of the risk of melanoma. However, the following factors are also strongly correlated with the risk of developing melanoma: (1) family history of melanoma, (2) blond or red hair, (3) marked freckling on the upper back, (4) three or more blistering sunburns before the age of 20, (5) outdoor employment for 3 or more years during adolescence, and (6) precancerous actinic keratosis. Typically developing after the age of 40, actinic keratosis is defined by small scaling patches that are more easily felt than seen, blending as they do with the surrounding skin. This condition results from cumulative exposure to sunlight.

Any person claiming two of these factors runs a melanoma risk that is 3.5 times greater than that of the general population; three or more of these factors increases the probability to 20 times the average risk.

Another group that has recently been identified at high risk for melanoma are persons with the *dysplastic nevus syndrome.* Dysplastic means atypical or unusual, and nevus is a medical term for skin mole. Persons with this syndrome have many large moles, some of which are melanomalike in appearance. The definition of this syndrome is still evolving, but these features are generally present in each patient: (1) more than 100 moles, (2) at least one mole measuring 8 mm in diameter, and (3) one mole with features that are considered *atypical,* that is, suggestive of melanoma. Medical experts believe that the risk of melanoma in persons with the dysplastic nevus syndrome increases if either the patient or the family has a history of melanoma.

The prevention of melanoma essentially hinges on the protection of the skin from sunlight. Parents must vigilantly shield their young children with protective coverings and sunscreens during outdoor play. Moreover, people of all ages must be alert to the hazards of overexposure to sunlight and take the necessary precautions. Individuals at increased risk for melanoma must regularly practice the procedures for self-screening and consult their doctors regarding suspicious skin changes.

An area of confusion for patients and even doctors is the difference between an ordinary mole and melanoma. At times, only the trained eye of a dermatologist can distinguish between the two. Although biopsies should be performed for suspicious skin changes, the following *ABCD rule* can be helpful in distinguishing between moles and melanomas.

- Asymmetry. Most benign moles are symmetrical; a line drawn through the middle of a mole would produce two halves that are mirror images of one another. Melanomas are typically asymmetrical; a line drawn through the middle of a melanoma would produce two halves that are different from one another.
- Border. Most moles have a distinct border, whereas the border of a melanoma is likely to be blurred or indistinct.
- Color. A mole is usually uniform in color, whereas a melanoma is often uneven in color.
- Diameter. A mole with a diameter greater than the width of a pencil head eraser can be an early sign of melanoma.

Prognosis

At the time of initial diagnosis, most melanomas are localized exclusively in the area of the skin. The predominant prognostic feature of a localized melanoma is the measured thickness of the cancer. In the laboratory, the pathologist simply measures the vertical dimension of the cancer in millimeters. The thinner the melanoma is, the better the prognosis. Localized melanomas measuring less than 0.95 mm in thickness have a cure rate of more than 95%. In contrast, the cure rate of melanomas measuring more than 4 mm is approximately 30%. Obviously, the best treatment for melanoma is the prompt detection and removal of the cancer in its earliest stage.

Another prognostic feature of melanoma is its location in the patient's body. Melanomas originating in the lower limbs actually carry the most favorable diagnosis. The sex of the melanoma patient is also a prognostic factor in that women generally have a better prognosis than do men. Other features contributing to a less favorable prognosis are the advanced age of the patient and the presence of skin ulceration at the time of diagnosis.

Table 6-1

Survival of Melanoma Patients According to Stage at Diagnosis

	All melanoma patients (%)	Survival rate after 15 years (%)
Stage I	47[a]	86[b]
Stage II	38	53
Stage III	13	25
Stage IV	2	Less than 5

[a] Today, 75% of all patients are diagnosed in stage I.
[b] Patients with stage IA melanoma have a survival rate that is greater than 95%.
SOURCE: Adapted from Figure 44-3 in DeVita VT (ed). *Cancer Principles and Practice of Oncology*, 3rd ed. Philadelphia: Lippincott, 1989.

A set of guidelines known as a *staging system* is used to determine a patient's prognosis and recommended course of treatment. To stage a melanoma, both the thickness of the melanoma and the status of the local lymph nodes must be considered.

Lymph nodes are pea-like structures that are located throughout the body to fight infection. During a patient's physical examination, the physician searches for enlarged, melanoma-containing lymph nodes. Such lymph nodes are firm to the touch, are often 2 to 3 times larger than normal lymph nodes, and virtually always contain melanoma cells. In the absence of involved lymph nodes, the stage of the melanoma is based on the thickness of the melanoma. When the lymph nodes are believed to contain melanoma cells, the stage is determined by both the thickness of the melanoma and the status of the lymph nodes. Melanomas are categorized into four stages:

- Stage IA. Localized melanoma less than 0.75 mm in thickness.
- Stage IB. Localized melanoma of 0.76 to 1.5 mm in thickness.
- Stage II. Localized melanoma more than 1.5 mm in thickness.
- Stage III. Melanoma of any thickness with involved lymph nodes.
- Stage IV. Melanoma that has spread to a distant site in the body.

Table 6-1 illustrates the survival rates of melanoma patients by stage, 15 years after diagnosis. Because these statistics were collected from 1955 to 1980, they fail to indicate the greater number of patients now being diagnosed in the early stages of melanoma. Today, 75% of melanoma patients are diagnosed in stage I.

Treatment of Localized Melanoma

Stages I and II

The traditional therapy for early melanoma is the surgical removal of the primary cancer, a procedure known as *wide local excision*. This type of excision requires that the surgeon remove the tumor as well as 1.5 to 3 inches of normal surrounding skin. Although wide local excision is quite effective in controlling the melanoma, this surgery can, depending on the tumor's location, result in disfigurement to the patient.

In the late 1970s, leading cancer authorities began to question the need for such extensive surgery. Thereafter, Dr. Umberto Veronesi of Milan, Italy, compared the efficacy of wide local excision to that of moderate surgery—excising the tumor and only 0.5 inches of surrounding skin. For melanomas less than 1 mm in thickness, moderate excision proved as effective as wide local excision. Consequently, many experts recommend moderate excision for early-stage melanomas. However, wide local excision continues to be regarded as the optimal surgery for melanomas greater than 2 mm in thickness. As no consensus yet exists regarding surgery for melanomas greater than 1 mm but less than 2 mm, this particular decision is best made on a patient-by-patient basis.

Unlike some cancers that are responsive to preventive (adjuvant) chemotherapy following surgery, melanomas are resistant to this type of therapy. (See Chapter 14, Chemotherapy and Hormonal Therapy.) As a result, postsurgical melanoma patients are urged to perform regular self-examinations of the skin and to visit their physicians routinely for follow-up care.

The case of L.W. is typical of early-stage melanoma patients.

L.W. is a 34-year-old man whose wife had noted a slight increase in the dime-sized mole located above his left shoulder blade. He was examined by a dermatologist, who initially suspected melanoma. A biopsy performed in the office confirmed the diagnosis of a melanoma measuring 0.85 mm in thickness.

L.W. showed no evidence of the melanoma's spread; his lymph nodes, x rays, and blood tests were entirely normal. A surgeon then performed a moderate reexcision of the site, a procedure that entailed removing 0.5 inch of surrounding tissue.

L.W. was subsequently seen by an oncologist. During this visit, L.W. was extremely nervous about his diagnosis. The oncologist informed L.W. that no additional therapy was necessary. L.W. was advised simply to be examined regularly by his dermatologist and family doctor. He was also taught how to perform a thorough self-examination of the skin. Four years later, L.W. continues to enjoy good health.

L.W. is representative of most early-stage melanoma patients whose chances of surgical cure are excellent. As these patients are advised to practice regular self-examinations of the skin and visit their personal physicians routinely, they do not require the care of an oncologist.

Stage III

Patients with stage III melanoma have enlarged lymph nodes that are believed to contain melanoma cells. Characteristically, involved nodes are located in the groin, the underarm, and the neck region. The standard treatment for stage III melanoma includes a wide excision of the primary site, followed by a removal of the cancerous lymph nodes. This surgery is done in two steps, with the initial excision being followed by the removal of lymph nodes.

The surgical removal of lymph nodes is called a *lymph node dissection*. As a result of this rather extensive procedure, the patient often develops significant swelling of the involved leg or arm, called *lymphedema*. For instance, a lymph node dissection of the right groin often induces lymphedema of the entire right leg.

Some cancer authorities go so far as to advocate aggressive lymph node dissection for all high-risk melanoma patients, including those whose stage II melanomas are greater than 2 mm in thickness. Because of the extent of surgery and the possibility of lymphedema, however, most doctors recommend lymph node dissection only for patients with obviously abnormal lymph glands. Certainly, this recommendation is standard for stage III patients whose physical condition is good and whose lymph nodes are easily accessible. Moreover, this procedure is recommended whenever it can accomplish the complete removal of all discernible evidence of the cancer. Like earlier stages of melanoma, stage III melanomas are believed to be resistant to preventive (adjuvant) chemotherapy.

Stage IV

In patients with stage IV melanoma, the disease has spread to a distant site (undergone *metastasis*). At the time of diagnosis, only 2% of melanoma patients are found to be in this stage. However, 20% of melanoma patients do eventually develop metastatic disease.

Melanoma is an unusual type of cancer in that it is not particularly responsive to two normally effective cancer treatments, chemotherapy and radiation. Consequently, consideration is sometimes given to the surgical removal of stage IV cancers. A candidate for surgery must have a cancer that has metastasized in only one area, quite typically in the brain or lungs. If metastasis has occurred in more than one organ, surgery is not considered a treatment option.

In an attempt to control rather than cure the cancer, chemotherapy is often administered when surgery is not a viable option for stage IV melanoma patients. At present, chemotherapy succeeds in shrinking metastatic melanomas in about 20% of patients and effects complete remission in nearly 5% of patients. Whenever a metastatic melanoma causes distressing, localized symptoms, radiation therapy is given to control them. Admittedly, stage IV melanoma is quite a difficult cancer to treat. However, one of the most promising areas of melanoma treatment is to be found in biological therapy or immunotherapy. (See Chapter 13, Radiation Therapy, and Chapter 16, Biological Therapy.)

Biological therapy is a treatment method that utilizes the body's natural defense system to destroy cancer cells. Research has revealed that substances known as *cytokines* control the production of white blood cells (WBCs), the body's primary defense against infection. In biological therapy, cytokines are administered to stimulate the body's immune system to fight the cancer.

During the 1980s, biological therapy was largely experimental and still constitutes an active area of research. The first commercially available form of biological therapy was the drug interferon. This is a natural substance produced by WBCs to fight viral infections. Modestly successful against melanoma, interferon is reported to reduce tumors in approximately 30% of patients.

Another biological therapy presently under investigation at a number of research centers is the drug interleukin. Like interferon, interleukin stimulates WBCs to destroy melanoma cells. Preliminary studies indicate that interleukin is particularly effective against melanoma cancers. The response rate for such cancers has been reported to be as high as 45%, with a significant percentage of patients registering complete remissions.

Although most biological treatments are now investigational, this therapy holds considerable promise for the successful treatment of melanoma. As the case of D.K. illustrates, biological therapy can yield excellent results for some melanoma patients.

D.K. is a 37-year-old woman of fair complexion. She had a suspicious mole on her right arm removed by a dermatologist. As there was controversy regarding the pathology report, the material from the biopsy was sent to a second pathologist for expert review. The second pathologist concluded that the mole was a malignant melanoma, 1.8 mm in thickness. As there was no evidence of the melanoma's having spread to another site, D.K. underwent a wide local excision by a surgeon.

After surgery, D.K. was examined periodically by her family physician. Six years after diagnosis, a routine chest x ray showed a shadow 2 inches in diameter on the left lung. A physical examination as well as scans of the chest, abdomen, head, and bone revealed no further abnormalities. Moreover, D.K. felt quite well. D.K.'s physicians recommended surgery. Surgical exploration of the left chest confirmed the presence of a single tumor, which was removed. Pathological analysis determined it to be melanoma. As D.K. showed no evidence of spread, her physicians decided against further treatment, opting instead to monitor her closely.

Eight months after lung surgery, a painful lump developed in D.K.'s left breast over a period of several days. She was examined by a surgeon, who immediately removed the mass. Again, the tumor proved to be melanoma.

A thorough evaluation, including scans of the bone, brain, chest, and abdomen, showed no other area of involvement. As D.K.'s risk of recurrence was extremely high, the oncologist recommended a preventive course of chemotherapy. D.K., however, refused this therapy, opting to be followed monthly by her physicians.

Three months after breast surgery, D.K. developed abdominal pain. On evaluation, she was found to have an isolated mass in her right kidney. A biopsy confirmed that the tumor was melanoma. At this point, the oncologist believed that D.K. had two viable options: surgical removal of the mass or biological therapy. After discussing these options, D.K. decided to apply at the National Cancer Institute (NCI), which is located in Bethesda, Maryland, in order to be considered for investigational biological therapy.

At the NCI, D.K. was admitted to a study evaluating the efficacy of tumor-infiltrating lymphocytes. After receiving a 5-week course of this therapy, D.K. returned home. She was scheduled to return to the NCI in 3 weeks for reevaluation and, quite possibly, a second course of treatment.

While at home, however, D.K. developed an inflammation of the pancreas with abdominal pain and fever that necessitated her admission to a local hospital. An abdominal scan revealed not only that the pancreas was inflamed but that the mass in the right kidney had entirely disappeared! After recovering from the inflammation, D.K. eventually returned to the NCI for further evaluation. As the biological therapy may have caused the pancreas inflammation, she did not receive a second course of treatment at that time.

Three years after her initial lung surgery, D.K. continues to do well with only regular follow-up care by her oncologist.

D.K.'s case is rather unusual in that she received treatment at the NCI rather than at a regional or local medical center. Nevertheless, D.K.'s experience illustrates that melanoma can recur years after initial diagnosis. Because of the limited effectiveness of chemotherapy with melanoma, D.K.'s original treatment was aggressive surgery, followed by investigational biological therapy.

Until more effective therapy for melanoma is developed, the population must continue to rely on time-tested methods of prevention and early detection. This requires an acute awareness of the dangers of excessive sun exposure and perhaps a rather radical adjustment in life style. The public also must become knowledgeable about the appearance of skin cancer and practice self-examination of the skin.

7

Lymphoma: Hodgkin's Disease and Non-Hodgkin's Lymphoma

Cancers originating in the lymph nodes, pea-sized glands found throughout the body that fight infection, are classified as lymphomas. Literally hundreds of these glands harbor lymphocytes or white blood cells that circulate through the bloodstream to combat infectious organisms like viruses and bacteria.

Under microscopic examination, the cancerous lymph node is found to contain malignant-appearing lymphocytes. Although other types of cancers, like breast or colon cancers, often spread to the lymph glands, the cells of such metastasized cancers resemble those produced by the organ of origin rather than lymphoma cells.

Extensive research during the past 20 years has resulted in an increased understanding of lymphoma as well as drastically changed modes of treatment for it. With the discovery that Hodgkin's disease behaves and responds to treatment quite differently than do other types of lymphomas, physicians now classify lymphomas into two categories: Hodgkin's disease and non-Hodgkin's lymphoma. Before specifying these differences, however, the many shared features of lymphoma are considered.

Incidence of and Risk Factors for Lymphoma

In the United States, lymphoma is diagnosed in approximately 45,000 patients yearly; of this number, roughly 37,000 patients are classified with non-Hodgkin's lymphoma and the remaining 8,000, with Hodgkin's disease. The latter disease is especially common in young adults between the ages of 20 and 35, 60% of whom are men, whereas non-Hodgkin's lymphoma is primarily a disease of older adults, with the incidence beginning to rise in the 4th decade of life.

The cause of Hodgkin's disease is unknown. In developed countries, this particular cancer is associated with higher social class, advanced education, and small families. There are many reports of multiple siblings with the disease.

In contrast, non-Hodgkin's lymphomas are often associated with certain viruses and defects in immunity. For example, the onset of African Burkitt's lymphoma is linked to the Epstein–Barr virus. The incidence of non-Hodgkin's lymphoma rises in patients whose immune systems are altered as a result of organ transplantation, congenital deficiency, acquired immunodeficiency syndrome (AIDS), or lupus. Exactly how these viruses and immune deficiencies induce this type of lymphoma is still unknown.

Symptoms and Screening

The most common sign of lymphoma is a painless enlargement of the lymph nodes, usually in the neck, underarm, or groin. Lymph glands normally enlarge during an episode of infection, but such benign enlargement generally resolves over a period of 6 weeks. Certainly, any lymph node that remains noticably enlarged for more than several weeks should be examined by a physician. In addition to sustained enlargement of the lymph glands, other symptoms of lymphoma include fever, weight loss, decreased appetite, night sweats, and fatigue.

Unfortunately, no reliable screening test exists yet for lymphoma. Whereas mammograms can detect early breast cancer, no one test can accurately determine the status of the body's numerous lymph nodes. Nonetheless, patients claiming any of the primary risk factors for this disease should undergo periodic physical examinations by their doctors.

Diagnosis

A biopsy must be performed on any persistently enlarged lymph node to determine the definitive cause of enlargement. A biopsy, of course, involves the surgical removal of the lymph gland. In cases where the lymph nodes are readily accessible, such as the neck or groin, the biopsy can be performed under local anesthetic. When the questionable lymph nodes are located in less accessible areas such as the chest or abdomen, however, more involved surgery is required, usually exploratory in nature.

After the lymph node is removed, it is processed in the laboratory and then studied under the microscope by a pathologist, that is, a physician who specializes in reading slides and making diagnoses. The pathologist must first determine whether the cancer is a lymphoma or some other kind of tumor. If a lymphoma is identified, the architecture of the lymph node must then be studied in order to classify the type of lymphoma. This is a difficult task at best, as there are four subtypes of Hodgkin's disease and more than 10 subtypes of non-Hodgkin's lymphoma. Because the differences between types may be extremely subtle, biopsy slides are often sent to expert pathologists specializing in the classification of lymphomas. Such precise classification is crucial because the type of lymphoma determines the method of treatment.

Once the lymphoma diagnosis is established, further testing is performed to ascertain the extent or stage of the tumor. Routine tests include computed tomography (CT) scans of the abdomen and chest, a bone marrow biopsy of the pelvic bones, and blood tests. In some cases of Hodgkin's disease, the lymph nodes are injected with dye in a test known as a *lymphangiogram*.

Stages and Prognosis of Lymphoma

Physicians use a set of guidelines known as a *staging system* to classify cancers and determine appropriate therapies. The stage of a lymphoma is a function of both its position in the body and its extensiveness. The stages of both Hodgkin's and non-Hodgkin's lymphoma are as follows:

- Stage I. The lymphoma is confined to a single area or group of lymph nodes.
- Stage II. The lymphoma involves two distinct groups of lymph nodes on the same side of the diaphragm. (The diaphragm is a muscle that facilitates breathing and separates the chest from the abdomen.)
- Stage III. The lymphoma is present on both sides of the diaphragm.
- Stage IV. The lymphoma extends beyond the lymph nodes, involving such organs as the lung, liver, or bone marrow.

Each stage is also characterized by telling symptoms known as *B symptoms*, the existence of which generally signifies a worsened prognosis. Included among these symptoms are fevers, night sweats, and weight loss encompassing at least 10% of total body weight. For example, a patient with lymphoma on both sides of the diaphragm who experiences fevers and significant weight loss is classified as stage IIIB.

As noted earlier, the behavior of the two types of lymphoma is quite different. Because Hodgkin's disease tends to spread in a predictable manner from one group of lymph nodes to another, the stage of the lymphoma is the dominant prognostic factor of this cancer, with each advancing stage bearing a more serious prognosis. In contrast, non-Hodgkin's lymphoma tends to spread erratically with vast differences in the growth rate among subtypes. For these reasons, subtype is the primary prognostic factor of non-Hodgkin's lymphoma.

The contrasting behaviors of these two lymphomas also necessitate differing modes of treatment. Whereas Hodgkin's disease is usually treated according to its stage, non-Hodgkin's lymphoma is often treated according to its subtype.

Treatment

Hodgkin's Disease

The treatment of Hodgkin's disease constitutes one of the true successes of modern oncology. In the late 1960s, Dr. Vincent Devita of the National Cancer Institute developed a chemotherapy program that effected cures in patients with advanced Hodgkin's disease. At present, more than 75% of patients diagnosed with Hodgkin's disease can be cured.

Hodgkins' disease is known to be responsive to both radiation therapy and chemotherapy. Although therapy selection ultimately depends on the individual patient, radiation therapy is typically used in the early stages of the disease, and chemotherapy is employed in the later stages.

In the majority of Hodgkin's patients, the stage of the lymphoma is readily established through the aforementioned protocol of tests. Should the stage remain questionable, however, the patient may require a surgical exploration of the abdomen during which representative lymph nodes are removed and biopsies are subsequently performed. In this procedure, which is known as a *staging laparotomy*, as many as 15% of patients with apparent early-stage Hodgkin's disease are found to have cancer below the diaphragm. Once the stage is definitively established, the appropriate therapy can be planned.

Therapy for Hodgkin's disease is typically selected on the basis of the stage as well as the absence (designated by A) or presence (designated by B) of B symptoms.

- Stage IA. Usually treated with radiation therapy.
- Stage IB. Treated with either radiation therapy or a combination of radiation therapy and chemotherapy. The cure rate for stages IA and IB is 90%.

- Stage IIA. Commonly treated with radiation therapy.
- Stage IIB. Treated with either radiation therapy or chemotherapy followed by radiation therapy. The cure rate for stages IIA and IIB is approximately 80%.
- Stage IIIA. Optimal therapy remains controversial. Some experts advocate radiation to all lymph nodes of the body, whereas other authorities recommend chemotherapy. The cure rate for this stage is 65–85%.
- Stage IIIB. This stage is treated with chemotherapy and the cure rate is 50–75%.
- Stages IVA and IVB. These stages are treated with chemotherapy. Additional radiation may be given to specific, highly cancerous areas. The role of bone marrow transplantation is presently being evaluated. The cure rate for this stage is 50–60%.

Although stage and B symptoms primarily determine the treatment of Hodgkin's disease, other factors must also be considered. For example, whenever this lymphoma affects a large percentage of the chest region, the patient is usually treated with both chemotherapy and radiation therapy (See Chapters 13, Radiation Therapy; 14, Chemotherapy and Hormonal Therapy; and 15, Bone Marrow Transplantation.)

Special consideration must also be given to cases of recurrence, that is, the return of the disease after initial therapy. Patients who initially receive radiation therapy often receive chemotherapy during recurrence, whereas patients who initially receive chemotherapy often receive additional chemotherapy or bone marrow transplantation.

Non-Hodgkin's Lymphoma

Non-Hodgkin's lymphoma can be a confusing diagnosis for both doctor and patient as there are six different systems of classification with each system claiming many subtypes. The behaviors of these lymphomas are also variable, because the growth rate ranges from slow to rapid.

In an attempt to simplify the situation, the World Health Organization in 1982 proposed a system of classification based on the subtypes' rate of growth. Widely used today, this system classifies non-Hodgkin's lymphomas into three categories: low grade, intermediate grade, and high grade. As the lymphomas in each category or grade behave similarly, they are, in effect, considered as separate "species" and treated similarly. In other words, the grade of the lymphoma determines treatment. For example, a low-grade non-Hodgkin's lymphoma is treated differently from a high-grade non-Hodgkin's lymphoma in the same stage.

Low-Grade Non-Hodgkin's Lymphoma

Two aspects of the behavior of low-grade lymphomas are particularly unusual. First, even though such lymphomas are typically diagnosed in an advanced stage, life expectancy averages 4 to 8 years. Second, although low-grade lymphomas are initially quite responsive to both chemotherapy and radiation therapy, treatment does not result in increased survival, as these tumors typically shrink only to recur years later.

Whenever appropriate, these paradoxical cancers are treated solely by observation. Whereas patients do receive limited therapy to alleviate troublesome symptoms that may develop, patients without symptoms simply receive routine follow-up care every 3 months. Symptoms commonly necessitating therapy include persistent fevers, weakness, low blood counts, and physically disfiguring enlargement of the lymph nodes. The case of J.F. illustrates the typical treatment received by a patient with a low-grade lymphoma.

J.F. is a 65-year-old woman who noted swelling of the left neck for many months. She eventually consulted her family doctor, who confirmed the existence of multiple enlarged lymph nodes in the neck and advised a biopsy.

When the biopsy revealed a low-grade lymphoma, J.F. was referred to an oncologist. After undergoing routine staging studies, including a bone marrow biopsy that was normal and a CT scan of the abdomen that confirmed enlarged lymph nodes in the abdomen, J.F. was determined to have stage III.

The oncologist advised no therapy. Subsequently, J.F. was examined every 3 months for the next 2 years. Eventually, the lymph nodes in the neck enlarged to the point that J.F. disliked her appearance. Although J.F.'s blood work remained acceptable, and a CT scan of the abdominal lymph nodes revealed little change, the oncologist advised radiation therapy to the neck lymph nodes for cosmetic reasons. The radiation therapy resulted in prompt resolution of the swelling in the neck.

Two years after radiation therapy, J.F. exhibits no further symptoms.

The course of J.F.'s disease illustrates the slow growth typifying low-grade lymphomas as well as the accepted mode of treatment, that is, observation followed by limited therapy as warranted. Radiation therapy may be employed to control any troublesome symptom that may develop, such as J.F.'s unsightly neck swelling. Most patients with advanced-stage, low-grade lymphoma do eventually develop symptoms that require treatment.

Intermediate-Grade Non-Hodgkin's Lymphoma

Intermediate-grade lymphomas are life threatening and, unlike low-grade lymphomas, are treated with chemotherapy at diagnosis. As this type of lymphoma is extremely responsive to chemotherapy, claiming a cure rate of 70%, patients in all stages receive it. In addition, patients in stages I and II receive radiation in areas of known tumor, whereas patients in stages III and IV may receive radiation in areas of extensive involvement. Chemotherapy is typically administered in monthly cycles, numbering between 4 and 12. Once a remission is obtained, treatment ends, and the patient simply begins routine follow-up.

Should the lymphoma recur, more chemotherapy may be administered. Another increasingly employed treatment for such recurrence is bone marrow transplantation.

High-Grade Non-Hodgkin's Lymphoma

High-grade non-Hodgkin's lymphomas are extremely aggressive cancers that require intensive chemotherapy in order to be cured. Peculiar to this type of lymphoma is the tendency to spread to the brain. Consequently, patients are usually given preventive treatment, either radiation therapy or chemotherapy instilled into the spinal fluid, immediately after remission has been obtained. Although the chemotherapy drugs used in the treatment of high-grade lymphomas are similar to those used for intermediate-grade lymphomas, the cure rate for high-grade lymphoma is considerably lower, ranging from 40 to 60%.

Because of the aggressive nature of high-grade lymphomas, some research centers are currently exploring the possible role of bone marrow transplantation in initial therapy. As a precautionary measure in case of recurrence, some centers already advocate the harvesting and storage of patient bone marrow whenever remission is obtained. F.G. is one such patient who agreed to this procedure.

F.G. is a 27-year-old auto parts salesman who consulted his family doctor after experiencing general weakness and abdominal pain for 3 weeks. Laboratory tests showed abnormalities of the blood and liver.

Subsequently, a CT scan revealed a tumor in the liver, an upper GI test revealed a mass in the stomach, and a biopsy of the bone marrow revealed a high-grade lymphoma in the bone. Diagnosed with a stage IV high-grade lymphoma, F.G. immediately began a regimen of chemotherapy. As the chance of cure for this type of aggressive lymphoma is 40–50%, F.G.'s oncologist consulted with a transplantation expert. The decision was made to complete the initial schedule of chemotherapy. As F.G. has no siblings to donate compatible bone marrow, plans were also made to store his marrow in the event of remission.

After six cycles of chemotherapy, tests confirmed that F.G. was in remission. Consequently, his bone marrow was harvested at the transplantation center and stored in a freezer there in case the lymphoma recurred.

After this procedure, F.G. received two additional cycles of chemotherapy as well as direct injections of chemotherapy drugs into the spinal fluid to prevent spread to the brain. Two years later, F.G. continues to do well and shows no evidence of lymphoma.

The role of transplantation in the treatment of high-grade lymphomas is presently evolving. Given the high risk of recurrence, F.G. opted to prepare for the possibility of bone marrow transplantation, although it is hoped that he will remain in remission and will have no need to use the stored bone marrow.

8

Leukemia

Although leukemia is generally regarded as a disease of the blood, it is actually a disease of the bone marrow, the cell-producing substance contained within the bones' cavities. Bone marrow manufactures the three types of cells composing the blood: red cells, white cells, and platelets. Furthermore, bone marrow functions as a kind of incubator for newly produced cells, harboring cells until they become mature enough to enter the bloodstream. Leukemia results when malignant white cells uncontrollably multiply, crowding out the normal blood-forming cells of the bone marrow and thereby disrupting the essential processes performed by the bone marrow and blood.

Red blood cells (RBCs), which impart color to the blood, carry oxygen and carbon dioxide. In the lungs, RBCs pick up oxygen, the cells' energizer, and deliver it via the bloodstream to the organs. In the same manner, RBCs then retrieve the waste gas, carbon dioxide, from the organs and carry it to the lungs for exhalation. Too few RBCs in a person's blood results in *anemia*, a condition that can cause weakness, headaches, and dizziness. Because leukemia disrupts the body's normal production of RBCs, patients with this disease frequently suffer from anemia.

Platelets are cells that circulate in the blood for the purpose of clotting. Whenever a person is cut, platelets initiate the formation of a blood clot, which stops the loss of blood. An extremely low count of platelets may even result in unprovoked or spontaneous bleeding. Because the leukemic patient is unable to produce a sufficient number of platelets, such a patient often bruises easily and bleeds excessively.

White blood cells (WBCs) are produced in the bone marrow. On maturation, they leave the bone marrow to circulate in the bloodstream, where they destroy any infection invading the body. WBCs consist of two major types, neutrophils and lymphocytes. Neutrophils, which constitute 65% of WBCs, are the body's primary defense against such bacterial infections as pneumonia, urine infections, and skin boils. Lymphocytes, composing 30% of WBCs, combat viruses and regulate the body's response to infections.

Leukemia is a condition that results from the uncontrolled growth of malignant WBCs in the bone marrow. As these malignant cells multiply, the marrow can no longer produce its normal quota of RBCs and platelets. Furthermore, because malignant WBCs are defective, leukemic patients are particularly susceptible to infections.

Incidence and Risk Factors

Leukemia is diagnosed in nearly 28,000 people yearly in the United States. Although leukemia ranks as the most common childhood cancer, with 4000 cases diagnosed each year, the majority of patients with this disease are adults. Moreover, the incidence of leukemia is 30% higher in men than in women. As with most cancers, the risk of this disease increases for both men and women older than 40 years and rises significantly with each decade of life.

The cause of leukemia remains unknown, but many risk factors have come to be strongly associated with the disease. A primary risk factor appears to be exposure to massive doses of radiation, as evidenced by the increased incidence of leukemia in Japanese survivors of the atomic bomb. This elevated risk continued for 20 years following the exposure. Fortunately, the minimal exposure encountered by patients in the course of routine x-ray exams has not been shown to increase the risk of leukemia or other cancers.

A risk factor that appears to play a somewhat limited role in the development of leukemia is heredity. For example, should an identical twin develop leukemia, the other twin has a 20% chance of developing the disease within 1 year of the first twin's diagnosis. In fact, siblings of patients with leukemia run a leukemic risk 4 times greater than that of the general population. People with Down's syndrome are also at increased risk for this disease.

Since researchers discovered that leukemia in birds is caused by viruses that alter WBC chromosomes, many experts believe that the chromosomes of human leukemic WBCs undergo a similar type of alteration that causes them to divide uncontrollably. In fact, chromosome abnormalities in WBCs, also known as *oncogenes*, have been found in many human leukemias. Although neither the cause of the chromosomes' alteration nor the ensuing process of their proliferation is yet understood, current oncogene research promises exciting possibilities for the future.

Symptoms, Screening, and Diagnosis

Leukemia induces a number of nonspecific symptoms. Initially, many patients experience flulike symptoms. Patients also frequently complain of weakness, typically caused by anemia. As a result of low platelet counts, leukemic patients often bruise easily, reporting bleeding from the gums or blood in the urine. Because of the ineffectiveness of leukemic white cells to fight infection, patients tend to have subnormal immunity and experience repeated infections. Such patients can also develop bone and joint pain resulting from the proliferation of leukemic white cells in the marrow.

Unfortunately, no proven screening test yet exists for leukemia. Only after a patient reports any of the previously mentioned symptoms does the physician order a diagnostic blood test, that is, a complete blood count measuring the number of RBCs, WBCs, and platelets. In most leukemic cases, the WBC count is high or the RBC and platelet count is low. Once the abnormalities of the blood count are discovered, the bone marrow must be examined.

The diagnosis of leukemia can be made only by microscopic examination known as a *bone marrow aspirate and biopsy*. During this procedure, the physician removes a few drops of marrow from either the breast bone or lower back for slide analysis and performs a small biopsy of the bone. For such a biopsy, the patient usually receives local anesthesia, and the test can be performed in the doctor's office. Although normal bone marrow reveals a mix of maturing RBCs, WBCs, and platelets, leukemic marrow shows a marked increase in WBCs. By studying the appearance of the WBCs, the pathologist is able to classify the leukemia.

Classification of Leukemia

Leukemias are classified and treated according to two distinctive features of these abnormal WBCs. The first feature is derived from the cells' origin: if the malignant cells resemble lymphocytes, the leukemia is considered *lymphocytic*, and if the malignant cells resemble neutrophils, the leukemia is considered *myelogenous*. As differentiating these two types of cells can be quite difficult, further testing is sometimes required to classify the leukemia accurately. Such testing may involve coating the slides with special stains, studying the chromosomes of the bone marrow cells, or obtaining a second pathological opinion.

The second cellular feature used to classify leukemias is growth rate. Malignant WBCs that multiply rapidly are classified as *acute* leukemias, whereas cells that increase slowly are classified as *chronic* leukemias. Based on these divisions of cellular origin and growth rate, there are four common categories of leukemia: acute lymphocytic leukemia, chronic lymphocytic leukemia, acute myelogenous leukemia, and chronic myelogenous leukemia.

The exact type of leukemia is critical in determining both the prognosis and therapy. Whereas the acute types demand immediate therapy, the chronic variants often require less intensive treatment. As each type of leukemia behaves as a distinct entity, the four types will be considered separately.

Leukemia Treatments

Because the ensuing discussion of leukemic therapies builds on information contained in other Part II chapters (specifically, Chapter 14, Chemotherapy and Hormonal Therapy; Chapter 13, Radiation Therapy; and Chapter 15, Bone Marrow Transplantation), the reader is encouraged to review these chapters before reading the following section. The three most common types of leukemia therapies include

1. Chemotherapy, a treatment denoting a class of cancer-fighting drugs that travel throughout the bloodstream to destroy cancer cells. Highly responsive to chemotherapy, leukemia is most commonly treated with such drugs.
2. Bone marrow transplantation (BMT), a form of high-dose chemotherapy that was developed initially to treat relapsed leukemia. BMT is now a common treatment for a variety of leukemias, particularly acute myelogenous leukemia.
3. Radiation therapy (RT), a treatment utilizing powerful x rays to destroy cancer cells. In the treatment of leukemia, RT is used to destroy cancer cells in specific sites, such as the brain, that are not readily accessible to chemotherapy.

Unlike other cancers in which surgery is often used as a diagnostic tool or treatment option, leukemic cancers are neither diagnosed nor treated surgically. However, patients with leukemia do commonly undergo a limited surgical procedure involving the placement of a permanent venous catheter. Known as the Hickman catheter, this soft flexible tube is inserted into the large vein of the upper body to permit the simultaneous infusion of drugs, fluids, and blood, thus sparing the patient repeated jabs with needles.

Acute Lymphocytic Leukemia

Acute lymphocytic leukemia (ALL) ranks as the most common fatal illness in children between the ages of 2 and 15. Accounting for 20% of leukemias, this disease strikes adults less frequently than it does children. As a rapidly growing malignancy, it causes enlarged lymph nodes in 80% of patients. Unlike other forms of leukemia, ALL tends to spread to the spinal fluid surrounding the brain. Instead of classification by stage, ALL is characterized according to its subtypes: L-1 (85% of patients), L-2 (15% of patients), and L-3 (less than 1% of patients.) Prognosis is related to the presence of certain characteristics. Favorable prognostic features of ALL at diagnosis include age from 2 to 7 years, the female sex, a WBC count of less than 30,000, the subtype of L-1, and normal spinal fluid.

The two phases of ALL therapy are divided into induction and maintenance. Induction therapy is aimed at eliminating all detectable leukemic cells in the bone marrow. During this period, which generally lasts 4 to 6 weeks, most patients are hospitalized for such supportive measures as intravenous antibiotics and transfusions of RBCs and platelets. Chemotherapy drugs given during this phase include vincristine, prednisone, daunomycin, and L-asparaginase. Once the cycle of drugs is completed, another examination of the bone marrow is performed. If no leukemic cells remain, the patient is determined to be in remission.

Because ALL tends to spread to the spinal fluid surrounding the brain, patients routinely receive preventive therapy to the spinal fluid. This therapy involves either RT to the spine and brain or direct injections of chemotherapy drugs into the spinal fluid.

Once remission is established, the patient receives maintenance therapy, that is, treatment aimed at eliminating any stray or undetected leukemic cells in the body. Maintenance therapy requires that the patient receive low doses of chemotherapy drugs weekly for 18 to 36 months. The most commonly prescribed maintenance drugs are methotrexate and 6-mercaptopurine, the minimal doses of which rarely induce side effects.

Although ALL is extremely responsive to chemotherapy, the prognosis in children is generally more favorable than that in adults. More than 90% of children will achieve remission; after a 5-year interval, nearly 60% remain cancer free. In contrast, whereas 80% of treated adults have a resolution, only 33% are cured.

After achieving remission, high-risk ALL patients may receive another cycle of high-dose chemotherapy in an interim phase known as *intensification.* Similar to induction therapy in terms of dosage and side effects, such intensified chemotherapy is followed with a course of maintenance therapy.

Should ALL return after a period of remission, the relapsed leukemia is generally treated again with induction chemotherapy. Unfortunately, remissions following such relapses are usually temporary. Consideration may then be given to either BMT or a course of intensified maintenance therapy.

Acute Myelogenous Leukemia

Acute myelogenous leukemia (AML) is a rapidly growing leukemia that commonly affects adults, particularly in the 5th and 6th decades of life. In contrast to ALL, AML rarely strikes children or metastasizes to the spinal fluid. Although five subtypes of AML actually exist, their behaviors as well as treatments are markedly similar; consequently, for the purposes of this discussion, these subtypes are considered as one.

Because AML is highly responsive to chemotherapy, 75% of patients experience remission. Because of complications arising from both the disease and intense treatments, patients are typically hospitalized for 4 to 6 weeks after diagnosis. The two standard chemotherapy drugs used to treat AML are cytosine arabinoside (ara-C) and daunorubicin. Patients generally require intravenous antibiotics as well as platelet and RBC transfusions. When the bone marrow recovers from chemotherapy, a bone marrow examination is normally performed to establish the existence of remission. Between 66 and 75% of patients will obtain a remission.

Unfortunately, only 25% of patients who experience remission are actually cured. Therefore, in order to improve the chance of cure, many patients are advised to have intensive therapy following remission. The two types of recommended treatment following remission are BMT and high-dose intensification therapy. Patients younger than 50 years are often likely candidates for BMT. When this option is not considered appropriate, however, intensification therapy is recommended.

Should the leukemia recur, patients are generally retreated with induction therapy. Unfortunately, remissions in relapsed AML are frequently short.

Chronic Myelogenous Leukemia

Chronic myelogenous leukemia (CML), which constitutes 20% of all leukemias, usually develops in patients older than 40 years. In fact, CML accounts for fewer than 3% of childhood leukemias. Although the life expectancy of patients with CML averages 3 to 4 years, a number of patients with this disease have been known to survive more than 8 years.

As in all leukemias, CML is diagnosed through a bone marrow aspirate and biopsy. In patients suspected of CML, genetic material of the leukemic cells is also routinely analyzed, because 95% of CML patients possess an abnormal genetic trait known as the Philadelphia chromosome. As this altered gene is believed somehow to effect the development of CML, it is currently a focus of intense research.

In contrast to acute types of leukemia, CML tends to progress slowly through predictable stages. In the earliest stage, which is known as the *chronic phase* because it lasts an average of 40 months, patients are often symptom free, with the only sign of disease being an elevated WBC count. Eventually, however, the leukemia cells become increasingly active in both the blood and bone marrow, causing fevers and nonspecific symptoms such as weakness and weight loss. This *accelerated* phase typically lasts 2 to 6 months. In the final stage of CML, termed *blast crisis,* the WBC count becomes extremely elevated, and leukemic cells spread to the lymph glands and other organs. During this critical stage that lasts only a period of weeks, patients are generally quite sick and usually require frequent hospitalization.

Unlike the acute leukemias requiring immediate and intensive treatment, CML is treated according to stage. The stage-by-stage therapy of CML is as follows.

Chronic Stage

Therapy is generally delayed until the WBC count reaches an elevated range greater than 50,000. This stage lasts for 2 to 4 years, and patients generally feel well. To control the WBC count, oral chemotherapy in the form of hydroxyurea (Hydrea) or busulfan is commonly prescribed in daily doses. Interferon, a protein manufactured by the body to fight infection, is also commonly administered in injection form three times a week to control the WBC count. (See Chapter 18, Biological Therapy of Cancer.)

Accelerated Stage

During this stage, a rapidly rising WBC count usually requires intensive chemotherapy similar to the induction therapy used to treat acute leukemias. Patients also often benefit from blood transfusions that alleviate symptoms such as fatigue. This stage lasts for 2 to 6 months.

Blast Crisis

In addition to intensive chemotherapy, the ailing patient typically requires comfort measures during this final stage. Twenty percent of patients can be treated with the same induction therapy drugs used for patients with ALL.

The only method of therapy currently known to cure CML is allogeneic BMT. Consequently, this particular type of BMT can be considered a viable treatment option for all stages of CML in patients younger than 50 years. Unfortunately, advanced age precludes the majority of CML patients from this arduous procedure. The following is the case study of J.S., a likely candidate for transplantation whose first-hand account of actually selecting a transplant center is also included in Chapter 15:

> J.S. is a 33-year-old man who was found to have an elevated WBC count in the course of a routine physical exam. His family doctor referred him to an oncologist, who performed a bone marrow aspirate and biopsy, the results of which indicated the possibility of CML. The marrow was subsequently tested for the Philadelphia chromosome. When this test proved positive, the diagnosis of CML was firmly established.

> J.S. was in the chronic stage of CML which, while not imminently harmful, would become life threatening within 3 to 4 years. J.S. expressed an interest in pursuing aggressive treatment. Because he was 33 years old and had five siblings, a fact that improved his chances of locating a compatible donor, J.S. was a likely candidate for an allogeneic BMT. When J.S.'s youngest brother proved a suitable donor, J.S. decided to proceed with the transplant. Two years following the procedure, J.S. is free of cancer and is working full-time.

J.S.'s case illustrates that eligibly aged CML patients are well advised to explore BMT as a treatment option. Unfortunately, many patients are too old at diagnosis to be candidates for BMT.

Chronic Lymphatic Leukemia

Chronic lymphatic leukemia (CLL) is the most common form of leukemia in the industrialized world, accounting for 30% of leukemias. Increasing in incidence with advancing age, CLL primarily strikes adults older than 60 years and men twice as frequently as women. Approximately 30% of patients experience no symptoms with this slow-growing leukemia.

Unlike that of other types of leukemia, the diagnosis of CLL is usually straightforward in that the WBC count and bone marrow examination reveal a marked increase in the number of lymphocytes. Although these malignant lymphocytes are quite normal in appearance, they function improperly, predisposing the patient to infection.

Like CML, CLL progresses through predictable stages. In the early stages, only an enlargement of the lymph nodes or spleen is evident. Later, the weakened bone marrow can produce such symptoms as weakness due to anemia or easy bleeding and bruising due to a low platelet count. The development of a low platelet count is often a serious prognostic sign. Based on these features, the staging system for CLL is as follows.

- Stage 0. An elevation in the lymphocyte count is the only detectable abnormality. The average length of survival is approximately 12 years.
- Stage I. Both an elevated lymphocyte count and enlarged lymph nodes are evident. The average length of survival is more than 8 years.
- Stage 2. An elevated lymphocyte count as well as an enlarged liver or spleen are present. The average length of survival is approximately 6 years.
- Stage 3. An elevated lymphocyte count with resultant anemia as well as possible enlargement of lymph nodes, liver, or spleen exist. The average length of survival is more than 2 years.
- Stage 4. An elevated lymphocyte count and a low platelet count are evident. Moreover, anemia or enlarged lymph nodes and spleen may be present. The average length of survival is more than 1 year.

The slowest growing and most predictable of all leukemias, CLL typically causes no symptoms in the earlier stages and consequently requires no treatment. Patients in these stages are generally monitored closely with periodic bloodwork and physical examinations. Usually within several years, however, CLL progresses to the later, symptomatic stages.

Patients in stages III and IV often receive treatment in order to alleviate troublesome symptoms such as fevers, general weakness, and abdominal pain due to the enlargement of the spleen. Whereas patients receiving intense therapy for acute leukemias require hospitalization, CLL patients tolerate the lower-dose cycles of chemotherapy and radiation therapy quite well as outpatients. Common chemotherapy drugs include prednisone, vincristine, and cyclophosphamide given intravenously each month. Rather than experiencing side effects from this therapy, patients generally report feeling much improved.

In a minority of patients, CLL can cause enlargement of the lymph nodes and spleen without causing an elevated WBC count. In such cases, CLL behaves similarly to low-grade lymphomas and requires analogous treatment. (See Chapter 7 for information on low-grade non-Hodgkin's lymphoma.)

9

Urinary Tract Cancers: Bladder and Kidney

Cancers of the urinary system account for 9% of all cancers in men and 4% of all cancers in women. Often regarded as a single entity, urinary cancers actually refer to two distinct types of cancer, kidney and bladder cancers. Because these organs are related in anatomy, function, and symptoms, a discussion of these common features will precede the discussion of the individual cancers.

Function and Anatomy of the Urinary Tract

The kidney and bladder are the major organs of the urinary tract, the system that removes body waste through the production and excretion of urine. In the process of filtering waste products from the blood, the kidney produces urine, which is then stored in the reservoir of the bladder.

The kidneys are paired organs located in the upper abdomen on either side of the spinal column. Shaped like kidney beans, each organ measures 5 inches in length and weighs approximately 1 lb. The urine produced by the kidneys drains continually into tubes known as ureters for transport to the storage receptacle of the blad-

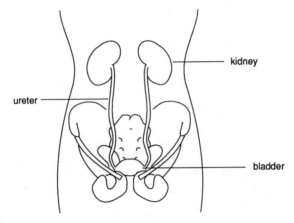

Figure 9-1. Anatomy of urinary system.

der. After prodding by voluntary muscles, the bladder empties its contents into a slender canal called the urethra, through which urine is discharged from the body. Figure 9-1 details the general anatomy of the urinary system.

Symptoms

The symptom most commonly associated with cancer of the urinary tract is the presence of blood in the urine. Although this symptom is typically induced by other benign conditions such as urinary tract infection, bloody urine always warrants investigation, as does any pain experienced during urination.

Urinary tract cancers also infrequently cause other nonspecific symptoms such as weight loss, decreased appetite, and unexplained fevers. Occasionally, kidney cancer causes diffuse pain in the region of the lower back. Like blood in the urine, these symptoms are very often caused by other unrelated medical conditions.

Diagnosis

The first diagnostic test used to evaluate any urinary symptom is urinalysis, a microscopic examination of a urine sample. Usually performed in the office of the family physician, the urinalysis reveals the presence of abnormalities in the urine, often leading to a diagnosis like infection. In fact, in most cases the patient is initially treated for a urinary tract infection. Should abnormal urinalyses persist, however, the patient is generally referred to a urologist, a physician who specializes in treatment of urinary tract diseases.

A test frequently ordered is the intravenous pyelogram (IVP), a procedure in which dye is injected into the bloodstream, collecting in concentrated levels throughout the urinary system. Via x-ray imaging, the urologist is then able to examine the entire urinary tract. Should a suspicious mass be detected, a biopsy is required. Another simple diagnostic test for the urinary tract is *cytology*, that is, the microscopic examination of the urine for malignant cells.

Should cytology studies or the IVP indicate the presence of abnormalities, further diagnostic tests are needed. One such cardinal test known as *cystoscopy* provides a direct visualization of the bladder. In this procedure, the urologist inserts a flexible, lighted scope through the urethra into the bladder and ureters in order to inspect the lining of these organs. A biopsy of any detected abnormality can be simultaneously performed with this instrument. As the kidneys are inaccessible to cystoscopy, a kidney abnormality revealed by IVP typically involves some type of surgery. Frequently, the entire kidney is removed in the operating room under general anesthesia in a procedure known as a *nephrectomy.*

The two major types of urinary cancer are transitional cell carcinoma and adenocarcinoma. Whereas adenocarcinoma usually develops in the kidney, transitional cell cancer originates in the bladder, arising less often in the ureter and urethra. Because these cancers differ widely in terms of prognostic features and treatment, it is best to consider cancers of the bladder and kidney separately.

Bladder Cancer

In 1993, bladder cancer was diagnosed in 53,000 Americans, 75% of whom were men. Such an elevated incidence of bladder cancer in men may be attributable to their greater exposure to two known risk factors, smoking and industrial hazards such as dyes, benzene, paint, and rubber. In ways not yet understood, repeated bladder infections also predispose patients to bladder cancer.

Common symptoms of bladder cancer include bloody urine, burning on urination, and resistant or recurring urinary infections. The screening tests presently used to detect this type of cancer are urinalysis and the IVP.

Any suspicious findings are then further evaluated through cystoscopy and a computed tomography (CT) scan. In the course of cystoscopy, the urologist carefully inspects the entire bladder and biopsies any abnormal areas while also attempting to determine the extent of the abnormality. A pathologist then examines the tissue from the biopsy under the microscope for cancer cells.

Prognosis

In addition to confirming the presence of cancer, the pathologist makes a determination regarding two important features of the bladder cancer: its depth of invasion into the organ's tissues and its grade. These features influence prognosis as well as the treatment plan.

Structurally and functionally, the bladder resembles an inflatable tube whose walls expand and contract according to the amount of urine present. The bladder wall consists of four layers of tissue. The innermost layer, called the *mucosa,* is extremely thin. Encompassing the mucosa is a layer of connective tissue, surrounded by a layer of muscle and an outermost layer of fat. The *depth of invasion* refers to the penetration of the cancer into these layers of wall tissue with deeper penetrations yielding poorer prognoses.

The grade of a bladder cancer is an estimate of its aggressiveness on a scale of 1 to 4 based on its appearance under the micro-scope. The low-grade cancers, grades I and II, maintain a cellular resemblance to normal bladder tissue. As low-grade cancers tend to invade only the mucosal and connective layers of wall tissue, such cancers claim a favorable prognosis. In contrast, cancers with grades of III and IV differ markedly from normal bladder tissue. Typically, these cancers grow rapidly, invading the layer of muscle and, at times, extending through the bladder wall. As a result, the prognosis of these high-grade cancers is usually less favorable.

Staging

Physicians use a set of guidelines known as a *staging system* to classify cancers and determine therapy. The stage of a bladder cancer is established mainly by the depth of penetration into the bladder wall. The stages of bladder cancer are as follows:

- Stage 0. The cancer is confined to the mucosal layer of bladder tissue. It is the earliest form of bladder cancer.
- Stage A. The cancer extends through the mucosa into the layer of connective tissue.
- Stage B is generally divided into two types: stage B1, the cancer has penetrated superficially into the muscle layer of the bladder; stage B2, the cancer has penetrated deeply into the muscle layer of the bladder.
- Stage C. The cancer has penetrated the entire wall of the bladder and is now found in the layer of fat that surrounds the bladder.
- Stage D is generally divided into two types: stage D1, the cancer has spread beyond the bladder to the pelvic organs or lymph nodes; stage D2, the cancer has spread to distant sites such as the liver, bone, or lung.

Figure 9-2 schematically illustrates the staging system for bladder cancer according to the depth of invasion.

Treatment

The treatment of bladder cancer is based on the stage and overall condition of the patient. As this particular area of cancer

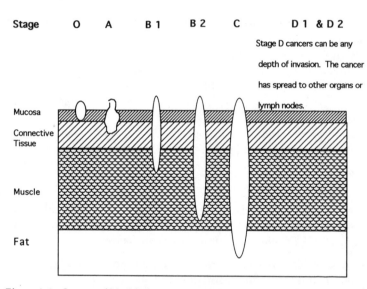

Figure 9-2. Stages of bladder cancer as established by depth of invasion of the bladder wall.

treatment is currently undergoing significant change, any description of therapies according to stage is necessarily less than inclusive.

Stage 0. Employing cystoscopy, the urologist removes the tumor as well as other suspicious sites in the bladder through the process of *cauterization,* that is, the application of electric current to destroy cancerous tissue. This form of treatment is generally quite effective: the 5-year survival rate is 90%.

Because the risk of bladder cancer recurrence is high in such patients, however, they are routinely scheduled for surveillance cystoscopies at 3-month intervals. In addition to this preventive measure, chemotherapy drugs are commonly administered directly into the bladder. This technique, called *intravesical chemotherapy,* has been shown to further reduce the rate of recurrence. It requires that the patient receive weekly doses of agents such as bacille Calmette–Guérin (BCG), thiotepa, and mitomycin for 6–12 weeks.

Stage A. Treatment involves the cystoscopic removal of the tumor, usually followed by intravesical chemotherapy. Surveillance cystoscopy is an integral factor in follow-up care, because nearly 73% of patients with superficial bladder cancers (stages O and A) eventually develop recurrences. The case of K.S. illustrates the crucial importance of surveillance measures.

> K.S. is a 45-year-old manager of the service department in a car dealership. After suddenly noting a brownish cast to his urine, he consulted a urologist, who performed a physical examination, urinalysis, and blood tests. Finally, a cystoscopy confirmed the diagnosis of an early-stage bladder cancer.
>
> When informed that he would require intravesical chemotherapy and surveillance cystoscopies for life, K.S. was troubled by the businesslike approach of the physician. Consequently, K.S. sought a second opinion from a urologist on staff at another hospital. This urologist reviewed K.S.'s situation, including the microscopic slides of the cancer, and concurred with the original diagnosis of stage 0 bladder cancer as well as the recommended treatment. In addition, he addressed K.S.'s fears about extended follow-up care and answered questions both clearly and simply.
>
> Electing to be treated by the second urologist, K.S. received 12 weeks of intravesical chemotherapy and repeat cystoscopies every 3 months. Nine months after the initial diagnosis, K.S. developed another stage 0 bladder cancer for which he received further intravesical chemotherapy. One year later, K.S. continues to have periodic cystoscopies and currently shows no evidence of cancer.

K.S.'s experience underscores how crucial follow-up care is in the prudent management of bladder cancer. In the absence of such monitoring cystoscopies, subsequent cancers can easily reach advanced, less treatable stages. Furthermore, although the treatment prescribed by the first urologist whom K.S. consulted was entirely appropriate, K.S. was able to relate on a more personal level with the second-opinion urologist. His final choice of a physician was a wise one in that a patient is always best treated by the physician who merits the patient's trust.

Stage B1. By definition, this stage cancer displays only superficial invasion of the bladder muscle, a fact that introduces the possibility of understaging the cancer. Although many cases of B1 bladder cancer are effectively controlled by cystoscopic removal of the tumor and intravesical chemotherapy, other cases do require more aggressive treatment (e.g., large tumors, multiple tumors, and high-grade cancers). In such instances, patients receive the same treatment as do those with stage B2 and C cancers.

Stages B2 and C. Treatment for these cancers is aggressive. Given the evolving status of this particular area of treatment, however, it is difficult to generalize about appropriate therapies. Currently, the role of bladder-sparing surgery as well as the benefit of presurgical chemotherapy is being investigated. In actual practice, a patient often receives two or more of the following therapies on the recommendation of a team of doctors including a urologist, a medical oncologist, and a radiation therapist.

A technique commonly used to treat bladder cancer in stages B2 and C is a *radical cystectomy*. In this extensive procedure, the urologist removes the bladder as well as contiguous tissue or organs. In women, a radical cystectomy involves removal of the pelvic organs, including the ovaries, uterus, and upper portion of the vagina. In men, this procedure involves removal of the prostate. In order to provide for the elimination of urine, the urologist then proceeds to reconstruct the urinary system. One method called a *urostomy* involves utilizing a section of intestine to serve as a conduit through which urine can drain to the ureters. The rerouted ureters then empty urine through a permanent hole in the abdominal wall and into a collection bag maintained outside the body.

Radiation therapy is often used in the treatment of advanced bladder cancer despite the fact that its role remains somewhat controversial. (See Chapter 13, Radiation Therapy.) In an effort to improve the patient's chance of survival, radiation therapy is commonly administered before a radical cystectomy. Moreover, high-dose radiation therapy may be given to patients unable to tolerate the rigors of surgery.

Recently, chemotherapy has been proven effective in the treatment of advanced bladder cancer. (See Chapter 14, Chemotherapy and Hormonal Therapy.) After either surgery or radiation therapy, such preventive chemotherapy is given to minimize the risk of recurrent cancer. Unlike intravesical chemotherapy, this form of therapy is given intravenously so that the drugs can travel systemically and thereby destroy stray cancer cells throughout the body. A combination of drugs known as M-VAC (methotrexate, vinblastine, adriamycin, and cisplatin) has been proven effective in the treatment of stage C bladder cancers; presently, this combination is being evaluated for the treatment of B2 cancers.

Stage D1. Treatment typically involves radical cystectomy, followed by chemotherapy, radiation therapy, or a combination of both therapies.

Stage D2. Because of the distant spread of this stage cancer, treatment is palliative rather than curative. For example, a patient who experiences localized bone pain as a result of tumor pressure may be given radiation therapy in an attempt to shrink the size of the tumor and thus reduce pain. M-VAC chemotherapy likewise causes shrinkage of the cancer in about 65% of patients.

Table 9-1 summarizes the treatment of bladder cancer by stage.

Kidney Cancer (Renal Adenocarcinoma)

In 1992, approximately 25,000 cases of kidney cancer were diagnosed in the United States. Like bladder cancer, kidney cancer occurs three times as often in men as it does in women, and most particularly in men between the ages of 40 and 70.

Although the exact cause of kidney cancer remains unknown, certain risk factors have been noted. For example, city dwellers have a higher incidence of this disease than do non–city dwellers. Moreover, some studies have established an association between kidney cancer and tobacco use, whereas others have implicated the chronic exposure to low doses of radiation in this disease.

Fully 60% of patients who are diagnosed with kidney cancer initially experience the symptom of blood in the urine. Many patients complain of either a dull backache or flank pain, a symptom often caused by a blood clot in the ureter. Such painful symptoms frequently mimic those that are caused by kidney stones. As with

Table 9-1

Survival Rate and Treatment of Bladder Cancer by Stage

Stage	5-Year survival (%)	Therapy
0	90	Cystoscopic removal of tumor, surveillance
A	75	cystoscopies and, for many patients, intravesical chemotherapy
B1	55	Depending on the presence of certain factors, treatment is similar to that for either stage A or stage B2
B2	35	A combination of radical cystectomy and
C	20	either radiation therapy or adjuvant chemotherapy. Recommendations are best made on an individual basis
D	5	Radiation therapy, chemotherapy, and, for some patients, surgery. Recommendations are best made on an individual basis

SOURCE: *Bladder Cancer, Information for Physicians.* National Cancer Institute's PDQ System Cancer Fax, 1993.

any cancer, patients also often report a loss of appetite, weakness, fatigue, and localized bone pain at the time of diagnosis.

The initial tests used to evaluate a patient for kidney cancer are the same as those used for bladder cancer: a physical examination, a urinalysis, and an IVP. The latter is a key test in evaluating the symptom of bloody urine: if the IVP is normal, the urologist usually proceeds with a cystoscopy in order to examine the bladder; however, if the IVP shows an abnormality in the kidney, the urologist focuses further testing in the area of the kidney. In fact, most kidney cancers are first detected through the IVP.

When a kidney cancer is suspected, the patient routinely undergoes three diagnostic tests. The first test is a sonogram of the kidney. Noninvasive in nature, the sonogram employs sound waves to determine whether the abnormality is either a solid mass or a fluid-filled cyst. Whereas cysts are typically benign, solid masses require further investigation.

Another commonly administered test is the kidney angiogram. In this procedure, an x-ray catheter is inserted into the artery of the kidney so that dye can be directly injected into the blood supply of the kidney. In this way, the urologist is able to examine the anatomy of the suspicious mass as well as adjacent tissues. The angiogram effectively detects kidney cancer in 90% of patients. Should a kidney cancer be strongly suspected, a CT scan of the abdomen is performed in order to determine whether the cancer has spread beyond the kidney.

Staging

Physicians employ a set of guidelines known as a *staging system* to classify cancers and determine therapy. The dominant prognostic feature of kidney cancer is its stage. The four stages of kidney cancer are as follows.

- Stage I. The cancer is confined exclusively to the kidney.
- Stage II. The cancer has spread outside the kidney but not beyond the capsule of fibrous tissue, known as Gerota's fascia, that envelops the kidney.
- Stage III. The cancer has spread to the lymph nodes surrounding the kidney or to the vein that drains the blood from the kidney. Evidence of spread may also appear in the large blood vessel known as the inferior vena cava that carries blood to the heart.
- Stage IV. The cancer has spread to other organs such as the lung or bones.

Treatment

Treatment of kidney cancer is determined according to stage. Quite typically, treatment involves the surgical removal of the cancer. The standard procedure used to treat kidney cancer is the *radical nephrectomy*, a procedure that entails the removal of the kidney and adjacent lymph nodes. After surgery, patients in the later stages are usually treated with chemotherapy, radiation, or a combination of both therapies. The following is a stage-by-stage summary of the treatment of kidney cancer.

Stages I and II. The most common treatment involves some type of nephrectomy with the extent of surgery determined by the specific situation of the patient. Although selected stage I patients may qualify for a partial nephrectomy, nearly all stage II patients require a radical nephrectomy. Subsequent therapy is not routinely administered to patients whose surgeries are deemed successful.

For those patients who are unable to tolerate the rigors of surgery, radiation therapy to the kidney is a treatment option. Another viable approach for such patients is *arterial embolization.* This procedure entails injecting small amounts of gelatinous material into the kidney's main artery in an attempt to block the blood supply to malignant cells and thereby destroy them.

Stage III. Surgical removal of the cancer is the standard treatment. Because of the frequent involvement of abdominal vessels, surgery is typically extensive. In fact, a radical nephrectomy constitutes the least invasive of the surgeries for this stage. Often, the surgery involves the repair or partial removal of the inferior vena cava. Naturally, such extensive surgery is recommended only for patients in good physical condition. When surgery is not feasible, however, patients may be given either radiation therapy or arterial embolization to alleviate troublesome symptoms caused the cancer.

Stage IV. Because these cancers constitute such a diverse group, it is difficult to generalize about optimal therapies. Whereas some cancers grow slowly and induce only occasional symptoms over the course of many months, other cancers behave aggressively and cause life-threatening problems in a matter of weeks. For many patients in this stage, the aim of treatment is to control any distressing symptoms of the cancer. Treatment recommendations, which may include one or more of the following options, are best made on a patient-by-patient basis.

A therapy that continues to be somewhat controversial for

stage IV patients is the surgical option. Nephrectomy is typically performed today to control symptoms, the most common of which is urinary bleeding; this surgery was traditionally employed to treat widely disseminated kidney cancer. A few studies in the medical literature of the 1940s even claimed that kidney cancer that had metastasized to the lungs disappeared in that site following nephrectomy. As the accuracy of such studies is now disputed, most authorities do not recommend radical nephrectomy as an acceptable method of treating widespread kidney cancer.

However, a treatment option commonly employed for such cancers is radiation therapy. It is used to control specific symptoms like pain or bleeding in the urinary tract. Chemotherapy and hormonal therapy are also frequently used in the treatment of stage IV kidney cancers. As only 15% of such cancers respond well to chemotherapy, however, it is employed judiciously on a patient-by-patient basis. Hormonal therapy utilizes the female hormone, progesterone, to retard the growth of malignant cells. Because this treatment has few side effects and can sometimes physiologically promote the feeling of well-being in patients, hormonal therapy is ideally suited for patients who are unable to tolerate aggressive forms of therapy.

A particularly promising area of research for stage IV patients is biological therapy. This therapy seeks to achieve antitumor effects through stimulation of the body's immune mechanisms. One such biological therapy uses interferon, a substance produced by the body to fight viruses. As one of the few biological therapies commercially available now, interferon proves effective in 15% of patients. At present, researchers continue to evaluate the benefits of other biological therapies including interleukin, tumor-infiltrating lymphocytes, and monoclonal antibodies. When appropriate, patients with advanced kidney cancer are encouraged to participate in these studies. (See Chapters 13, Radiation Therapy; 14, Chemotherapy and Hormonal Therapy; and 16, Biological Therapy.)

A well-described occurrence is the objective regression of kidney cancer in patients who receive no treatment whatsoever. Such

Table 9-2
Survival Rate and Treatment of Kidney Cancer by Stage

Stage	5-Year survival (%)	Therapy
I	70	Surgical removal of the cancer. Chemotherapy
II	50	and radiation are not given after surgery
III	35	Aggressive surgery whenever possible
IV	5	Treatment recommendations are individualized. Possible options include surgery, radiation, chemotherapy, hormonal therapy, and biological therapy

SOURCE: *Kidney Cancer, Information for Physicians.* National Cancer Institute's PDQ System Cancer Fax, 1993.

spontaneous regression is reported to occur in no more than 3% of patients, but this phenomenon does serve to underscore the unpredictable behavior of any kidney cancer. In view of the limited efficacy of standard therapies for stage IV kidney cancers, a period of treatment-free observation may certainly be a legitimate option for some patients.

Table 9-2 lists the 5-year survival rates and treatment recommendations for kidney cancers according to stage.

10

Testicular Cancer

Testicular cancer is a rather rare malignancy that accounts for only 1% of cancers in men. Essentially a "young man's" cancer, this disease ranks as the most common cancer among men aged 15 to 35 years. Fortunately, self-examination constitutes a proven method of early detection for this type of cancer. Moreover, with the advent of effective chemotherapy in the 1970s, testicular cancer is highly treatable and curable.

Risk Factors, Symptoms, and Screening

Although the cause of testicular cancer is unknown, a major risk factor of this particular cancer is an undescended testicle. During the course of male fetal development, the testicle typically migrates from the lower back into the scrotum. In men whose testicles have failed to descend in this manner, a 40-fold risk of developing testicular cancer exists, with an estimated 12% of such cancers arising from this condition. It should be noted, however, that surgical correction of this abnormality decreases the risk of testicular cancer.

The role of socioeconomic factors in the development of this cancer is less defined. Only the factor of race is clearly established;

the incidence of testicular cancer in the white American populace is double that of the black American populace. White-collar workers claim a slightly more elevated risk than do their blue-collar counterparts, but related factors such as heredity, geography, and trauma appear to play no role at all in the development of testicular cancer.

The most common symptom of this cancer is a painless swelling or mass in the testicle. However, approximately 40% of patients report a type of dull pain in the groin or lower abdomen. Barring infection in the testicle, severe pain is rare.

The best method of early detection for this particular cancer is a monthly self-examination of the testicles by all men past the age of puberty. The routine practice of testicular self-examination (TSE) will result in early detection and cure of this malignancy. The American Cancer Society recommends that men perform TSE once a month, typically after a warm bath or shower, which relaxes the scrotum. One method of performing TSE is as follows.

1. While standing in front of a mirror, the man inspects his scrotum for any sign of swelling.
2. Using both hands, he rolls each testicle between the fingers and thumb to search for any hard lumps.
3. The epididymis, the cordlike structure that carries sperm, should be found. This is a normal structure and should not be mistaken for a lump. All lumps should be promptly shown to a physician.

Figure 4-1 illustrates the male anatomy including the testicle, epididymis, and scrotum.

Diagnosis

Any mass or abnormality of the testicle detected during TSE must be examined by a physician. A rock-hard mass is frequently indicative of testicular cancer, but a less defined abnormality can be much more difficult to diagnose. For example, the results of one study showed that nearly 50% of testicular cancer patients initially received the diagnosis of testicular infection. Whenever the abnormality remains questionable, the physician may request a *sonogram* of the testicles. In this test, sound waves are employed to provide a two-dimensional image of tissue, a process that can reveal evidence of cancer.

When the suspicion of testicular cancer arises, the patient is immediately referred to a urologist, that is, a specialist of the urinary system. In order to confirm the presence of cancer through laboratory analysis, the urologist must remove the abnormal testicle in a surgical procedure known as a *radical inguinal orchiectomy.* A less invasive biopsy or testicle-sparing surgery is not performed because of the risk of spreading the cancer during the procedure itself. In a radical inguinal orchiectomy, the urologist makes an incision in the groin and removes the abnormal testicle, thus leaving the scrotum intact.

Types of Testicular Cancer

Based on appearance under the microscope, testicular cancers are classified into two types: seminoma or nonseminoma. Whereas both types are quite sensitive to chemotherapy, only seminoma is responsive to radiation therapy. For this reason, it is imperative that the type be clearly established.

One blood test widely employed in the diagnosis and treatment of testicular cancer is that for *tumor markers.* Actually, tumor markers are substances produced by normal as well as cancerous human cells. The two tumor markers commonly produced by testicular cancer cells are alpha-fetoprotein (AFP) and beta-human chorionic gonadotropin hormone (BHCG). As an elevation of the latter normally occurs with pregnancy, the measurement of BHCG is a common test for pregnancy. In 85% of testicular cancer patients, an abnormal elevation of either AFP or BHCG is detected. Whenever the type of testicular cancer remains uncertain, tumor markers prove especially helpful because an elevated AFP occurs only in nonseminoma testicular cancer.

In addition to tumor markers, routine diagnostic testing includes a thorough physical examination, chest x ray, blood work, and computed tomography (CT) scan of the abdomen and pelvis. These tests determine whether the cancer has spread to other parts of the body.

Staging

Physicians use a set of guidelines known as a *staging system* to classify testicular cancers into three groups. Whether seminoma or nonseminoma, stage is determined by extent of the cancer. The three stages of testicle cancer follow.

- Stage I. The cancer is confined to the testicle. More than 95% of such patients are cured.
- Stage II. The cancer has spread beyond the testicle to the adjacent lymph nodes of the pelvis or abdomen. (Lymph nodes are pea-like structures that fight infection throughout the body.) More than 95% of such patients are cured. However, if the lymph node tumor is considered "bulky," that is, measures more than 5 cm, the patient's prognosis is slightly more serious.
- Stage III. The cancer has spread beyond the testicle and adjacent lymph nodes to distant sites such as the lung or bones. Fully 75% of these patients are cured.

Treatment

All patients with testicular cancer undergo a radical inguinal orchiectomy. Depending on the stage and type of cancer, the patient may receive either radiation therapy or chemotherapy. Radiation therapy employs x rays to destroy cancer cells; chemotherapy refers to a class of cancer-fighting drugs that travel throughout the bloodstream to destroy cancer cells. (See Chapters 13, Radiation Therapy; and 14, Chemotherapy and Hormonal Therapy.) Because the two types of testicular cancer are generally treated quite differently, these cancers will be discussed separately.

Seminoma

Seminoma testicular cancer has several unique characteristics. First, this cancer is unusually sensitive to radiation, a fact resulting in the sole use of this therapy to treat it. Actually, few other types of cancer can claim the distinction of being so responsive to radiation therapy. Second, seminoma rarely produces tumor markers. Although seminoma never produces AFP, this type of testicular cancer produces BHCG in only 10% of patients.

The stage-by-stage treatment of seminoma is as follows.

- Stage I. Treatment consists of a radical orchiectomy followed by radiation therapy. Because fully 15% of stage I patients have undetected cancer in the lymph nodes, all patients receive preventive radiation to the abdominal lymph nodes. As the dosage is relatively low, patients generally tolerate this therapy quite well. One such patient with stage I seminoma is G.H.

G.H. is a 39-year-old man who consulted his family doctor after noting a lump in his right testicle. On referral to a urologist, G.H. was found to have a mass the size of a golf ball in the right scrotum. The urologist strongly suspected a testicular cancer.

On hospitalization, all diagnostic tests proved normal, including a physical examination, blood work, CT scan of the abdomen, and chest x ray. The AFP and BHCG were not detectable. Subsequently, G.H. underwent a right radical inguinal orchiectomy; this procedure yielded the diagnosis of a stage I seminoma.

Preventive radiation of the abdominal lymph nodes was recommended. G.H. completed this 5-week course of radiation without experiencing side effects. Follow-up care included monthly examinations by his urologist for 2 years, after which time G.H. began to be examined every 3 months. Four years following diagnosis, G.H. is cancer free.

Like most patients with testicular cancer, G.H. is young and very active. After tolerating radiation therapy quite well, he is considered to be cured.

- Stage 2. Treatment is dependent on the size or bulkiness of the tumor. When the tumor is small, the patient is typically treated with a radical orchiectomy followed by radiation of the abdominal lymph nodes. However, a patient with a bulky stage II tumor, that is, a malignancy measuring more than 5 cm in diameter, may be treated with either radiation therapy or chemotherapy. Presently, many leading authorities advocate chemotherapy for patients with bulky stage II seminoma.
- Stage III. Treatment typically consists of a radical orchiectomy followed by chemotherapy. As the cancer in this stage is widespread, radiation therapy is not routinely given. On completion of chemotherapy, all of the staging tests are repeated. Whenever feasible, any remaining tumors are surgically removed.

Nonseminoma

Until the late 1970s, most nonseminoma testicular cancers were treated surgically. During this period, Dr. Lawrence Einhorn of Indiana University discovered that patients with widespread nonseminoma could actually be cured with a new chemotherapy drug known as cisplatin.

One potentially serious side effect of chemotherapy is the destruction of the body's white blood cells (WBCs), that is, cells produced by the bone marrow to fight infection. Because a low WBC count predisposes the patient to infection, chemotherapy doses are traditionally reduced whenever this count plummets. However, Dr. Einhorn introduced a counterprinciple of treatment for nonseminoma patients by establishing that cures could be effected by disregarding a dangerously low WBC and adhering to the chemotherapy schedule. His specific combination of drugs included vinblastine, cisplatin, and bleomycin (VPB) to be given every 3 weeks for approximately 12 weeks. In the most recent chemotherapy programs, the drug VP-16 has been substituted for vinblastine.

Unlike seminoma cancers, in which only 10% of patients have a detectable tumor marker, nonseminoma cancers typically produce tumor markers. Because these markers accurately reflect the condition of the cancer, they prove extremely important during both therapy and follow-up care. As the cancer shrinks, the marker proportionally decreases, thus confirming the effectiveness of treatment. Once therapy is completed, the markers are measured monthly for 2 years.

A surgical procedure used to treat nonseminoma cancer is a *retroperitoneal lymph node dissection*. Regarded as a major surgery, this procedure entails the removal of the lymph nodes of the abdomen and pelvis. Because impotence can develop when the dissection is extensive, fertility-sparing techniques are now used whenever appropriate. Retroperitoneal lymph node dissection was the standard treatment for nonseminoma before the development of effective chemotherapy, but this surgery is still used today for staging purposes and as a treatment for certain stage II patients.

The following is a stage-by-stage approach to the treatment of nonseminoma cancers.

- Stage I. Treatment consists of a radical inguinal orchiectomy followed by either lymph node dissection or observation. Because lymph node involvement occurs in only 27% of patients, some cancer authorities believe that, after orchiectomy, patients should have their tumor markers monitored and that only those patients who register elevations or evidence further spread should receive a lymph node dissection. At present, the optimal treatment of this staged cancer remains controversial.
- Stage II. Treatment depends on the amount of cancer in the abdominal lymph nodes. Patients with a lymph node malignancy measuring less than 5 cm receive a radical orchiectomy followed by lymph node dissection. Because 50% of such surgical patients experience relapse, further treatment routinely entails either close observation or two cycles of VPB chemotherapy. Patients wishing to preserve fertility usually choose the former approach. Although the cure rate for both approaches is equal, nearly half

of patients who choose observation eventually experience relapse and receive chemotherapy.

Treatment for patients with "bulky" stage II nonseminoma cancer is a radical orchiectomy followed by three cycles of chemotherapy. On completion of chemotherapy, the patient is restaged with x rays and blood tests. If test results are negative, the patient simply receives monthly follow-up care for 2 years. However, if test results are positive, the patient may undergo

Table 10-1
Treatment of Testicular Cancers by Type and Stage

Type and stage	Treatment after radical inguinal orchiectomy	5-Year cure rate (%)
Seminoma		
Stage I	Radiation therapy to pelvic and abdominal lymph nodes	90+
Stage II	Same as stage I. Some authorities favor chemotherapy for "bulky" tumor patients	90+
Stage III	Chemotherapy followed by surgical removal of any remaining tumor	90+
Nonseminoma		
Stage I	Surgical removal of lymph nodes of the abdomen	95
	Monthly observation in lieu of surgery is an option for selected patients	
Stage II	Nonbulky: Surgical removal of lymph nodes followed by either monthly observation or chemotherapy	95
	Bulky: Chemotherapy followed by surgical removal of any remaining tumor	95
Stage III	Chemotherapy followed by surgical removal of any remaining tumor	75

SOURCE: *Testicular Cancer, Information for Physicians,* National Cancer Institute PDQ System, Cancer Fax, 1993.

surgical removal of any residual cancer that is detected by the test.

- Stage III. Treatment is a radical orchiectomy followed by three cycles of chemotherapy. On completion of chemotherapy, the patient is restaged. Any remaining tumors are surgically removed. However, if the patient is cancer free after chemotherapy, he simply receives routine follow-up care for 2 years.

Because the type of chemotherapy used to treat testicular cancer is extremely powerful, fully 25% of patients require hospitalization for side effects, particularly high fever and low WBC count. (See case study D.C. in Chapter 14, Chemotherapy and Hormonal Therapy.)

It should be emphasized that all nonseminoma patients require follow-up care for at least 2 years after diagnosis. Such care includes a monthly physical examination, blood test, tumor marker study, and whenever appropriate, CT scan. Table 10-1 summarizes the treatment of seminoma and nonseminoma testicular cancers by stage.

11

Cancer of Unknown Primary Site

In the vast majority of cancer patients, the original source of a cancer is easily established. Based on all available information including x rays, blood tests, physical examination, and microscopic analysis, the cancer diagnosed is believed to have originated in a specific organ, otherwise known as the *primary site*. For example, a patient's malignant breast mass is diagnosed as a primary breast cancer; a man's malignant nodule in the prostate is diagnosed as primary prostate cancer. The primary site of origin determines both the treatment and the prognosis.

In as many as 10% of cancer patients, however, the primary site is not established with certainty. These patients are said to have a cancer of unknown primary site (CUPS). Doctors believe that patients with CUPS have microscopic cancers that escape detection. By the time of diagnosis, such a cancer has spread beyond its organ of origin and has reached an advanced stage.

A CUPS diagnosis differs from that of other cancers in several notable ways. First, there are no accepted risk factors for CUPS. Neither gender, diet, geography, occupational exposure, nor heredity influences the development of CUPS. Second, there are no screening tests of proven benefit; by definition, these cancers have indeterminate primary sites.

Third, the diagnosis of CUPS is essentially arrived at by exclusion, that is, only when no strong evidence exists to identify an organ of primary origin. Unfortunately, the primary site of such a cancer is often never detected; only in approximately 50% of CUPS patients does a likely primary site ever become apparent. So difficult is this determination of primary sites that even autopsy examination fails to yield a conclusive identification in nearly one third of patients who die of CUPS.

Fourth, the ambiguity inherent with the CUPS diagnosis is a source of tremendous frustration for the patient, family, and physician. Families have a difficult time accepting that, with all of the recent improvements in modern diagnostic testing, the primary site cannot be detected.

This uncertainty influences treatment recommendations. Patients with CUPS are often given a trial of therapy "as if" the primary site were established. This "as if" approach to treatment is based on the cancer's anatomic location and its appearance under the microscope. The oncologist asks. "What treatable type of cancer can appear in this fashion?" Although the primary site of the cancer is not established, the patient is treated as if a known and treatable primary cancer has been identified.

The Evaluation of Patients with CUPS

By definition, patients with CUPS have no obvious source of the cancer. Practically speaking, this means that the routine studies, physical examination, blood work, and x rays are unrevealing. Additional testing is usually done at the discretion of the doctor, although most patients receive a computed tomography (CT) scan of the chest and the abdomen.

Tests aimed at detecting responsive cancers are also performed. These usually include x rays to evaluate the thyroid and the reproductive organs. Any suspicious symptom is investigated.

For example, a CUPS patients who is hoarse may benefit from an examination of the throat, whereas another patient with blood in the stool should have the intestinal tract investigated.

Unfortunately, in most patients these extra tests do not establish the primary source. As a result, special attention is given to the pathological diagnosis. In fact, review of the biopsy material becomes one of the most crucial steps in evaluating a patient with CUPS. When the diagnosis is uncertain, the biopsy material is often sent to an expert pathologist for a second opinion.

It is the pathologist's job to classify cancers according to the cancer's appearance under the microscope; this classification provides information as to the primary site of the cancer. Cancers are generally classified into two broad categories, *lymphoid* and *nonlymphoid*. Lymphoid cancers arise in the bone marrow and lymph nodes, whereas nonlymphoid cancers arise in all other organs of the body. Hodgkin's disease and non-Hodgkin's lymphoma are common lymphoid cancers that are extremely responsive to chemotherapy.

Nonlymphoid cancers are classified into five types based on their microscopic appearance: adenocarcinoma, squamous carcinoma, large-cell carcinoma, small-cell carcinoma, and undifferentiated carcinoma. Because specific organs often give rise to specific cell types, cellular information is critical in evaluating a likely primary source of the cancer. For example, most primary breast, prostate, and colon cancers are adenocarcinomas. In contrast, head and neck cancers as well as cervical cancer are most often squamous cancers. Table 11-1 illustrates the relationship between microscopic classification and possible primary cancers.

Highly sophisticated tests can be performed on the biopsy material to determine classification. These special stains, can provide clues about the origin of the cancer, because each stain is specific for a diagnostic *tumor marker* of a primary cancer. If the cancer cells contain the marker, the special stain will detect it. When positive, these special stains provide valuable information, as in the case of K.L.

K.L. is a 65-year-old man who noted a lump on the right side of his neck. He was examined by his family doctor, who referred K.L. to a surgeon. The surgeon removed the mass, which was diagnosed an undifferentiated cancer. The remainder of his examination was normal. Additional normal studies included routine blood work and CT scans of the neck, chest, and abdomen.

In an attempt to determine the primary site, special stains were done and proved negative for thyroid, melanoma, and prostate. However, the lymphoid stains were positive, raising the possibility of Hodgkin's disease or lymphoma. The material was sent for a second opinion to a pathologist expert in lymphoid cancers, who diagnosed the cancer as a lymphoma. Instead of further surgery, K.L. began a regimen of chemotherapy for lymphoma. Three years later, K.L. shows no evidence of tumor.

The case of K.L. illustrates how the use of special stains can improve diagnostic accuracy. The special stains supported the diagnosis of lymphoma and indicated the need for an expert opinion. K.L.'s case also illustrates the crucial role of a second opinion when the diagnosis is uncertain.

The Treatment of CUPS

Unfortunately, in too many CUPS patients, treatment is of marginal benefit. This is due to the uncertainty concerning the

Table 11-1
Cancer Classification and Possible Primary Organ

Classification	Possible primary organ
Lymphoid	Blood (leukemia) and lymph nodes (Hodgkin's disease, non-Hodgkin's lymphoma)
Nonlymphoid adenocarcinoma	Breast, colon and rectum, stomach, ovary, prostate, some lung cancers
Squamous carcinoma	Cervix, anus, head and neck cancer, some skin cancers, some lung cancers
Large-cell carcinoma	Some lung cancers
Small-cell carcinoma	Some lung cancers, some skin cancers
Undifferentiated carcinoma	Can arise from virtually any organ

true primary source of the cancer as well as to the cancer's spread. However, there are distinct groups of CUPS patients, possessing unique features that predict a positive response to therapy, who respond favorably to treatment. In the presence of one of these features, aggressive treatment is usually recommended.

Patients who develop a squamous cancer of the neck region are considered to have a potentially responsive cancer. A thorough head and neck exam is generally performed by an ear, nose, and throat (ENT) specialist, who utilizes mirrors to inspect the throat. Even when there is no obvious primary source, such a patient is treated with either surgery or radiation for a possible head and neck primary cancer.

When an adenocarcinoma is found in the underarm of a female patient, she is treated for a possible primary breast cancer. Samples of malignant tissue are stained for estrogen receptors, frequently present in breast cancers. Most authorities recommend either radiation therapy for the involved breast or a modified mastectomy.

Ovarian cancer often causes abdominal swelling due to a collection of fluid known as *ascites* that often contains cancer cells. Women with CUPS who develop cancerous ascites, but have normal ovaries, are often treated for a probable primary ovarian cancer with cisplatin chemotherapy.

Drs. Anthony Greco and John Hainsworth at Vanderbilt University have described yet another group of CUPS patients who respond to chemotherapy. These patients, whose diagnosis is a poorly differentiated carcinoma, claim one or more of the following features: younger than 50 years, rapid tumor growth, a good response to prior treatment, or an elevation of tumor markers that is usually associated with testicular cancer. A high percentage of these CUPS patients respond to cisplatin chemotherapy.

Unfortunately, the majority of patients with CUPS have no findings indicative of a primary cancer. Treatment choices for these patients are especially difficult because chemotherapy infrequently proves beneficial, and the chance of cure is remote.

However, many oncologists do recommend a trial of chemo-

Table 11-2
Significant Findings in CUPS That Direct Treatment

Finding	Therapy
Special stains	Therapy is directed according to the type of primary that is discovered by the stains
Squamous carcinoma in the neck region	Surgery or radiation for a primary head and neck cancer
Adenocarcinoma of the underarm	Mastectomy or radiation "as if" a primary breast cancer
Malignant cells in abdomen	Chemotherapy "as if" a primary ovarian cancer
Poorly differentiated cancer	Cisplatin chemotherapy
None of the above findings	A trial of chemotherapy or hormonal therapy is a consideration. Sometimes treatment of problems as they arise is most appropriate

SOURCE: Sporin JR, Greenberg BR. Empiric chemotherapy in patients with carcinoma of unknown primary site. *American Journal of Medicine* 88:49–55, 1990.

therapy for CUPS patients. A combination of drugs commonly used for CUPS is fluorouracil, adriamycin, and mitomycin. The chemotherapy is continued as long as the cancer proves responsive. For CUPS patients who have no symptoms, a trial of observation is certainly a reasonable approach. Because of limited side effects, hormone therapy is also employed in the treatment of CUPS.

Supportive care, the treatment of specific problems as they arise, is often a reasonable approach for patients unable to tolerate chemotherapy. As CUPS patients experience the same cancer-induced symptoms as do those patients with well-defined cancers, the treatment of such complications is identical for both groups. The decision not to treat a CUPS cancer can be exceptionally trying for the patient, family, and doctor. Ultimately, such a decision often comes down to a value judgment on the part of both the oncologist and the patient. (These problems are discussed in depth in the Chapters 18, No Therapy, and 21, Day-to-Day Symptoms.)

Table 11-2 summarizes the treatment of CUPS patients according to significant hints that point to a treatable primary cancer.

II

Cancer Treatments

12

Surgical Therapy of Cancer

with John A. McKeating, M.D.

Surgery is actually the oldest method of cancer treatment; its use dates back to the ancient Egyptians. Even as recently as the 1930s, radical surgical procedures were believed to hold the promise of cancer cure. Today, as the behaviors of multiple cancers are better understood and the alternative treatments of chemotherapy and radiation are well established, surgery has assumed a more defined role in cancer treatment.

For most cancer patients, surgery is essentially used to treat localized cancers. Such a procedure usually involves the removal of the primary source of the cancer as well as any cancer cells that may have spread to nearby lymph glands and organs. Surgery, however, is only rarely employed to contain cancer cells that have spread to remote parts of the body, the treatment of which generally involves chemotherapy, radiation therapy, or both. At present, surgery remains the single best treatment for many cancers, particularly skin cancer, non–small-cell lung cancer, and colon cancer. Moreover, surgery plays a vital role in the diagnosis, staging, and treatment of numerous other cancers.

The surgeon who treats cancer patients is one member of the

medical team that might include a doctor of internal medicine, a pathologist, a medical oncologist, a radiation therapist, a plastic surgeon, and a rehabilitation specialist. In this capacity, the surgeon is involved in the entire spectrum of the patient's care, whether it be diagnosis, staging of the cancer, curative and noncurative (palliative) treatment, surgical emergencies, or insertion of a venous catheter for the administration of chemotherapy.

Diagnosis

A patient who evidences a suspicious "lump," "mass," or "x-ray abnormality" is usually referred by the primary physician to a surgeon. Although a presumptive diagnosis may often be made on the basis of a thorough medical history and a physical examination, the surgeon is typically asked to obtain a tissue or fluid sample for diagnosis.

The type and extent of surgery performed depends on the location of the mass. For tumors of the throat, esophagus, stomach, colon, and rectum, a technique known as *endoscopy* may be used. In this examination, a flexible lighted tube with the capacity to excise tissue samples is passed into the organ containing the mass. Superficial tumors of the breast, thyroid, skin, muscle, and fat may be accessible by biopsies that utilize either a fine needle or small incision. Biopsies can sometimes be performed on tumors situated in deeper body cavities by passing a very thin slender needle into the area with the aid of a computed tomography (CT) scan or ultrasound machine. In other situations, an operation may be needed for the purpose of biopsy.

In some instances, an analysis of the biopsy sample may be accomplished immediately with the use of a *frozen section*. In this method, the pathologist freezes a generally pea-sized sample of tissue in a specialized machine and afterwards slices the frozen tissue into wafer-like sections that can be immediately studied under the microscope. When this type of analysis is not possible, permanent slides of tissue must be prepared and evaluated, a process that may

Table 12-1
Common Diagnostic Surgical Techniques

Type of biopsy	Description of process	Organ
Endoscopy	Inspection of organ with lighted tube	Colon, stomach, throat rectum, colon, lung
Cytology	Examination of body, fluid, sputum, or scrapings	Pap smear of cervix, fluid from abdominal or chest cavity, nipple drainage, bone marrow
TRU-CUT® needle	Larger bore needle inserted into organ	Breast, liver, lymph nodes
Fine needle	Tiny needle inserted into an organ, often via x-ray guidance	Thyroid, breast
Incisional biopsy	Removal of a piece, but usually not all, of the cancer	Muscle, fat, skin, lymph nodes, breast
Excisional biopsy	Removal of entire cancer	Any location or area

require several days. In order to diagnose certain types of cancer, special stains may also need to be applied to the slides of tissue, a procedure that may further delay the diagnosis by several days.

Should an *excisional biopsy* be performed, that is, removal of the entire tumor, the pathologist carefully notes the tumor's features such as size, depth of penetration into surrounding normal tissue, the margin of adjacent normal tissue, presence or absence of abnormal lymph nodes, and degree of spread into nearby structures. Table 12-1 lists the commonly used diagnostic techniques.

Staging

Physicians use a set of guidelines known as a *staging system* to classify cancers and gauge prognosis. In fact, proper treatment usually depends on careful staging of the cancer. Whereas some cancers can be staged by a physical examination and a few simple x-ray tests, other cancers must be staged by surgical exploration.

Prime examples of cancers that require staging surgery are breast cancer and Hodgkin's disease. A patient with breast cancer routinely undergoes a procedure known as an *axillary lymph node dissection*. In this procedure, which is increasingly performed on an outpatient basis, the patient receives general anesthesia, and the surgeon proceeds to make a small incision in the underarm to remove the lymph nodes located there.

In contrast, the staging of Hodgkin's disease sometimes requires a major abdominal operation known as a *staging laparotomy*. In this setting, the surgeon makes an incision in midabdomen from the breast bone to the navel. The spleen as well as multiple small lymph nodes within the abdomen are removed, and biopsies of the liver are taken. Based on information gained by the staging studies, physicians are able to determine the optimal treatment for the patient. (See Chapter 1, Breast Cancer, and Chapter 7, Hodgkin's and Non-Hodgkin's Lymphoma.)

Curative Surgical Therapy

Whereas a *palliative* operation is performed to control troublesome symptoms of a patient's cancer, a *curative* operation is performed with the possibility of curing the patient's cancer. However, a curative surgical procedure cannot control tumor cells that may have already spread to other parts of the body, and such a procedure can certainly not guarantee that the patient will be cured of the disease. In fact, cure can be established only with the passage of time.

In order to undergo curative surgery, the cancer patient must qualify in two essential ways. First, the given disease must show no evidence of distant spread; this prerequisite is established through blood tests and x rays. Second, the patient must be physically strong enough to tolerate the rigors of the planned procedure. Frequently, preexisting medical conditions preclude the use of aggressive surgery. For patients whose physical condition is questionable, preoperative testing may be performed in order to establish the safety of the planned procedure.

A type of surgery generally performed with a curative intent is breast cancer surgery. The following cases of D.M. and J.M. illustrate that the surgical treatment of breast cancer is now highly individualized.

D.M. is a 70-year-old healthy woman who, after noting a large painless lump in her right breast, postponed seeking medical attention for several months. In D.M.'s immediate family, both her mother and sister have had breast cancer. The surgeon's examination revealed a 6-cm mass, movable and nontender, in the upper outer quadrant of the breast. Neither skin involvement nor swollen lymph nodes in the underarm area were evident. The surgeon recommended that a small incisional biopsy be taken immediately in the office under local anesthesia (Novocaine), after which the patient returned home.

Two days later, the pathology report confirmed the diagnosis of breast cancer. The surgeon met with D.M. and her family to discuss the treatment options thoroughly. Because of the large size of the tumor and the relatively small amount of breast tissue surrounding it, the surgeon advised a modified radical mastectomy, because the cosmetic results of breast-conserving surgery would be poor. When D.M. decided in favor of this procedure, the surgeon contacted D.M.'s family doctor, who confirmed that D.M.'s overall medical condition was good, an indicator that she could well tolerate such surgery.

Several days later, D.M. was admitted to the hospital for the procedure. In the operating room, she received a general anesthetic. The surgeon proceeded to make two long incisions above and below the nipple; these incisions extended from the breastbone to the armpit. Raising the skin flaps, the surgeon then removed breast tissue from the chest wall and removed all lymph-bearing tissue from the underarm area. With minimal blood loss, the incisions were closed, and two flexible plastic drains were positioned beneath the skin in order to facilitate the drainage of small amounts of blood and serum over the next few days.

On the evening after the operation, D.M. was alert and walking. She was discharged on the second postoperative day. Three days later, the drains were removed in the surgeon's office. Five days after that, the sutures were removed.

As the pathological analysis revealed that several of the lymph nodes were involved with tumor, D.M. was referred to a medical oncologist for further treatment with either chemotherapy or hormonal therapy. She was also advised to be somewhat protective of her right arm because, with the removal of the lymph nodes, it was more susceptible to infection. For example, she was counseled to have blood drawn from the other arm and to wear gloves when performing rough chores such as gardening in order to prevent lacerations. When fully healed, D.M. began an exercise regimen in order to regain shoulder mobility. Fortunately, as complications from this procedure are quite rare, D.M. was able to resume her normal range of activity within 5 weeks. In the future, she has the option of choosing either breast reconstruction or a prosthesis, that is, a fitting for an artificial breast to be worn inside a bra.

J.M.'s situation was quite different from that of D.M.

J.M. is a 50-year-old woman whose most recent mammogram revealed an abnormality of the right breast. Her medical history showed no risk factors for breast cancer; the physical examination of the breast proved entirely normal.

Because the abnormality could not be manually located by the surgeon, the suspicious area had to be "localized" by a radiologist before a biopsy could be taken. Consequently, on the morning of the scheduled surgery, the radiologist employed a mammography machine to locate the tiny site of microcalcification and mark it with the placement of a small wire. J.M. was then taken to the operating room where, under local anesthesia, the marked breast tissue was removed. In order to confirm that the tissue did, in fact, contain the abnormality, the radiologist immediately took another mammogram of the specimen—which had been removed—and relayed the affirmative results to the surgeon. After the incision was sutured, J.M. was sent to the recovery room and was discharged later in the day.

Within 2 days, the pathologist confirmed the diagnosis of a small breast cancer. The surgeon fully explained the treatment options, which included the modified radical mastectomy as well as a type of breast-conserving surgery. J.M. was a candidate for the latter as her lone tumor was small and the size of the breast allowed for radiation, a therapy that must be given in conjunction with breast-sparing surgery. After some deliberation, J.M. elected to have the axillary node dissection. In the course of this outpatient procedure, the lymph nodes proved cancer free. After the incision's temporary drain was removed in the surgeon's office on the fifth postoperative day, J.M. proceeded to make an uneventful recovery. She was then referred to a radiation therapist for radiation therapy as well as a medical oncologist for possible treatment involving chemotherapy, hormonal therapy, or both.

Despite obvious differences in the cases of D.M. and J.M., surgery offered both patients the potential for cure. Both women were in good medical condition and showed no evidence of distant spread. Although their elected surgeries differed significantly, it is important to emphasize that each woman was fully involved in making the treatment decision regarding her disease.

Palliative Surgical Therapy

Patients whose diseases are widespread may benefit from palliative rather than curative surgery. For example, patients with advanced colon cancer whose disease has metastasized to the lungs and liver sometimes experience painful obstructions in the colon. Although an operation cannot cure such patients, a localized procedure can bypass or remove the tumor, thus providing relief from the obstruction.

In a palliative operation, the surgeon attempts to maximize the patient's comfort by relieving troublesome symptoms with the least amount of surgery possible. To achieve this aim, the surgeon actually scales down or limits the scope of the given procedure, the priority being to enable the patient to leave the hospital as quickly as possible and to maintain a certain quality of life. Of course, surgical complications must be vigilantly dealt with as these, too, may affect the quality of a patient's life. The case of M.W. illustrates an appropriate use of palliative surgery.

M.W. is a 72-year-old man who consulted his family doctor when disturbed by constipation and small amounts of rectal bleeding. A barium enema test revealed a mass on the left side of the colon. Because the colon narrowed at the site of the mass, it appeared that the mass was partially obstructing the colon. Although a CT scan of the abdomen revealed cancer spots in the liver, thus establishing an advanced stage of disease, M.W. felt surprisingly well. The results of the physical examination were entirely normal.

At this juncture, the surgeon to whom M.W. had been referred held a conference with the patient and his family. As the cancer in the liver was deemed inoperable, the surgeon recommended removal of the cancerous obstruction in the colon, eliminating the possibility of intestinal obstruction. As M.W. expressly desired to live as normal a life as possible, it was decided that the goal of surgery was to maintain his quality of life by palliative surgery, that is, removal of the colon mass.

M.W. was immediately placed on a bowel-cleansing regimen including a clear liquid diet, oral antibiotics, and laxatives. On the morning of the planned surgery, he was admitted to the hospital. In the course of the procedure, a vertical incision was made in the abdomen from the breast bone to the pubic bone. For the purpose of confirmation, biopsies were taken of the small nodules of the liver and found cancerous. The segment of the colon containing the tumor was then removed and the ends of the colon reattached. After the abdomen was closed with sutures and staples, a tube known as a *nasogastric* tube was inserted into the stomach via the nostrils to ensure that the stomach remained empty, and the bladder was then catheterized to drain urine.

On the first postoperative day, M.W. was walking and his pain well controlled by medication. On the following day, the nasogastric tube was removed and, within 24 hours, his bowels began to function, and he was able to eat. M.W. was discharged on the sixth postoperative day.

M.W. resumed his normal level of activity in approximately 6 weeks. He was referred to a medical oncologist in order to consider the benefit of further therapy and, in fact, M.W. did experience a temporary response to chemotherapy for 4 months. Because of a relapse of the liver cancer, however, M.W. died 7 months after surgery.

M.W.'s case exemplifies how palliative surgery can contribute to the quality of a cancer patient's life. After being relieved of the colon tumor that would have eventually caused an intestinal obstruction, M.W. was able to live in relative comfort for some months following surgery.

Another type of palliative surgery required by cancer patients addresses the problem of nutritional deficiencies that may emanate from either treatment or the disease itself. When chemotherapy induces severe nausea and vomiting or when intestinal tumors impede digestion, aggressive and creative surgery may be necessary to ensure proper nutrition. For example, a patient whose tumor blocks the esophagus may benefit from a feeding tube placed directly into the stomach until radiation treatments succeed in shrinking the tumor. For various periods during or after treatment, other patients may require intravenous feeding. Today, this method of feeding is refined to the point that it is both extremely safe and effective. Of course, the patient's prognosis and overall condition determine the extent of surgical intervention. Such treatment decisions invariably demand judgment as well as compassion on the part of the physicians.

Surgical Emergencies in Cancer Patients

In surviving cancer, patients are subject to standard health problems such as appendicitis, diverticulitis, and gallbladder disease that can require surgical attention. However, cancer survivors are also subject to problems peculiar to their cancer status. Such problems may arise during the treatment itself or may develop years after therapy is completed. In many cases, the prior history of cancer may complicate an otherwise simple surgical procedure.

In rare instances, chemotherapy has been known to cause or aggravate surgical problems. For example, patients with intestinal lymphoma may suffer from perforation of the bowel as chemotherapy "melts away" the tumor. This condition requires immediate surgical intervention to prevent the development of a life-threatening infection in the abdomen. Moreover, chemotherapy commonly causes depression of bone marrow, resulting in a very low white blood cell count. As such patients are prone to infections, surgery must often be postponed until the white blood cell count rises to a safe level.

Radiation to various parts of the body may also cause problems in surgical candidates long after treatment is completed. High doses of radiation to a patient's pelvic area sometimes result in deterioration of the intestinal walls, a condition that demands particular care from the surgeon and one that may, in fact, influence decisions during the course of surgery. For example, attaching the colon to the rectum after the removal of a colon cancer may be patently unsafe for a patient who has received large doses of pelvic radiation. For such a patient, the formation of a colostomy may be necessary. Acting with full awareness of such potential pitfalls, the surgeon who treats the cancer survivor must exercise care and judgment in attempting to minimize the complications resulting from any surgical procedure.

Permanent Venous Catheters

In the course of treatment, the cancer patient may require intravenous (IV) tubes for the regular administration of chemotherapy drugs and, on occasion, antibiotics and nutritional solutions. Multiple IVs, apart from causing pain during each insertion, also tend to deplete usable veins in the arms. To avoid such problems, a tube known as a *large-bore indwelling IV catheter* is often permanently placed in the large veins of the upper chest or neck.

Most types of permanent catheters available today must be inserted by the surgeon under sterile conditions in the operating room with the aid of a local anesthetic and some sedation. Some of these catheters are implanted beneath the skin and easily accessed with a needle through the skin of the chest wall. A small receptacle residing under the skin is attached to flexible tubing that enters the vein beneath the collar bone and travels down into the great vessels of the chest. As these vessels have a decidedly high rate of blood flow, they can accommodate chemotherapy drugs and concentrated nutritional solutions.

Other implanted devices protrude through the skin with one or two IV lines that can be accessed by a needle without puncturing the skin. However, the disadvantage of this device as well as permanent catheters in general is a susceptibility to infection. In order to prevent clotting, permanent venous catheters require routine flushes with heparin, a blood thinner. Other complications that can arise from the placement of these catheters include the introduction of air into the lung (pneumothorax) and bleeding in the chest (hemothorax). Each type of catheter has advantages and disadvantages, but these devices are relatively safe, very convenient, and easily removable.

The cancer patient benefits most from surgical procedures when they are individualized to respond to the patient's overall medical condition. As an integral member of the treatment team, the surgeon may be required in a host of situations, and it can accurately be said that the surgeon is involved in all aspects of the patient's care. Like medical decisions, surgical decisions in cancer therapy are based on experience, sound judgment, and compassion.

13

Radiation Therapy

Radiation therapy (RT) employs x rays in the treatment of cancer. Over the past 20 years, as the medical understanding and use of radiation has greatly increased, RT has developed into a sophisticated science. It must now be administered by doctors, called radiation oncologists, who specialize in this mode of treatment. At present, nearly 50% of cancer patients receive RT at some time during treatment.

What Is Radiation?

From a scientific standpoint, radiation is energy in the form of electromagnetic waves. The concept of electromagnetic waves may initially appear complex, but electromagnetic waves are actually as familiar as sunlight or the sound of a radio. As it turns out, sunlight, radio waves, and radiation are all electromagnetic waves. Radio waves, for example, exist in different frequencies; tuning in a particular radio station simply entails selecting the proper frequency. The higher the frequency of the electromagnetic wave, the greater its form of energy. Radiation, then, is essentially a series of high-frequency radio waves that possess sufficient energy to destroy cancer cells.

Two types of radiation are used in the treatment of cancer. The first, external RT, utilizes x rays with extremely high levels of energy. After being produced by a machine, these x-ray beams are aimed at specific areas of a patient's body, delivering their energy immediately on contact. The second type of radiation used in the treatment of cancer is implant RT. In implant RT, a radioactive material is placed as close to the tumor as possible in order to facilitate the delivery of lethal doses of radiation directly to the cancer.

How Does Radiation Work?

Radiation is an effective cancer treatment because of its capacity to damage rapidly growing cells. Cancer cells grow more rapidly than the cells of normal tissues do, so cancer cells are particularly sensitive to the effects of radiation. In fact, the faster a cancer grows, the more effective radiation is in arresting it.

Radiation, however, poses risks for normal tissue as well, a reality that greatly complicates the planning of RT. After studying the x rays, the radiation oncologist must map a target area. These calculations are frequently done with the aid of a computer. Actually, this process is analogous to the destruction of a military target. Just as the task of a fighter pilot is to bomb the target without harming the civilian population, the job of a radiation oncologist is to destroy the cancer while sparing healthy tissue.

How Is Radiation Measured?

The effects of radiation, on both normal and cancerous cells, depend on the amount of radiation given. Radiation is customarily measured in *rads*. A rad is a unit of energy that measures the heat of an x ray, a measurement employed by the radiation oncologist to calculate a precise and safe amount of radiation for the cancer patient. Radiation, like medication, must be given in safe doses. Typically, a patient receives 180 to 200 rads daily for a few weeks, with the total dose of rads often numbering between 3000 and 6000 rads.

Factors That Determine a Patient's Radiation Therapy

Like all other types of cancer treatment, RT must be individualized for each patient. Of course, the patient's safety is always a primary concern in formulating a plan. Within these safety parameters, certain factors determine the type and amount of RT given to the patient.

The first significant factor considered in planning RT is the patient's specific *type of cancer.* Every type of cancer possesses a predictable response to RT, which is defined as the amount of radiation required to control the growth of a specific cancer. Because of differences in growth rates, some cancers are more susceptible than others to radiation. For example, seminoma is a type of testicular cancer that is extremely responsive to radiation therapy. Consequently, radiation is routinely given to such testicular cancer patients after surgery.

A second critical factor in formulating a plan for RT is the *location of the cancer.* Location identifies normal body tissues that will be exposed to the effects of radiation during the course of RT. Normal tissue can be damaged by radiation in much the same way that cancerous tissue is. As was mentioned earlier, the growth rate of a tissue largely determines its sensitivity to radiation. Rapidly replenishing cells, such as those in hair, blood, and sperm, have an extremely high rate of growth. Consequently, they are particularly susceptible to the damaging effects of radiation. Tissues that are very sensitive to radiation must be shielded from the radiation. Actually, the radiation tolerance of adjacent normal tissue is as crucial to the planning of RT as is the type of cancer.

The third consideration in formulating a plan for radiation is the *purpose* of RT. The two purposes of radiation are cure and control of the cancer. When the potential for cure of the cancer exists, the maximal amount of radiation possible is given. Of course, the higher this dose of radiation is, the higher the risk of damaging nearby normal tissues. Frequently, however, the goal of RT is to control rather than to cure the cancer. In this situation, RT is employed to eliminate cancer-induced symptoms such as pain or headache. As noncurative RT requires lower doses of radiation, it is generally tolerated quite well.

A factor that often limits or precludes the use of RT is a *history of radiation* to an area of the body. Unlike other cancer treatments, such as chemotherapy, which can be given to a patient repeatedly, RT is commonly administered only once to any given area. Any patient who has received maximal radiation cannot receive more to that area. In some instances, however, a patient may receive a booster dose of radiation if surrounding normal tissues can tolerate it.

As with other forms of cancer treatment, the overall *medical condition* of the patient is a crucial factor in formulating a plan for RT. Physically, patients must be strong enough to tolerate radiation. Because radiation can further damage an already diseased organ, RT is sometimes not recommended for patients with serious medical conditions. B.L. is such an example, a patient whose lungs could not tolerate the appropriate RT.

> For years, B.L. had been treated by his family doctor for "black lung." Needing multiple medications for this condition, B.L. also required continuous oxygen in order to sleep. After B.L. complained of difficulty in breathing, a chest x ray revealed a spot on the lung that proved cancerous. Given his generally poor physical condition, surgery was not an option.

> B.L. consulted a radiation oncologist for possible radiation therapy. However, the radiation oncologist calculated that the amount of radiation needed to control the lung cancer would damage the remaining normal lung, causing the patient more harm than good. As B.L.'s underlying lung condition precluded both surgery and radiation, the decision was made to treat him with chemotherapy.

The case of B.L. underscores the importance of patient safety in the planning of RT. The administration of RT involves extremely sophisticated calculations, and the most important calculation is essentially a judgment on the part of the radiation oncologist that

Table 13-1
Important Factors in Planning Radiation Therapy

Factor	Comments
Type of cancer	The type of cancer determines the amount of radiation required to treat the cancer
Location of the cancer	The location of the cancer determines which normal tissues are exposed to the risks of radiation. Normal tissues vary widely in their capacity to tolerate RT
Purpose of RT	Less RT is required to control a cancer than to cure it
Prior RT	There is a limit to the amount of RT that a patient can safely receive in only one area
Medical condition of patient	The patient must be able to tolerate RT. An organ already damaged by an unrelated illness may not be able to withstand RT to that organ

the patient can be given radiation with a high degree of safety. Table 13-1 summarizes the five factors essential to the safe administration of RT.

Administration of Radiation Therapy

Each of the two types of RT, external beam RT and implant RT, requires a distinct process of administration. As a result, the experience of a patient receiving external beam RT is vastly different from that of a patient receiving implant RT.

External Beam Radiation Therapy

For the patient who is scheduled to receive external beam RT, the first visit to a radiation unit is generally a day of preparations. The radiation oncologist examines the patient and studies the chart. The dose of radiation (number of rads) is then calculated, frequently with the aid of a physicist. Once the area to be radiated has been precisely located, permanent tattoos are applied to the patient's skin as guidelines for the radiation beam. Whenever normal tissues need to be protected from the radiation beam, customized shields are made to protect that area.

External beam RT is administered in much the same manner as a routine x ray. A radiation technologist, the specialist who actually administers RT, accompanies the patient into the treatment room. After positioning the patient before the machine, the radiation technologist "lines up" the radiation beam with the tattooed area, adjusts any shields, and exits to commence treatment. Typically, a session of RT lasts a few minutes. Most patients receive external beam RT Monday through Friday as outpatients. Depending on the amount of radiation planned, the duration of RT varies from 2 to 10 weeks.

Implant RT

Although implant RT works in the same way as external beam RT, the processes are decidedly different. Implant RT involves the surgical insertion of a radioactive implant, often under general anesthesia, in or near the cancerous tissue. The radiation is then delivered over a period of a few days directly to the nearby tissues. During this process, the patient stays in hospital isolation to avoid exposing others to the elevated levels of radiation. Once the radioactivity is spent, the implant is removed, and the patient can be safely discharged.

Because of its complexity, implant RT is limited in its uses. Cancers that are anatomically accessible are most often treated in this manner. One such example is cervical cancer, for which radioactive material is inserted through the vagina and placed directly on the cancerous tissue. Cancers likewise treated with implant RT are breast cancers and cancers of the head and neck. The choice between external beam RT and implant RT often depends on the location of the cancer and the area that needs to be treated.

Common Uses of Radiation Therapy

RT can be used to treat virtually all cancers and is so effective that nearly 50% of cancer patients eventually receive it. Because

RT is such a versatile cancer treatment, it is difficult to describe its many uses both briefly and accurately. Consequently, the common uses of RT will be discussed according to its two primary purposes, the cure and the control of cancer.

Two features that distinguish curative RT from noncurative RT are the timing and the dose of radiation. When RT can cure a patient, treatment is given immediately. In contrast, noncurative RT, which is aimed at controlling a specific symptom, is given only when the symptom develops. Because the dose of radiation required to control a cancer is usually less than that given to cure a cancer, the patient receiving noncurative RT is likely to experience fewer and less severe side effects.

Types of cancers that spread in a predictable manner and respond well to RT are frequently treated for cure. Head and neck cancer and Hodgkin's disease are two examples of such cancers. Head and neck cancers appear in the area of the body above the collar bone and below the eyebrow. As these cancers tend to remain in this area, they are radiated following surgery with a high probability of cure. Because early stage (I and II) Hodgkin's disease also predictably spreads, the lymph nodes are routinely radiated with an excellent chance of cure. (See Chapter 7, Hodgkin's and Non-Hodgkin's Lymphoma.) An example of such a patient is N.C.

N.C. is a 40-year-old woman who visited her doctor after finding a lump on the left side of her neck. He recommended a biopsy, which confirmed Hodgkin's disease. After further testing, the cancer was found only on the left side of the neck and chest. However, as N.C. had a 20% chance of having Hodgkin's disease in the abdomen, she underwent exploratory surgery. Fortunately, no cancer was found.

N.C. received external beam RT to her neck, chest, and upper abdomen. She was able to continue her job as a nurse during treatment, experiencing only occasional nausea that dissipated after completion of RT. N.C. is now examined every 3 months and, as 5 years have elapsed since the initial diagnosis, she is considered to be cured.

In certain types of cancer, RT is so effective that it can be used instead of surgery. For example, early-stage uterine cancer is often treated with implant RT rather than hysterectomy. Breast cancer,

Table 13-2
Selected Cancers Frequently Cured by Radiation Therapy

Type of cancer	Comment
Cervical and uterine	These cancers are frequently treated with external and implant RT in lieu of surgery
Breast	Lumpectomy followed by RT to the affected breast is considered as effective as mastectomy
Early-stage prostate	Although RT is considered by many experts as effective as radical surgery, controversy continues
Early-stage Hodgkin's disease	RT is the standard treatment for this disease and cures the majority of patients
Seminoma (testicular cancer)	RT is given to abdomen after surgery of the testicle

too, is now increasingly treated with a combination of restricted surgery and RT in lieu of traditional mastectomy. Table 13-2 lists cancers frequently treated and cured with RT; however, it should be noted that not every cancer in these general categories can be effectively treated with RT.

RT is frequently given with the intention of controlling symptoms rather than curing the cancer, when the cancer has spread to an organ and is causing a troublesome symptom. The purpose of RT here is not to extend the quantity of life but rather to improve the quality of life. Consequently, only the area that is causing the symptom receives radiation. Especially well treated by RT are certain organs of the body, including the bone, brain, and skin.

Cancers that have spread to the bone typically cause well-localized pain. Patients can often locate their tumors by pointing to the specific spots on their bones. Radiating this precise location thus controls both the cancer and the pain. Initially, the patient is given pain medication in tandem with RT. Once RT effectively shrinks the cancer, the pain medication is either reduced or stopped entirely. (See Chapter 23, Control of Cancer Pain.)

So effective is RT as a treatment for brain tumors that it is the treatment of choice for the majority of brain cancer patients. Because of the location of these tumors, surgery is often impossible to perform. Moreover, most types of chemotherapy do not penetrate the brain. Brain tumors characteristically cause obvious symptoms such as weakness in the arms or headaches. With the aid of brain scans, RT can be directed to the precise location of the cancer, producing an improvement of symptoms in more than 80% of patients.

Skin cancers, in particular, can be successfully treated with a special type of external RT known as *electron beam* RT. Never penetrating deeply, electron beam RT expends its total energy in the body's outer layers, thus sparing the internal organs any harmful radiation. Because skin cancers are so superficial, they are often easily and effectively treated with electron beam RT. Lymph nodes are pea-like structures spread throughout the body whose job it is to fight infection. When cancerous lymph nodes enlarge and cause symptoms, external beam RT is usually quite effective in shrinking such tumor-bearing nodes.

Side Effects of Radiation Therapy

The possibility of side effects resulting from RT quite naturally generates anxiety and fear in patients. To combat these negative feelings, the wise patient views side effects as a necessary part of a greater whole, that is, the control or cure of cancer. A number of "commonsense" points need to be emphasized about radiation's side effects.

First, side effects are *normal* consequences of powerful therapies. Often, patients assume that they have personally caused these symptoms when, in fact, side effects are the results of the treatment. Undesirable symptoms can and should be expected during the treatment process.

Second, side effects tend to *improve with time* with the vast majority resolving completely when the patient is given sufficient time to rest and heal. Whenever RT is even temporarily stopped, a patient's symptoms typically begin to improve.

Third, *counteractive measures* can be taken to eliminate or control RT's side effects. Many medications can effectively alleviate undesirable symptoms.

Last, it is important for patients undergoing RT to *self-monitor* their bodies. Only the patient knows his or her own body intimately enough to be able to detect an emerging problem. Any questions or problems should be promptly reported to the doctor. As with all areas of health, the early detection of radiation's symptoms results in the most effective care.

RT's side effects can be broadly grouped into two categories, nonspecific and site-specific symptoms. Nonspecific side effects are generalized symptoms, like fatigue, which can develop regardless of where the body receives RT. Site-specific side effects are symptoms that develop within borders of the radiated area.

Nonspecific Side Effects of Radiation Therapy

A common side effect in patients receiving RT and one that can occur at any time during treatments is loss of appetite. As cancer patients may have multiple reasons for developing loss of appetite, attributing the onset of this symptom to RT is inherently difficult. Other reasons for a patient's loss of appetite include depression or reaction to the diagnosis of cancer, infection, pain, side effects of medications, and even the cancer itself. Relying on a process of elimination, the doctor attempts to isolate the cause of the appetite loss. Sometimes, suspending RT can determine whether RT is, indeed, the primary cause. Regardless of cause, however, patients must try to maintain a healthy nutritional status during treatment by "forcing foods." In an attempt to stimulate appetite, some doctors prescribe a short course of steroids.

Another side effect commonly experienced by patients receiving RT is fatigue. Like loss of appetite, fatigue can be caused by many conditions other than RT, such as infection, anemia, and depression. Once again, the doctor attempts to isolate the cause.

Whenever RT is the cause of fatigue, however, the side effect generally resolves on completion of therapy.

A frequent side effect of RT is nausea. Whereas loss of appetite and fatigue can develop at any time during the course of treatments, nausea predictably occurs at the outset of RT. Such nausea is easily controlled with medication and resolves soon after RT is completed. (See Table 14-1, Common Antinausea Medications.)

Site-Specific Side Effects of Radiation Therapy

Developing exclusively in the area of RT, site-specific side effects are the expected negative effects of radiation on normal tissues. Given the vulnerability of radiated tissue, both patient and doctor need to give special attention to the RT site.

A side effect of RT that many patients find especially traumatic is hair loss. Unfortunately, most patients assume that all RT causes inevitable baldness when, in fact, RT causes hair loss only within the area of RT. If the scalp is not radiated, the patient does not become bald. However, when the scalp does lie within the treatment area, the patient is advised to be fitted with a wig before treatment.

As the skin is particularly susceptible to radiation damage, nearly all patients develop some degree of burn from external RT, though fair-skinned patients are especially vulnerable. Initially, the skin appears and feels sunburned. As the dose of radiation increases, the skin can appear swollen and become quite painful. Should the patient's skin reaction become severe, RT is usually stopped until the condition of the skin improves.

Radiation to the area of mouth and neck can cause a number of problems for the patient. Dryness of mouth, resulting from damage to the salivary glands, typically develops within the first 2 weeks of therapy and creates difficulty in chewing and swallowing. (See Table 14-2, Treatment of Mouth Sores.) If the dose of RT has been high, such dryness of mouth may be permanent. To counter this side effect, patients can rely on artificial salivas and increase the daily intake of fluids. As saliva's role is crucial in preventing tooth decay, patients experiencing dryness of mouth must practice good dental hygiene. RT to the mouth and neck area can also alter the sense of taste, thus requiring the patient to cultivate new preferences in food.

Like the skin, the membranes of the throat can be burned by RT. Whereas the initial reaction resembles a sore throat, in more serious reactions, the membrane develops painful sores that can impede swallowing. For mild to moderate soreness, the patient is encouraged to force fluids and is given pain medication, sometimes in the form of oral xylocaine to numb the membranes. If the pain persists, however, RT may be suspended to allow for a period of healing.

The most common side effects of RT in the chest area are difficulty in swallowing and the sensation of heartburn. These symptoms are due to an irritation of the esophagus, the tube connecting the mouth and stomach. Swallowing difficulty and heartburn are treated in the same way as mouth and throat irritations.

RT in the region of the abdomen frequently causes diarrhea. Beginning a week or two after RT is initiated, this symptom may persist several weeks after RT is completed. Mild cases can generally be treated with antidiarrhea medications such as a kaolin and pectin mixture (Kaopectate) or diphenoxylate hydrochloride (Lomotil), but severe cases require that RT be suspended until patients develop a normal bowel habit. Although nausea is also a frequent side effect with abdominal RT, this symptom is usually well controlled with medication.

Major organs that can be permanently damaged by RT require additional considerations. Organs such as the lungs, kidneys, and liver must be shielded during treatment or else given comparatively small doses of radiation. Consequently, these particular organs rarely develop side effects.

The bone marrow is an organ that generally tolerates RT quite well. However, side effects do develop when more than 25% of the marrow is radiated or when areas are repeatedly treated. Blood counts are monitored during RT to avoid any seriously low counts.

Most patients tolerate RT very well, developing only minor, easily controlled side effects. Z.M. is just such an example.

Z.M. is a 57-year-old woman who noted a lump in her right breast. Biopsy was performed; the mass was found to be cancerous. After discussing treatment options with her doctor, she elected to have a lumpectomy with external beam RT.

After 3 weeks of external RT, she noted that her right breast was warm and tender. The radiation oncologist recommended a 10-day rest period. When the pain and tenderness resolved, RT was resumed. She completed her radiation without further problems. Z.M. believes that the cosmetic result of surgery is excellent and is doing well 4 years after her diagnosis.

Z.M. is representative of most patients who receive RT. She developed minor side effects that resolved after a temporary suspension of radiation.

14

Chemotherapy and Hormonal Therapy

with Alfred P. Doyle, M.D.

Chemotherapy and hormonal therapy are often jointly considered in discussions of cancer treatment because these therapies have many similar characteristics. In contrast to surgery and radiation, which are used to treat localized areas of the body, both chemotherapy and hormonal therapy are systemic treatments used to treat the entire body. Two important differences, however, do exist between chemotherapy and hormonal therapy: First, chemotherapy can cause significantly more side effects than hormonal therapy. Second, hormonal therapy is used to treat only a few types of cancer. For these reasons, chemotherapy and hormonal therapy will be independently considered.

Chemotherapy

Chemotherapy uses a class of cancer-fighting drugs that travel throughout the bloodstream to destroy cancer. Chemotherapy drugs, however, vary widely in terms of composition, administration, side effects, and applicability to specific cancers.

Several scientific laws govern the administration of chemotherapy. First, all living tissue is composed of cells and is sustained by the process of cell reproduction. As a cancer is living tissue, any cure of a cancer depends on the destruction of its cells.

Second, chemotherapy destroys both normal and cancerous cells. Such unavoidable damage to normal cells can result in side effects for the patient undergoing this therapy. Consequently, each administration of chemotherapy involves a delicate balance between the intended destruction of the cancer and the control of undesirable side effects.

Third, chemotherapy's potency is greatest in cells that rapidly reproduce. Rapidly growing cancers are usually responsive to chemotherapy, whereas slow-growing ones generally prove resistant to it. This characteristic also explains why chemotherapy's side effects occur predominantly in the hair, bone marrow, and intestinal lining. Because cells in these organs divide more rapidly than those in other body areas, these particular organs are extremely susceptible to chemotherapy and resultant adverse reactions.

Fourth, each chemotherapy drug has distinct side effects. Consequently, several drugs with different side effects can be given in varying combinations, thus maximizing the patient's total dose of chemotherapy. When the multiple side effects of these drugs are monitored carefully, such combinations are both safe and effective.

Fifth, every type of cancer possesses a predictable response to chemotherapy. Obviously, a cancer's responsiveness to chemotherapy is an important factor in planning treatment. For example, small-cell lung cancer is so responsive to chemotherapy that this treatment is generally recommended in lieu of surgery. In contrast, prostate cancer is markedly less responsive to chemotherapy and, as a result, either radiation or surgery is often the preferred treatment.

A patient receives chemotherapy by one of three routes: orally, by injection, or by infusion into a vein. Relying on an established schedule called a *protocol*, the doctor chooses a combination of chemotherapy drugs that has been proven both safe and effective against the specific type of cancer. The protocol designates the standard dosages of chemotherapy drugs and the intervals at which they should be given, usually either weekly or monthly.

Purposes of Chemotherapy

The three standard purposes of chemotherapy are the prevention, the cure, and the control of cancer.

Chemotherapy that is preventive in nature is commonly called *adjuvant* chemotherapy. The aim of adjuvant therapy is the destruction of stray cancer cells remaining in the body after surgery. Because these cells are too small to be detected, the patient shows no discernible evidence of cancer. Purely as a precautionary measure, however, adjuvant drugs are given to the patient to destroy any existing cancerous cells before they multiply. Drugs used in adjuvant chemotherapy are the same drugs used to treat extensive cancers. After surgery, the patient typically receives adjuvant chemotherapy for 4 to 12 months.

An especially encouraging medical breakthrough is the recent discovery that adjuvant chemotherapy significantly improves survival rates for patients with colon and breast cancers. Such adjuvant chemotherapy is now standard therapy for stage C colon cancers and many breast cancers.

The second purpose of chemotherapy, the cure of cancer, is frequently achieved with widespread cancers. Whenever the possibility of cure exists, the patient is typically given as much chemotherapy as can be safely tolerated. Expectedly, such maximal doses can result in serious side effects for which patients need to be hospitalized.

Two cancers requiring such intense curative therapy are acute leukemia and testicular cancer. Patients with acute leukemia receive a potent form of chemotherapy that suppresses the body's production of bone marrow. While receiving therapy, they are routinely hospitalized for 4 to 6 weeks. Chemotherapy for testicular cancer is so intense that 15% of patients need to be rehospitalized for the treatment of its side effects.

When chemotherapy cannot be employed in either a preventive or curative capacity, it can be given to control the cancer. Therapy is aimed at improving the patient's quality of life, and doses are often reduced to avoid side effects. Determining the appropriate dose, which is the amount of chemotherapy that can be comfortably tolerated by the patient, is essentially a matter of judgment on the part of the physician. As it is imperative that the treatment never becomes worse than the disease, the physician must balance the benefits of chemotherapy against its risks.

The following patient histories illustrate how a specific cancer determines the purpose and thus the intensity of chemotherapy.

> D.C. is a 33-year-old man who noted a mass in his right testicle and consulted his family doctor. The doctor immediately referred the patient to a urologist, who suspected a testicular cancer. Surgical removal of the mass confirmed this diagnosis. On evaluation, the cancer was found to have spread to the lungs.
>
> D.C. received intensive chemotherapy, a treatment offering a 90% chance of cure. However, after completing two full courses of chemotherapy, D.C. developed a low white cell count. Rather than suspending treatment to allow for the white count to increase, the oncologist recommended that D.C. continue with chemotherapy because testicular cancer is highly responsive to it. D.C. completed the therapy but later developed a bloodstream infection requiring his hospitalization. He remained extremely ill until the white cell count rose sufficiently to spur recovery. Three years later, D.C. is in remission.

In the treatment of testicular cancer, the medical consensus is that chemotherapy must be given completely on schedule to effect cure. For this reason, D.C. continued to receive intensive chemotherapy in spite of a threateningly low white blood cell count. In D.C.'s case, chemotherapy caused both his bloodstream infection and his cure.

In contrast, the case of B.G. illustrates how the dose of chemotherapy is reduced when the treatment aim is control of the cancer.

B.G. is a 65-year-old woman who had previously been treated for colon cancer. After doing well for 3 years, she began to experience abdominal pain. Her doctor noted an enlarged liver and, on further evaluation, determined that the colon cancer had spread to the liver. After a lengthy discussion during which the oncologist advised B.G. that chemotherapy offered a 50% chance of controlling the cancer, B.G. decided in favor of it.

Four courses of chemotherapy later, the treatment appeared to be working. Following the fifth treatment, however, B.G. developed such severe diarrhea and mouth sores that she required hospitalization for intravenous fluids. Chemotherapy was then delayed, and her situation improved. To lessen the possibility of further side effects, B.G.'s chemotherapy dose was decreased. With reduced dosage, troublesome side effects did not recur, while the liver tumors continued to be controlled.

The dual goals of treatment for B.G. were both to control the cancer and to improve her quality of life. In reality, dose reduction is often a matter of judgment on the part of the physician.

Common Side Effects of Chemotherapy

Chemotherapy drugs are extremely potent and require cautious administration. Protocols purposefully include a range of drugs with diverse side effects to improve the management of individual symptoms. Given the potency and multiplicity of drugs used in a chemotherapy protocol, the patient is likely to experience at least one side effect to some degree. As it is not feasible to discuss all of chemotherapy's possible side effects, some of which are unique to specific drugs, following is a discussion of only the most common and serious side effects of chemotherapy drugs.

One of the most emotionally disturbing side effects of chemotherapy is *hair loss*. Hair loss can occur at any time after chemotherapy is initiated, but it typically develops within the first 6 weeks. Moreover, it tends to be associated with drug combinations containing doxorubicin, vincristine, or cyclophosphamide. A practical strategy of coping with hair loss is for the patient to be fitted with a wig before hair loss occurs, thus assuring that the wig closely resembles the patient's natural hair. In lieu of wigs, male patients often choose baseball caps to conceal hair loss, whereas female patients opt for hats, scarves, and turbans.

A preventive technique used to minimize hair loss is the *cold cap.* During the administration of chemotherapy, ice packs are applied to the patient's scalp in an attempt to decrease the flow of blood-borne drugs to the scalp. Although use of the cold cap is widespread, its effectiveness has not been conclusively proven.

Nausea and *vomiting* are extremely common side effects of chemotherapy. Most of the chemotherapeutic drugs can agitate the digestive tract, and certain drugs, such as nitrogen mustard and cisplatin, are particularly apt to do so. In the vast majority of patients, nausea resolves within 30 hours of the drug's administration and can be effectively controlled by a number of antinausea medications. Occasionally, however, a patient's nausea lingers for as long as a week after therapy, requiring continued medication. Should nausea lead to repeated vomiting, a patient may experience added relief by taking the antinausea medication on the day before chemotherapy. In those rare instances when nausea leads to repeated vomiting, the patient can take the nausea medication in suppository form. Through the process of trial and error, the patient is usually able to discover a personal best regimen for controlling nausea. Table 14-1 provides a selected list of common antinausea medications.

A troublesome side effect that develops when chemotherapy affects the rapidly growing cells of the mouth lining is *mouth sores.* Similar in appearance to cold sores, mouth sores are often associated with protocols containing the drug methotrexate. Although these sores usually resolve within 5 to 7 days, persistent mouth sores can be quite painful, eventually impeding the intake of liquids and requiring medical attention. Table 14-2 provides a list of suggestions for patients experiencing mouth sores.

One of the most potentially serious side effects of chemotherapy is a weakening of the body's immune system known as *bone marrow suppression.* Chemotherapy drugs tend to destroy white blood cells (WBCs), the rapidly growing cells produced by the bone

Table 14-1
Common Antinausea Medications

Drug	Dose and route	Comments
Dexamethasone (*Decadron*)	2–8 mg orally or by injection	A steroid that is frequently given in conjunction with other antinausea medications
Haloperidol (*Haldol*)	2–20 mg orally or by injection	A sedative that has been found to be effective in controlling nausea
Lorazepam (*Ativan*) and Diazepam (*Valium*)	1–4 mg orally or by injection	Antianxiety drugs that apparently counteract nausea by calming the patient
Metoclopramide (*Reglan*)	20–60 mg orally or intravenously	One of the most effective antinausea drugs
Prochlorperazine (*Compazine*) and Thiethylperazine (*Torecan*)	10–25 mg orally, by injection, or by suppository	Two of the most widely used antinausea drugs
Ondansetron (*Zofran*)	2–10 mg orally or by injection	The newest and one of the most effective antinausea drugs. It is more expensive than the other drugs

All doses are in milligrams and in amounts commonly used by doctors. Drug names are generic with brand names in italics. This is only a partial listing of the many effective antinausea medications available today.

marrow, which serve as the body's primary defense against infection. This reduction in the body's WBC count usually occurs in 7 to 14 days after chemotherapy is administered.

When the WBC count is low, the patient is at risk of contracting serious infection. This problem is exacerbated by the fact that a low count masks the body's signs of infection. For example, a patient whose WBC count is low can have a urinary tract infection

Table 14-2
Treatment of Mouth Sores

1. Drink 3 quarts of fluid daily to avoid dehydration.
2. Brush teeth with a soft brush.
3. Avoid commercial mouthwashes with an alcohol content. Instead, use a homemade solution consisting of 1 tsp baking soda dissolved in 2 cups water.
4. Check that dentures fit properly.
5. Keep lips moist with cocoa butter, Chapstick, or Vaseline.
6. Eat soft bland foods like ice cream, yogurt, and applesauce. Puree other foods in a blender or rely on baby foods. Avoid alcohol and tobacco.
7. For pain relief, rinse mouth sores with viscous xylocaine before meals.
8. If mouth sores become severe, *contact your doctor.*

SOURCE: Adapted from Stomatitis/Mucositis. In Yasko JM. *Guidelines for Cancer Care.* Reston, VA: Reston, 1983.

without painful urination or can have pneumonia without a cough. In fact, the only reliable symptom of infection in such patients is fever. Therefore, as a precautionary measure, all chemotherapy patients are instructed to take their temperatures daily. Any patient registering a temperature higher than 101°F needs to be evaluated medically. Whenever a patient with a low WBC count registers such a fever, serious infection is assumed, and the patient is immediately hospitalized for a course of intravenous antibiotics. When the WBC count returns to normal, the fever typically resolves, and the patient can be discharged.

A recent and exciting medical advance is the development of bone marrow *factors* that act to combat chemotherapy's effect on the WBC count. Researchers had known for years that the human body makes a protein, called granulocyte colony-stimulating factor (G-CSF), which stimulates the bone marrow to make WBCs. The genetic material that controls the production of WBCs has now been isolated and inserted into a common bacterium. Laboratory grown, these bacteria presently produce unlimited amounts of G-CSF.

G-CSF (*Neupogen*) is commercially available and is injected daily following the completion of chemotherapy. G-CSF shortens the period of low WBC count for the patient, thus decreasing the chance of serious infection. Frequently, this protein permits the safe administration of higher doses of chemotherapy, thus intensifying the destruction of malignant cells. Several other bone marrow factors are currently under accelerated development.

A relatively rare side effect of chemotherapy is spontaneous *bleeding.* A result of damage to the bone marrow, this bleeding is specifically linked to the marrow's reduced production of platelets, the cell-like disks that promote clotting. When the number of platelets in the blood declines, the patient can bleed unexpectedly. Therefore, anyone receiving chemotherapy is cautioned to report instances of bruising or bleeding immediately to the doctor. If the platelet count is extremely low, the patient may require a platelet transfusion.

To prevent a threateningly low blood count, the patient periodically receives blood tests after chemotherapy. Such testing precisely identifies the status of the blood cells and enables the doctor to alert the patient of any impending danger. It is hoped that medical researchers will soon develop a bone marrow factor that will enhance the bone marrow's production of platelets.

Table 14-3 provides a list of drugs commonly used in chemotherapy. On a scale of 1 to 4, each drug is rated for its tendency to induce the primary side effects of hair loss, nausea, mouth sores, and bone marrow suppression. The table also includes the types of cancer typically treated with the drug, the drug's route of administration, and information unique to the drug.

Chemotherapy Protocols

Chemotherapy protocols are precise treatment programs that have been developed by cancer researchers. Much like a recipe, each protocol specifies the combination of drugs, the dosage, and the frequency of treatments. By referring to a published collection of these programs, a type of "chemotherapy cookbook," the oncologist chooses an accepted treatment protocol for the patient's particular cancer. Typically, the drugs are administered in cycles of 21

Table 14-3
Partial List of Common Chemotherapy Drugs

Drug[a]	Side effects	Scale[b]	Comments
Bleomycin	Hair loss	1	Types of cancer: testicular cancer and lymphoma
	Nausea	2	Route: injection or intravenous
	Mouth sores	2	Considerations: fever and chills immediately after administration. Can cause lung damage or discoloration of the skin.
	Bone marrow suppression	0	
Cisplatin (*Platinol*)	Hair loss	2	Types of cancers: ovarian, lung, and testicular cancer
	Nausea	4	Route: intravenous
	Mouth sores	1	Considerations: requires large urine output to prevent kidney damage. Can cause ear and nerve damage.
	Bone marrow suppression	2 to 3	
Cyclophosphamide (*Cytoxan*)	Hair loss	3	Types of cancer: breast, lung, ovarian, and bladder cancer
	Nausea	1 to 2	Widely used
	Mouth sores	1 to 2	Route: oral or intravenous
	Bone marrow suppression	3	Considerations: Can cause blood in urine and irritation of suppression of the bladder. An increased urine output helps to prevent bladder damage.
Cytarabine (*Cytosar*)	Hair loss	1–2	Types of cancer: leukemia and lymphoma
	Nausea	2	Route: injection or intravenous
	Mouth sores	1–2	Considerations: can cause rash
	Bone marrow suppression	4	

Table 14-3
(Continued)

Drug[a]	Side effects	Scale[b]	Comments
Doxorubicin (*Adriamycin*)	Hair loss	4	Types of cancer: lymphoma, breast, and lung cancers
	Nausea	4	Widely used
	Mouth sores	2	Route: intravenous
	Bone marrow suppression	3	Considerations: can discolor the urine. Can damage veins in the event of seepage during administration. Can cause heart damage.
Fluorouracil (*5-FU*)	Hair loss	2	Types of cancer: colon and breast cancers
	Nausea	2	Route: intravenous
	Mouth sores	2–3	Considerations: can cause a rash on palms of hands. Infrequently associated with heart problems. Can cause mouth sores when given on consecutive days.
	Bone marrow suppression	2	
Folinic acid	Hair loss	1	Types of cancer: colon and breast cancers.
	Nausea	1	Route: intravenous.
	Mouth sores	2	Considerations: not a chemotherapy drug, but folinic acid is used in conjunction with either methotrexate or fluorouracil. Can cause rash, mouth sores and diarrhea when given with methotrexate or fluorouracil.
	Bone marrow suppression	1 to 2	

(continued)

Table 14-3
(Continued)

Drug[a]	Side effects	Scale[b]	Comments
Mechlorethamine	Hair loss	3	Type of cancer: lymphoma
	Nausea	4	Route: intravenous
	Mouth sores	1	Considerations: can damage veins in the event of seepage during administration
	Bone marrow suppression	2 to 3	
Methotrexate (*Mexate*)	Hair loss	2	Types of cancer: lymphoma, bladder and breast cancer
	Nausea	2	Widely used
	Mouth sores	4	Route: intravenous or oral
	Bone marrow suppression	3	Considerations: requires large urine output to prevent side effects. Exposure to sunlight can precipitate rashes. Aspirin must be taken with caution.
Prednisone	Hair loss	1	Types of cancer: numerous cancers. Widely used
	Nausea	1	Route: intravenous or oral
	Mouth sores	1	Considerations: a steroid, potential side effects include mood swings, stomach irritation, weight gain, skin rash, and diabetes. **Must be used only as directed.** Used in conjunction with many chemotherapy drugs.
	Bone marrow suppression	1	
Procarbazine (*Matulane*)	Hair loss	2	Type of cancer: lymphoma
	Nausea	2	Route: oral.
	Mouth sores	1	Considerations: can interact adversely with milk products, alcoholic beverages and many medications.

(continued)

Table 14-3
(Continued)

Drug[a]	Side effects	Scale[b]	Comments
Procarbazine (*Matulane*) (continued)	Bone marrow suppression	3	
Taxol	Hair loss	4	Types of cancer: ovarian and breast
	Nausea	2	Route: intravenous
	Mouth sores	2	Considerations: allergic reactions often require premedication with prednisone and antihistamine. Can cause a slowing of the heart beat
	Bone marrow suppression	3	
Vincristine (*Oncovin*)	Hair loss	2 to 3	Types of cancer: lymphoma, breast, and lung cancers
	Nausea	1	Widely used
	Mouth sores	1	Route: intravenous.
	Bone marrow suppression	1	Considerations: can damage the nervous system, causing numbness in fingers and toes. Can cause tissue damage in the event of seepage during administration. Usually causes constipation.
VP-16 (*Vepecid*)	Hair loss	3	Common uses: lymphoma, lung and testicular cancers
	Nausea	1	Widely used
	Mouth sores	1	Route: intravenous and oral
	Bone marrow suppression	3	Considerations: can cause numbness and tingling of fingers and toes

SOURCE: Perry MC, Yarbro JW (eds). *Toxicity of Chemotherapy.* New York: Grune & Stratton, 1984.

[a] Drug names are generic with brand names in italics.

[b] Side effect scale is graded 0 to 4. Zero is the lowest degree of side effect and 4 is the highest.

to 28 days, with the dosage of each cycle adjusted to the patient's level of tolerance.

One such example of a chemotherapy treatment program is the original protocol developed in the 1960s to treat Hodgkin's disease. Known by the acronym, MOPP, whose letters represent the four chemotherapy drugs used in treatment (mechlorethamine, Oncovin, procarbazine, prednisone), this protocol specifies that the drugs be given on the first and eighth day of each 28-day cycle. Literally hundreds of protocols are used to treat various cancers.

Reproduction and Chemotherapy

Certain chemotherapy protocols can induce infertility in both sexes. This side effect should be fully discussed by doctor and patient before treatment. In men, chemotherapy can cause infertility by reducing the sperm count. When permanent sterility is likely, male patients may consider sperm banking before therapy.

Patients undergoing chemotherapy are encouraged to continue sexual relations in the routine fashion. However, chemotherapy may temporarily diminish sexual interest and drive. Women sometimes find that chemotherapy disrupts their menstrual cycles. Changing hormone levels can likewise result in vaginal dryness, necessitating the use of lubricating ointments. Impotence may occur in men receiving chemotherapy and last for several weeks following treatment. Concerns about sexual function should be discussed openly with the doctor.

As chemotherapy can precipitate birth defects, patients are strongly advised to avoid pregnancy during treatment. Patients of both sexes are urged to practice reliable methods of birth control. After the completion of treatment, genetic counseling can guide couples who desire to conceive.

The Use of Hormones in Cancer Treatment

Hormones are substances produced by specialized organs of the body to regulate specific bodily processes. Two of the most widely recognized are the sex hormones, testosterone and estrogen. Testosterone is the male hormone produced by the testicle to control sexual maturation and male characteristics: hair distribution, deepening voice, and sperm production. Likewise, estrogen is the female hormone produced by the ovaries to control sexual maturation and female characteristics: breast development, hair distribution, and menstruation.

Sex hormones have long been known to influence the growth of certain cancers. This condition was first discovered in 1885 when a young woman with a large breast cancer developed severe vaginal bleeding and required a hysterectomy. During the course of surgery, the ovaries were also removed, and the breast cancer shockingly disappeared. The doctors concluded that her breast cancer had been dependent on the female hormone, estrogen.

Following that celebrated observation, hormones began to be used to treat other breast and uterine cancers. Moreover, prostate cancer was later found to be dependent on the male hormone, testosterone. Castration, the surgical removal of the testicle to eliminate testosterone from the body, has commonly been used to treat prostate cancer since the 1940s.

Precisely how hormones function to counteract certain cancers remained a source of mystery for many years. In the 1960s, however, certain tissues were found to possess *receptors* for sex hormones. These receptors are structures in tissue that adhere to the hormone, an attachment analogous to the fit of a lock and key. The receptor is the lock that accepts the hormone's key. Statistically, hormone receptors are present in 50% of breast cancers and 90% of prostate cancers. This factor of hormone receptivity predicts which cancers will respond to hormonal therapy.

Like chemotherapy drugs, therapeutic hormones travel throughout the body. Altering the body's hormonal environment does not destroy the cancer; it does, however, retard the cancer's growth. Consequently, the typical aim of hormonal therapy is to control the cancer rather than to cure it. Approximately 20% of patients have cancers that are potentially dependent on hormones for growth.

Table 14-4

Hormonal Therapies Used in the Treatment of Cancer

Therapy[a]	Types of cancer	Comments
Androgen (male sex hormone)	Breast	Can cause fluid retention, nausea, facial hair and menstrual irregularities. Taken orally
Leuprolide acetate	Prostate	Eliminates the testicular ability to make testosterone. Given by injection
Orchiectomy (castration)	Prostate	Reduces testosterone by removal of the testicles. Results in impotence, breast development, and hot flashes. It is a surgical procedure
Progesterone (female hormone)	Breast, prostate, uterine, and kidney	Can cause fluid retention, nausea, and menstrual irregularities. Sometimes used to stimulate appetite. Taken orally
Tamoxifen (estrogen blocker)	Breast, uterine, and ovary	Widely used to treat breast cancer. Hot flashes and phlebitis are side effects. Taken orally.

[a] This list is not exhaustive.

An exceptional benefit of hormonal therapy is its minimal side effects. Unlike chemotherapy, hormonal therapy does not damage bone marrow, promote hair loss, or cause mouth sores. It does, however, induce weight gain by stimulating the appetite and, quite commonly, hormonal therapy provokes hot flashes in both men and women. Because of such comparatively mild side effects, hormonal therapy is often given to frail patients unable to tolerate chemotherapy.

Hormonal therapy actually constitutes a heterogeneous group

of cancer treatments. The common property of such treatments is the alteration of hormone levels in the patient's body. Although therapy usually involves the oral administration of the hormone two to three times a day, it can entail monthly injections or possibly the surgical removal of ovaries or testicles. (See Chapters 1, Breast Cancer; 4, Prostate Cancer; and 5, Gynecologic Cancers.) Table 14-4 lists hormonal therapies that are often used to treat specific cancers.

15

Bone Marrow Transplantation

The original crude attempt at bone marrow transplantation occurred in 1891 when bone marrow was reportedly "fed" to a patient. Since that first failed effort, transplantation procedures have greatly advanced!

The current method of bone marrow transplantation evolved in the early 1970s. Researchers at the University of Washington in Seattle were the first to report that bone marrow transplantation had effected cures in leukemic patients after standard treatments had been exhausted. Subsequently, transplantation was found effective in the treatment of such malignancies as Hodgkin's disease and non-Hodgkin's lymphoma. Today, bone marrow transplantation is used to cure many potentially fatal diseases. It is estimated that nearly 5000 bone marrow transplants will be performed worldwide in 1994.

The field of bone marrow transplantation is defined by both change and diversity. New drugs are introduced at an astonishingly rapid rate. Moreover, each transplant center tends to develop its "own" approach to specific problems. As such differences are often more a matter of style than substance, any discussion of transplantation must remain general in order to be helpful. Consequently, this discussion will focus on the process and concepts of transplantation rather than the specific details so subject to change.

What Is Bone Marrow?

Bone marrow is that rich substance made famous by chicken soup—long before the advent of transplantation! Actually, bone marrow is the soft material found within the cavities of the bones, containing the fibers, fat, and blood vessels that are required for bone growth. The bone marrow is the incubator of the blood; blood cells are "born" within the marrow and remain there until mature enough to enter the bloodstream. Bone marrow manufactures three types of blood cells: red cells, white cells, and platelets.

Red blood cells (RBCs) give blood its red color and are vital in the body's exchange of oxygen and carbon dioxide. RBCs pick up oxygen in the lungs and deliver it to the organs. These cells then carry back carbon dioxide from the organs to the lungs to be exhaled. A shortage of RBCs in the blood induces anemia, a condition that can cause weakness, dizziness, and headaches.

White blood cells (WBCs) are the policemen of the body, circulating in the blood to destroy any infection that arises. There are two types of WBCs: neutrophils and lymphocytes. Neutrophils, which constitute 60% of WBCs, supply the body's primary defense against bacterial infections such as pneumonia or urinary tract infections. Lymphocytes, composing 30% of WBCs, regulate the body's response to infection. If the blood is deficient in WBCs, therefore, a serious infection may develop. A subgroup of lymphocytes, known as T lymphocytes, play a pivotal role in bone marrow transplantation by controlling the body's ability to accept or reject foreign tissue.

Platelets are cells that circulate in the blood as clotting agents. Whenever the body is cut, platelets are needed to form a blood clot. A markedly low count of platelets may even result in bleeding without cause.

Chemotherapy and Bone Marrow Transplantation

Chemotherapy refers to the use of an entire class of drugs used to kill cancer cells. (See Chapter 14, Chemotherapy and Hormonal Therapy.) The destruction of these cells is dependent on the dose of chemotherapy, with higher doses resulting in greater percentages of destroyed cancer cells. The dilemma of chemotherapy, however, is that these potent drugs can also damage perfectly normal cells. At particular risk are the cells of rapidly growing tissue.

As the body's rapid producer of new blood cells, bone marrow is especially vulnerable tissue. Consequently, chemotherapy is routinely given in cycles to minimize damage to the bone marrow. As always, the maximum dose of chemotherapy that can be given to a patient is limited by the side effects it causes. The bone marrow, in particular, imposes limits on the amount of chemotherapy that can be given *safely*.

It is widely theorized that failure to cure a cancer results, in part, from insufficient amounts of chemotherapy. The reasoning is that markedly higher doses of chemotherapy can eliminate a greater number of cancer cells, thereby causing higher cure rates. As has been shown, however, the bone marrow of the cancer patient can tolerate only limited amounts of chemotherapy. Bone marrow damage is, in effect, the price paid to cure the cancer.

The aim of bone marrow transplantation is to enable the cancer patient to receive extremely high, possibly curative amounts of chemotherapy. Because the patient's bone marrow will necessarily be damaged by this process, healthy bone marrow tissue is then reintroduced or *transplanted* into the patient's body.

In the 1970s, bone marrow transplantation was initially used to treat "incurable" patients whose cancers had failed to respond to the standard treatment of chemotherapy. Agreeing to try bone marrow transplantation as a last resort, a small percentage of these patients were cured! Naturally, bone marrow transplantation came to be regarded as a promising cancer treatment, despite its multiple side effects. In fact, the elimination of these side effects accounts for many of the recent advances in transplantation. Today, this procedure is commonly used to treat such diseases as leukemia, Hodgkin's disease, non-Hodgkin's lymphoma, and some breast cancers.

Donor Bone Marrow

The donor bone marrow is the marrow given to a transplant recipient after treatment with chemotherapy. Because bone marrow must be readily available, it is typically stored in a frozen state, then thawed as needed. Donor marrow can aptly be described as the *seed of the blood system.* Just as flower seeds remain dormant in winter and bloom in spring, donor marrow remains dormant while frozen and blooms on transplantation.

Interestingly enough, the process of accumulating and storing donor bone marrow is called *harvesting.* During this procedure, the donor receives general anesthesia and lies face down on a table in the operating room. Employing multiple needles, the doctor then extracts marrow from the pelvis. Less than 10% of the donor's bone marrow is actually removed, an amount easily replaced by the body. As the risks of harvesting are minimal, the donor is typically discharged the next day.

The extracted marrow is strained and then mixed with a preservative. The actual freezing of the bone marrow is a time-consuming and technically sophisticated process. Once frozen, however, the marrow can be stored safely for years.

Transplants are classified by the three sources of available bone marrow. If the bone marrow given to a recipient comes from his or her identical twin, the transplant is termed *syngeneic.* If the donor bone marrow comes from either a sibling or a compatible unrelated donor, the transplant is termed *allogeneic.* If the patient receives his or her own marrow, the transplant is termed *autologous.* In an autologous transplant, the recipient is also the donor. It should be noted that the process of harvesting bone marrow is the same for all three types of transplantation.

In order for a transplant to be successful, the donor bone marrow and the body of the recipient must be compatible for a specific gene known as human leukocyte antigen (HLA). The HLA gene determines the type of T lymphocytes. If T lymphocytes and, more specifically, the HLA gene of the donor and recipient are not compatible, the recipient's body will identify the donor marrow as foreign and reject it.

The HLA gene is determined entirely by heredity; this gene is carried on the sixth human chromosome. Because bone marrow from an identical twin or from the patient, himself, is genetically identical to that of the recipient, both syngeneic and autologous transplants are always HLA compatible. HLA compatibility for an allogeneic transplant is more difficult to achieve. The most common source of marrow for this type of transplant is the sibling; a brother or sister has a 25% chance of having a compatible HLA gene. When no relative is a match, the search for an unrelated donor is initiated with the National Bone Marrow Registry. Once a compatible donor is found, the transplant can proceed.

The Stages of Bone Marrow Transplantation

The process of transplantation can be divided into five stages.

Stage 1: Preparation

During this stage, a number of important issues need to be resolved.

Is Transplantation an Option?

Not all cancer patients are candidates for transplantation. Two crucial factors are the patient's age and overall medical condition. Because this procedure is so arduous, only patients younger than 50 years who have no other medical problems are considered. A third critical factor is the responsiveness of the patient's cancer to transplantation therapy. This treatment is most frequently used with such cancers as leukemia, lymphoma, and neuroblastoma. A medical oncologist can best advise the patient concerning the possibility of transplantation.

Which Transplant Center Should the Patient Choose?

Currently, bone marrow transplants are being performed at many excellent transplant centers throughout all areas of the United States. It is in the patient's best interest to visit several of these centers before choosing one. Two especially important factors influencing this choice are the center's experience and its convenience for the patient. Certainly, a reputable center performs a minimum of 20 transplants yearly. Moreover, the center's medical staff should be specially trained in the process of transplantation.

In choosing a transplant center, many patients tend to underestimate the factor of convenience. It is important for the patient to realize, however, that the transplant process typically requires a full month of hospitalization and at least 3 months of frequent visits to the hospital on an outpatient basis. When the recipient undergoes this process without the continuing support of loved ones, emotional stress can increase. If the transplant process can be likened to fighting a war, traveling 2000 miles for transplantation is like fighting it on a distant front. As wars are more easily fought and won close to home, transplant patients should seriously consider the factor of proximity when choosing a center and thereby profit from the precious support of family and friends.

The case of J.S. illustrates how difficult the actual choosing of a transplant center can be. J.S. writes:

> I was 33 years old and in the best physical condition of my life when the news came—C.M.L.—chronic myelogenous leukemia, fatal in a few years if not aggressively treated. Bone marrow transplantation was strongly suggested as my best chance of cure.

> Bone marrow transplantation: What was it? How do we do it? Where do we do it? The first two questions were easily answered by my physician. The third question was not so easy to answer. The nearest transplant center was only 30 miles away in Pittsburgh, but should convenience be the only reason to choose a transplant center? What about reputation? Experience? Success rates?

> Our minds were still numb from the diagnosis. My wife and I were not sure where or how to start. The initial reaction is to go where your physician

suggests. However, after much thought and time, we realized that this was much too important a decision to make before reviewing all options.

We discussed many reasons to choose a center, but quickly came to the same conclusion. This was probably my only chance at cure and therefore we should choose a center with considerable experience, high success rates, and a real specialization in bone marrow transplants. Convenience, costs, and so on would be secondary concerns.

We began by questioning anyone who might have knowledge or experience with bone marrow transplants. We sent for literature from the American Cancer Society, Leukemia Society, and any organization that might be helpful. Over time, we narrowed our choices to four centers. A decision had to be made, and we decided to visit each transplant center to acquire a feel for each.

We went to the farthest center first. They were very receptive and seemed concerned for me. The second visit was to the closest center. The feeling was very different. We did not feel a sincere concern for us in this life-threatening situation. We visited a third center and came away with a similar feeling. By this time, we did not feel that it was necessary to visit the fourth center. We had been impressed with our first transplant center, and its reputation was outstanding. The decision was easily made; we would travel 3000 miles across the country.

Our search process worked for us. The center we chose was never a disappointment. There were many adjustments and preparations to make for such a long, extended trip, but we felt they were necessary in order for me to receive the best care. We evaluated our needs, set our priorities, and proceeded from there. We have no regrets.

That was 3 years ago and so far I am doing very well. We are expecting our first child in the spring.

J.S.'s case is a good example of how one couple went through the process of "choosing" a center. They were, in fact, advised by their physician to stay close to home. Instead, they decided to take an active role in finding the best center for them, a decision that ultimately worked out quite well.

What Type of Transplant Should the Patient Have?

The type of transplant, be it autologous, allogeneic, or syngeneic, is largely determined by the status of current medical knowledge. The field of transplantation changes so rapidly that it is difficult to discuss the recommended types of transplant with accuracy. For example, leukemias that were treated solely with allogeneic transplantation several years ago are treated with autologous transplantation today. Additional factors determining the type of transplant include the specific cancer, the complications and risks inherent in each type of transplant, and the personal wishes of the patient. As this decision is a medically complicated one, it is best deferred to the transplant center's staff.

How Is HLA-Compatible Bone Marrow Found for the Transplant Patient?

In autologous and syngeneic transplants, such compatible marrow is already available from either the patient or an identical twin. However, all allogeneic transplants require donors with HLA-compatible bone marrow. Because siblings have a 25% chance of being HLA compatible, the first step is to have these family members tested. When a patient's siblings are not HLA compatible, a donor search must be initiated through the federally funded National Marrow Donor Program. The time frame for this process can range from a few weeks to several years. For some unfortunate patients, donors are never located.

After compatible bone marrow is found, it must be harvested and then stored at the transplant site. A final preparatory step involves the placement of a permanent venous catheter, known as the Hickman catheter, in the recipient's body. This catheter is a soft flexible tube that a surgeon inserts into the large veins of the upper body. The catheter permits the simultaneous infusion of drugs, fluids, and blood throughout the process of transplantation, thus sparing the patient repeated sticks.

When the preparations are completed, the transplant can proceed as planned. A formal schedule for the transplant exists, similar to the countdown for the launching of a rocket. The date of "lift-off" or bone marrow infusion is known as day 0; preceding days are assigned negative numbers, and succeeding days are assigned positive numbers. For example, the seventh day before infusion is considered day (−7) and the 14th day following infusion is considered day (+14).

Stage 2: The Administration of High Doses of Chemotherapy (Days −7 to −1)

This stage constitutes the actual beginning of transplantation during which the patient receives extremely high doses of chemotherapy. The procedure at some centers also includes radiation of the recipient's entire body. Following the final dose of chemotherapy, a waiting period ensues to allow for the elimination of all chemotherapy drugs from the body. In general, patients tolerate this stage of the transplant quite well.

Stage 3: Infusion of the Donor Bone Marrow (Day 0)

A few days after chemotherapy is completed, the patient receives donor bone marrow through the Hickman catheter. The bags of frozen bone marrow are usually thawed at the patient's bedside. The marrow is then drawn into large syringes and simply injected into the catheter. After traveling through the bloodstream to the recipient's bone marrow, this donor marrow begins to grow and produce new WBCs, RBCs, and platelets. The entire process of bone marrow regeneration, called *engraftment*, takes 15 to 30 days.

Stage 4: Intensive Supportive Care (Day +1 to the Day of Engraftment)

In this critical stage of the transplant process, the recipient is profoundly weakened and vulnerable to infection. Because of the destruction of the original bone marrow, the recipient's blood counts plummet to dangerously low levels. Consequently, both platelets and RBCs are transfused periodically. However, as WBCs cannot be transfused, the body is unable to defend itself against infection. Once the WBC count dips under 1000, the patient is extremely susceptible to infection. To reduce this risk of such infection, the recipient is placed in protective isolation and given potent antibiotics.

Frequently, the transplant patient becomes so ill during this stage that he or she loses the desire to eat. Some patients develop severe diarrhea, causing the intestines to become too irritated to absorb nutrients. When a patient begins to experience such nutritional deficiency, food is administered through the Hickman catheter. In a process known as *total parenteral nutrition,* the patient receives all necessary requirements of proteins, carbohydrates, vitamins, minerals, and fats.

Until engraftment occurs and the marrow begins to generate its own blood cells, recipients are considered critically ill, requiring intensive support. Patients commonly suffer from rashes, liver inflammation, and periods of confusion, and some do require life-support measures. Regrettably, this stage of transplantation claims a mortality rate of 4–8%.

The earliest sign of engraftment occurs when the WBC count registers an increase. Shortly thereafter, the WBC count rises dramatically, and the platelet count typically follows. With a WBC count of 1000 or more, the patient is generally able to combat infection. Within the span of a few days, the transplant patient often improves remarkably, lessening the need for intensive support measures. To verify that regeneration of the cells is occurring, a biopsy of the bone marrow is performed. If the biopsy confirms engraftment, the transplant is considered successful.

Stage 5: Follow-up Period

Once the patient's condition continues to improve, the intensive support is removed. Gradually, the patient resumes normal activities; discharge then occurs within a few days. Of course, the transplant patient must be examined frequently for approximately 6 months to ascertain whether blood counts are normal and the cancer is still in remission. Sometimes, the patient continues to require RBC and platelet transfusions on an outpatient basis.

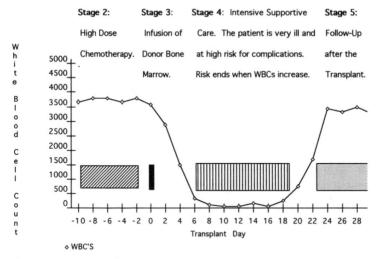

Figure 15-1. Stages of bone marrow transplantation: day and WBC count.

Transplantation is quite a predictable process. Using two key factors, day 0 of the transplant and the WBC, the transplant process can actually be charted on a graph. Such a graph can be helpful in anticipating potential problems for the transplant patient. Using the indexes of transplant days and WBC, Figure 15-1 illustrates the stages of transplantation. In stages 2, 3, and 5, the recipient's WBC count is adequate, indicating that the condition of the patient at these times is usually fair. In stage 4, however, the recipient's WBC count is markedly low, indicating that the patient is at risk.

Graft-versus-Host Disease

Graft-versus-host disease (GVHD) occurs when the donor T lymphocyte, a kind of WBC made by the transplanted marrow, regards the recipient's organs as foreign and proceeds to attack them. This reaction rarely occurs in autologous or syngeneic transplants because the donor and recipient are genetically identical. Although the donor and recipient in all allogeneic transplants are HLA matched to reduce the severity of this reaction, nearly all of these patients develop GVHD.

In GVHD, the donor T lymphocyte attacks the skin, liver, or intestines of the recipient. When GVHD develops early in the transplant process, the reaction is considered *acute GVHD*; when it develops as long as 1 year after the transplant, the reaction is considered *chronic GVHD*. Acute GVHD occurs in approximately 50% of all allogeneic transplants, causing skin rashes, liver abnormalities, or diarrhea. In contrast, chronic GVHD develops in only 25% of allogeneic transplants, resulting in leatherlike skin, weight loss, and susceptibility to infection.

If untreated, GVHD can be fatal. For this reason, drugs are given routinely during stages 3, 4, and 5 of transplantation to suppress or inhibit the donor T lymphocyte. The drugs frequently used in both the prevention and treatment of GVHD are methotrexate, cyclosporine, and prednisone.

A number of factors influence the recipient's risk of developing GVHD. Certainly, close HLA compatibility between donor and recipient minimizes the risk of GVHD, as does matching the sex between them. Although the risk of GVHD significantly increases with the age of the recipient, the donor's age does not appear to influence this risk.

Long-Term Side Effects of Bone Marrow Transplantation

Infertility is one of the most frequent and distressing side effects of transplantation. Infertility is actually a function of the patient's age as well as of the specific type and dose of chemotherapy that the patient receives during stage 2. Most patients who receive radiation to the entire body during this stage do become sterile. However, young women who receive only chemotherapy in stage 2 often experience temporary menstrual irregularities that resolve within 2 years. Women older than 26 years tend to experience early menopause, possibly requiring replacement hormones. To counter sterility, male patients may consider sperm banking before the transplant. Certainly, the issue of sterility should be thoroughly addressed by the patient, sexual partner, and physician before transplantation.

Patients with chronic GVHD may also develop other long-term side effects. In addition to encountering difficulty in maintaining normal weight, they may be more susceptible to such infections as pneumonia. Furthermore, 25% of patients receiving radiation develop cataracts within 2 to 6 years after the transplant. Fortunately, corrective surgery can often restore normal vision in these patients.

Financial Cost

Bone marrow transplantation is quite an expensive treatment; most transplants cost in excess of $100,000. To defray such enormous costs, many transplant centers require guarantees of reimbursement in advance. Insurance companies, which frequently refuse to underwrite experimental therapy, often adopt a case-by-case approach when evaluating transplants.

In addition to hospital bills, the transplant patient often incurs other considerable expenses. To receive follow-up care at the transplant center, the patient and family may need to find lodging for 3 months, an expense that may compel the recipient to choose a transplant center close to home.

Psychological Cost

The physical, emotional, and financial burdens of transplantation cause tremendous stress for both patient and family. The routine of family life is entirely disrupted as family members travel to the transplant center and arrange for child care. As few parties sleep well, fatigue quickly becomes habitual. Unfortunately, the patient's medical problems so totally dominate the transplant process that psychological problems sometimes receive scant attention.

Support groups, however, are available to help patients and their families deal with the stresses of transplantation. All involved parties should be strongly encouraged to participate in them and to seek, as well, the help of clergy and mental health professionals during this difficult time.

The Future of Bone Marrow Transplantation

The sole constant in the field of bone marrow transplantation is change. Some recent developments in transplant research offer exciting possibilities for the future. In fact, many experts believe that by the end of the decade, bone marrow transplants may be performed as outpatient procedures!

An area of intense research is the use of colony-stimulating factors (CSFs) in bone marrow transplantation. CSFs, which stimulate the bone marrow to produce WBCs, have recently become commercially available. Functioning as a type of "fertilizer" for bone marrow cells, CSFs are now used during transplantation to facilitate the process of engraftment (See Chapter 14, Common Side Effects of Chemotherapy.)

CSFs also cause bone marrow "seed" cells to circulate in the blood temporarily, a phenomenon that actually makes the donor's blood harvestable for transplantation. This technique, know as peripheral blood stem cell transplantation, offers several distinct advantages over conventional transplantation: (1) the bone marrow seed cells can be harvested on an outpatient basis, (2) patients with bone marrow malignancy can undergo harvesting in this manner, and (3) preliminary evidence indicates a more rapid engraftment of transplanted marrow.

Because the control or elimination of GVHD would make the transplant process much less toxic, many drugs are actively being investigated to counter GVHD. One such drug, XLO, which was developed to combat the body's rejection of a transplanted kidney, has recently been found helpful in preventing GVHD. Other research has focused on eliminating the major cause of GVHD by purging the donor bone marrow of its T lymphocytes.

Bone marrow transplantation is an established therapy for treating certain cancers. The National Cancer Institute estimates that if compatible donors had been available in 1991, 11,000 cancer patients could have been treated with allogeneic transplantation. Given the impetus of current research, transplantation is certain to become therapy for more types of cancers.

16

Biological Therapy of Cancer

with Richard M. Sherry, M.D.

Conventional therapy, including surgery, radiation therapy, and chemotherapy, is used to treat the vast majority of cancer patients today, 50% of whom are cured. In an effort to improve this cure rate, however, medical researchers are exploring a quite promising area of treatment known as *biological therapy*. Whereas conventional cancer therapies directly attack cancer cells, biological therapy (BT) utilizes the body's natural line of defense, its immune system, to fight or reject the cancer in much the same way that this system combats a cold or infection.

The Immune System

One apt analogy for the immune system is that of an army defending the body from invading viruses and bacteria. The "foot soldiers" of this army are the white blood cells (WBCs) that are produced in the bone marrow and then released into the bloodstream to intercept cells of infection. A type of "home base" for the WBCs is the lymph nodes, pea-sized glands scattered strategically throughout the body.

In the process of responding to an infection, WBCs can communicate with each other by using protein messengers known as *cytokines*. Cytokines enable WBCs to coordinate the body's defense against infection. For example, in a person with a strep throat, cytokines are released in the tonsils to recruit WBCs to fight the bacteria. Two cytokines presently being used to treat human cancers are alpha-interferon and interleukin-2.

Another important line of defense in the immune system is *antibodies*. Produced by WBCs, antibodies actually coat bacteria cells, thus making them vulnerable to the WBCs counterattack. After responding to an infection, the immune system "memorizes" the invader's cellular pattern, thus ensuring a rapid response to any subsequent attack. In this way, a person's resistance to common infections is formed.

Considerable evidence exists that the immune system plays an important role in combating cancer, especially because individuals with a weakened immune system are at particular risk of developing cancer. For example, kidney and heart transplant recipients, who must take immunity-suppressing drugs in order to avoid organ rejection, are known to have an elevated risk of cancer. Acquired immunodeficiency syndrome (AIDS) patients also are at increased risk for developing a number of cancers, especially Kaposi's sarcoma and non-Hodgkin's lymphoma.

In animals with cancer, experiments have shown that the immune system can be manipulated to reduce or eliminate cancer cells. For example, in the late 1970s, researchers found that certain liver cancers in mice were successfully controlled with BT.

This concept of fighting cancer by stimulating the body's natural defenses did not originate in the 20th century. Actually, as early as the 18th century, physicians described the disappearance of a breast cancer after the injection of bacteria into the tumor. However, exciting developments in biotechnology during the last decade have legitimized BT as a scientifically valid cancer treatment. Presently, researchers are introducing a variety of new BT approaches including vaccines, antibodies, and cytokines.

Vaccines

A vaccine involves the injection of either a dead or weakened virus into an unexposed individual so that the immune system can "recognize" the specific virus and thus develop a resistance to the disease. Vaccines are effective in eliminating certain diseases including measles, mumps, hepatitis B, and polio. Adopting a similar immunity-building rationale, researchers have attempted to immunize cancer patients with injections of tumor vaccines formulated from tumors of like kind.

For the past 20 years, both advanced melanomas and colon cancers have been treated with tumor vaccines. Although there is little evidence that patients with melanoma benefit from such therapy, several reliable clinical trials suggest that patients with colon cancer may benefit from such treatment.

Currently, research is focused on identifying the surface differences between malignant and normal cells. If consistent differences can be detected, then a more effective vaccine can be developed. Using biotechnology, it may also be possible to alter cancer cells and thus increase their detectability by the immune system.

Antibody Therapy

Produced by WBCs, antibodies are substances that coat foreign cells in the body. Once coated, such cells are destroyed by the immune system. Unfortunately, human cancer patients do not normally produce antibodies for cancer cells. One theory holds that cancer cells are able to evade detection because they undergo certain changes that are unidentifiable by the immune system.

Interestingly, mice that are exposed to human cancer cells can produce antibodies capable of recognizing and coating malignant cells. This mouse antibody can be collected, purified, and then injected into cancer patients in an effort to detect and eliminate tumors.

Although research has proven that injected antibodies can, indeed, destroy cancer cells, the amount of antibody eventually reaching the cancer is slight, with effectiveness ranging from moderate to negligible. Cancers in which antibody therapy has yielded modest reductions include lymphomas, ovarian cancers, and melanomas. The side effects of this therapy are minor and easily controlled.

Improvements in the area of antibody therapy are currently being intensively researched. In an effort to carry cancer therapy directly to malignant cells, antibodies known to be capable of reaching cancer sites are being linked with radioactive or chemotherapeutic agents. In yet another attempt to improve antibodies, genetic engineering is being employed. At present, the status of antibody therapy as a cancer treatment remains highly investigational.

Cytokine Therapy

Produced by WBCs, cytokines are protein messengers that direct and regulate the immune system. Although the biological functions of many cytokines show no apparent anticancer effect, two particular cytokines, alpha-interferon and interleukin-2, show considerable promise in combating some human cancers.

The functions of alpha-interferon are varied, including antiviral action as well as suppression of both the immune system and cancer cell growth. Alpha-interferon also causes the levels of many other cytokines to rise. Whereas interferon therapy has proven somewhat effective in the treatment of kidney cancer, melanoma, and lymphoma, this particular therapy has proven extremely effective in the treatment of a rare cancer known as *hairy cell leukemia*. Given by injection, interferon therapy has one major side effect, that is, flulike symptoms such as muscle aches, fever, skin rash, and fatigue.

Interleukin-2 (IL-2), has shown exciting activity in the treatment of kidney cancer and melanoma. In some patients, IL-2 promotes shrinkage or total elimination of even extensive cancers. However, effectively high doses often induce severe side effects such as fever, nausea, skin rash, kidney damage, and low blood pressure. For this reason, patients receiving IL-2 are closely monitored in an intensive care setting. Fortunately, these side effects typically subside following therapy and cause no residual harm. In Europe, IL-2 is currently approved for use in patients with advanced kidney cancer; in the United States, similar approval by the FDA appears to be imminent.

Cellular Therapy

Cellular therapy is a method of treatment involving the temporary removal of WBCs from the cancer patient's bloodstream. After these cells have been activated or energized with IL-2 in the laboratory, they become known as *lymphokine-activated killer* (LAK) cells. Having thus gained the capacity to destroy cancer cells, they are then reinfused into the patient's bloodstream.

The fact that cancerous tissue contains both malignant cells and normal WBCs forms the basis for another cellular therapy known as *tumor-infiltrating lymphocytes* (TIL). In this procedure, a portion of the patient's cancerous tissue is surgically removed and sent to the laboratory where the WBCs are extracted and grown in a test tube. These lymphocytes are treated with IL-2 to activate them for anticancer activity and then reinfused into the cancer patient.

Dr. Steven Rosenberg of the National Cancer Institute has pioneered the use of cellular therapy. During an initial trial, a 29-year-old woman with extensive melanoma was treated with LAK cells and IL-2 injections; she has remained free of disease for more than 5 years. Some patients with incurable kidney cancers and melanoma have also experienced dramatic effects with cellular therapy. The case study of D.K. in Chapter 6 is an example of the successful treatment of melanoma with TIL therapy at the National Cancer Institute.

As the side effects of cellular therapy are similar to those of IL-2 injections, patients receiving cellular therapy are closely monitored in intensive care units. Investigational and expensive, such treatment is usually administered under the supervision of research centers authorized by the National Cancer Institute. As in other forms of biological therapy, the full promise of cellular therapy has yet to be developed.

Although recent advances in the understanding of the immune response to cancer have been both rapid and impressive, the practical benefits of these efforts are still limited. Because experience to date has established that the body's natural defenses can, in fact, be manipulated to eliminate cancer cells, the goal of medical research is to translate this concept into viable procedures for the treatment of cancer patients.

17

Investigational Therapy: Clinical Trials in Cancer Treatment

with Richard M. Sherry, M.D.

A clinical trial in cancer treatment is a research study aimed at evaluating a new therapy. The goals of such research are to determine the safety as well as the effectiveness of a given treatment, particularly in relation to currently accepted methods. These goals are as difficult to achieve as they are worthy to accomplish.

Less than 15 years ago, many of today's standard or orthodox therapies were considered investigational. A case in point is the evolving treatment of breast cancer. Whereas a radical mastectomy, which is an operation that entails the removal of both the breast and chest muscles, was considered the standard treatment of breast cancer in the 1970s, numerous clinical trials in the interim have established that small breast cancers could be treated as effectively with breast-conserving surgery followed by radiation therapy. Other clinical trials have further determined that some breast cancer patients benefit from similar modified surgery followed by chemotherapy and hormone therapy. As a result, this former investigational therapy has now replaced the radical mastectomy as the standard treatment of many breast cancers. In fact, the majority of advances in cancer treatment result directly from such clinical research trials.

Typically, a clinical trial is suggested as a viable treatment option by the cancer patient's attending physician. It is estimated that as many as 10% of all cancer patients are potentially eligible for treatment under the auspices of a clinical trial.

Clinical trials are highly regulated by the U.S. Food and Drug Agency as well as the National Cancer Institute (NCI). A rigorous testing process that consists of four distinct phases is followed for all new cancer therapies.

During Phase I, researchers attempt to ascertain a safe and tolerable dose of the new drug. During this period of early evaluation, only those patients whose widespread cancers have proved unresponsive to standard therapies are accepted as trial candidates. Minimal doses of drug are given initially, with increments administered as knowledge of the drug increases.

Once a safe dose of drug has been established, research enters Phase II. The purpose of this phase is to determine the drug's effectiveness against the cancer. If found effective, the drug is evaluated further in a Phase III trial, during which the new drug's anticancer activity is compared with that of standard treatment approaches. In Phase IV trials, the investigational therapy becomes part of the standard treatment plan with the purpose of refining or possibly expanding the new therapy's role as a viable cancer treatment.

Clinical research trials necessarily employ strict eligibility guidelines for patients. The purpose of such guidelines is to reduce risk for patients who may not safely tolerate the given therapy, while ensuring the scientific validity of the treatment trial. Generally, any one of the following factors may serve to disqualify a patient from participation in a research trial: more than one primary cancer, a serious and preexisting medical condition, or advanced age.

A key provision of enrollment in a clinical trial entails the patient's informed consent. Consequently, before enrollment, the patient is given an *Informed Consent Form*, a document that clearly explains the trial's rationale and design as well as the known risks and possible benefits of treatment. Before entering a clinical trial, each patient must read, understand, and sign this form, a copy of which should be kept for review and reference. Signing a consent form does not constitute a binding contract because a participant is free to withdraw from the trial at any time.

The decision to participate in a clinical trial may be a difficult one for the patient to make. The truth of the matter is that some trials are better than others, some trials are newer than others, and some trials carry more risk than others. Before agreeing to participate in a clinical trial, the cancer patient might find it advantageous to consider the following questions.

1. *What is the goal of the study?* Because each trial is designed to evaluate particular scientific points, the patient is well served by understanding the exact purpose of the study.
2. *What are the potential risks and benefits of the trial?* How many patients have benefited or possibly been cured by this therapy? How many patients have suffered complications? Were these complications minor or severe? Have any patients died as a result of the treatment? What, if anything, is known about long-term side effects? Because consulting other patients who have undergone treatment may prove helpful, the candidate may quite appropriately request a list of former participants who have expressed a willingness to share their experiences regarding treatment.
3. *Apart from the clinical trial, what are the alternatives of treatment?* Candidates deserve to know the "track record" of both the new and standard therapy. In order to make an informed decision regarding therapy, all of the available treatment options should be considered. The patient should ask the doctor, "If I decide not to enroll in the study, what treatment would you advise?"

In many situations, a patient may be treatable with several

standard approaches, with the sole purpose of the proposed trial being to determine which treatment is optimal. Given this scenario, enrolling in a trial may be an entirely safe and reasonable decision.

4. *Who is the sponsor of the research?* Clinical trials can be sponsored by the NCI, national research groups such as the National Surgical Adjuvant Breast and Bowel Project, the Southwest Oncology Group, or a single institution/hospital. It is essential for the candidate to verify the sponsor's credentials in order to avoid those treatments bordering on quackery. Valid clinical trials are reviewed by an Institutional Review Board consisting of physicians, clergy, and respected community representatives who are responsible for determining whether the trial's objectives and methods are both reasonable and ethical. Patients should be extremely cautious of investigational therapies that are offered outside the parameters of a reputable medical institution utilizing such a board. (See Chapter 19, Cancer Quackery.) Certainly, the candidate has the right to ascertain the level of a treatment team's expertise. It is also fair to inquire if similar treatment might be obtained at a hospital whose personnel is more experienced with the therapy or whose trials have yielded more favorable results.

5. *How long will the trial last?* The duration of some clinical studies is several hours; other trials anticipate lifelong participation. Not only should the patient know the proposed length of the study, but each patient should also attempt to honor the initial commitment by completing the trial and thus help to ensure the accuracy of the results.

6. *What is the plan for future therapy?* The patient should consider treatment options in the event that the investigational therapy is unsuccessful. Sometimes, patients are reluctant to inquire about such back-up treatment, fearing to project a "negative attitude." Yet, the informed patient is better able to make wise treatment choices and control anxiety about the disease. By adopting reasonable expectations about treatment as well as specific contingency plans, the patient is free to become fully engaged in a chosen therapy.

It is equally important to establish the physician who will direct subsequent therapy as well as the location of therapy. Although patients often assume that participation in a clinical trial assures future medical care at the sponsoring institution, such provision is not always given.

7. *What is the cost of the therapy?* Billing procedures in clinical trials vary from the free-of-charge policy at the NCI to full-patient-pay policies at other institutions. Similarly, the coverage provided by medical insurance carriers varies for treatment received during the course of a clinical trial; many carriers refuse to cover procedures considered unorthodox or experimental. For these reasons, patients must determine the projected personal cost of treatment.

In addition to medical costs, patients must consider indirect expenses related to travel, lodging, medications, additional x rays, laboratory tests, and loss of income. Realistically, the cancer patient and family must determine what they are willing and able to sacrifice for a therapy that may ultimately be of little or no benefit.

Today, cancer research and treatment is defined by continual change. For patients as well as physicians seeking current cancer data, the NCI funds a computer information system known as *PDQ*. Updated monthly by cancer experts, PDQ provides listings of clinical trials and describes the status of current treatments. This service can be contacted via the NCI's Cancer Information Service by dialing 1-800-422-6237.

Recent advances in cancer therapy are largely attributable to the success of clinical trials. In fact, yesterday's investigational therapies are today's cancer cures. Because courageous patients are willing to venture into uncharted areas of treatment, medical researchers can persist in the clinical trials that continually expand the borders of treatment. Even as patients who elect to participate in clinical trials hope for cures or efficacious treatment, they are secure in the knowledge that they are making a personal contribution to the welfare of future generations.

18

No Therapy

The course of cancer treatment is a trying journey for patients; a crossroad faced by nearly everyone on this journey is *no therapy.* No therapy refers to that period during which the cancer patient receives no active treatment (i.e., surgery, radiation, or chemotherapy). Quite possibly, no therapy is the most common experience shared by cancer patients because almost all undergo periods of nontreatment at some time during illness.

No therapy is actually a foreign concept to the vast majority of people. Throughout training, nurses and doctors are continually asked **how** rather than **if** a patient should be treated. Consequently, the traditional medical approach is biased toward active or aggressive attempts to heal. Patients are equally uncomfortable with the concept of nontreatment because they equate treatment with cure. All biases aside, no therapy can be the best therapy for certain patients. Perhaps once the many benefits of this approach are better understood, no therapy can be appreciated as the valid cancer treatment that it is.

No Therapy Can Be a Time of Reevaluation

At times, a break from treatment aids the doctor in evaluating the patient. This is especially true when the source of a patient's problem can be attributed to either the cancer or treatment itself. In such cases, a break from treatment is helpful as a trial of observation. If the patient's condition improves while treatment is suspended, then continued observation is appropriate. If the patient's condition worsens, therapy can be resumed or changed. The two points in favor of no therapy in such situations are (1) the doctor cannot predict with certainty how a break from treatment will affect the patient, and (2) active therapy can be resumed at any time.

No Therapy Is an Integral Part of Routine Follow-up

Once therapy has been successfully completed, each patient requires routine follow-up care. The patient shows no evidence of cancer and is typically elated about ending treatment. If cancer treatment can be compared to the phases of an education, routine follow-up is a kind of graduation. The patient has completed all the "required courses" of therapy and can get on with life.

The aim of routine follow-up is to ensure the best possible outcome for the patient. Such follow-up generally involves a physical exam, x rays, and blood tests. Blood tests, of course, vary according to the type of cancer. For example, the blood of a prostate cancer patient is usually tested for a prostate-specific antigen and prostatic acid phosphatase, whereas the blood of a testicular cancer patient is tested for beta-human chorionic gonadotropin hormone. Each cancer also requires specific follow-up procedures. For instance, a patient with breast cancer receives a yearly mammogram; a patient with colon cancer receives a yearly colon exam.

Follow-up is aimed primarily at evaluating the cancer's status, but it does serve other purposes. Follow-up ensures that patients are regularly evaluated for delayed complications from therapy. For instance, patients whose necks have been radiated run an increased risk of hypothyroidism (i.e., an underactive thyroid). Some breast cancer patients develop swelling in their arms after breast surgery. It is illustrative to note that both of these complications can occur months or even years after treatment has ended.

One of the most important benefits of follow-up care is the psychological benefit. Follow-up reassures both the patient and family that all is well. Most patients, in fact, have a real need to know that the cancer is no longer detectable. With each uneventful visit, their confidence grows. Other cancer patients, however, experience depression after therapy has ended. Often, the anger and sadness associated with the original diagnosis surfaces only when the cancer is cured. For these patients, psychological counseling may be necessary to complete the healing process. (See Chapter 25, The Next Step: Being a Survivor.)

Former cancer patients tend to develop new cancers more frequently than does the general population, so routine follow-up is also intended to screen for unrelated cancers. For example, breast cancer patients run a slightly increased risk of developing ovarian and colon cancers. The surveillance of unrelated cancers is incorporated into the routine follow-up care of every patient.

No Therapy Can Sometimes Be the Recommended Therapy

Many patients interpret the medical decision not to treat a cancer aggressively as "quitting." This is simply not the case; the decision is always **when,** not **if,** to treat.

No therapy becomes the recommended therapy whenever it is best to let things happen as they may. Naturally, the patient is examined periodically to evaluate the status of the cancer. Surprising as it seems, many types of advanced cancer should not be actively treated. Some of these cancers are so slow-growing and non-threatening that treatment can be delayed indefinitely.

One class of cancers best treated by observation rather than by active therapy are low-grade lymph node cancers. Usually diagnosed in advanced stages, these lymphomas are quite responsive to both chemotherapy and radiation. One might presume, then, that active therapy would be beneficial. Research, however, has proven otherwise. Patients who do not receive therapy at the time of diagnosis fare as well as those who do receive it, with both patient groups surviving an average of 7 years. Another type of cancer best treated by observation is prostate cancer in the earliest stage because the majority of such patients never do develop cancer-related problems.

Sometimes a cancer is widespread at diagnosis but causes no symptoms to the patient. Whenever the possibility of curing such a cancer no longer exists, therapy is aimed solely at improving the quality of a patient's life. However, when the patient with advanced cancer is symptom free, treatment cannot improve and may drastically diminish the quality of the patient's life.

The most obvious situation warranting no therapy occurs when the cancer patient is unable to tolerate active treatment. Traditionally, doctors are cautioned to do no harm, and yet potent cancer treatments can frequently cause greater harm than benefit. Certainly the same patients who cannot tolerate the rigors of surgery may not be able to withstand radiation or chemotherapy, as was the case of the elderly patient M.L.

> M.L. was an 83-year-old matriarch of a large Italian family. She was diabetic, blind, and bedridden from progressive heart failure. On her most recent admission to the hospital, she was diagnosed with breast cancer. Concluding that breast cancer was not M.L.'s most serious illness and that her physical condition was poor, the physician recommended no therapy for the cancer. Several months later, M.L. died of a heart attack.

Some 83-year-old women can tolerate active treatment, but others cannot. M.L.'s case illustrates the need to evaluate and treat each patient on an individual basis.

No Therapy Can Be a Time of Recovery

Cancer treatments are often so physically demanding that patients are routinely counseled to take it easy while undergoing them. When severe fatigue develops, a break in treatment may be extremely beneficial, providing time for the patient and family to recover both physically and emotionally. It is advisable to regard such a break in the treatment schedule as a type of well-earned vacation.

No Therapy Can Be an Option after a Serious Side Effect of Treatment

Some side effects of cancer therapy are potentially life threatening. For example, chemotherapy reduces the number of white cells in the blood, thus predisposing the patient to serious infection. Approximately 3 to 4% of chemotherapy patients eventually require hospitalization for either pneumonia or a bloodstream infection. (See Chapter 14, Chemotherapy.)

After the patient recovers from such an infection, the treatment program must be reevaluated. Does the benefit of treatment outweigh the risk of yet another serious infection? If the chemotherapy appears to be effective, then the dose is typically reduced. However, if the benefit of chemotherapy is negligible, then stopping treatment altogether must be a consideration. Often the risks of chemotherapy prove greater than its benefits. The experiences of the following two patients illustrate the necessity of continually evaluating treatment.

> G.E. is a 72-year-old woman who was diagnosed with advanced Hodgkin's disease. After completing two courses of chemotherapy, she was hospitalized with a fever of 103°F. Her white blood count was markedly low, and she had developed a bloodstream infection. Quite ill, G.E. remained in the hospital for 3 weeks. Subsequent tests indicated that the cancer was responsive to treatment, and her physician believed that continued treatment could result in cure. In order to lessen the risk of serious infection, however, the dose of chemotherapy was reduced.

For G.E., the possible benefit of chemotherapy was greater than the risk of repeated infection. However, these risks are sometimes not justifiable, as shown in the case of B.R.

> B.R. is a 76-year-old woman who was diagnosed with advanced lung cancer. Chemotherapy had a 65% chance of effectiveness in B.R.'s type of cancer. After a conference with the physician and family, B.R. decided to try the treatments. After one course of chemotherapy, she was hospitalized with fever and severe diarrhea. She had a bloodstream infection and was extremely ill for 2 weeks. On recovery, the lung cancer showed no evidence of responding to chemotherapy. B.R. decided not to continue therapy, a choice which both the family and physician considered reasonable. Several months later, B.R. died as a result of lung cancer.

Whenever treatment causes serious side effects, the risk and benefits of continued treatment need to be evaluated. No therapy is a most appropriate course of action when, as in the case of B.R., the side effects of treatment offset its benefits.

No Therapy Can Be the Patient's Choice

Patients have many reasons for choosing not to treat their cancers actively. Some patients are reluctant to risk side effects such as hair loss or nausea; other patients have preconceived ideas about treatment that dissuade them. Occasionally, patients offer no explanations for refusing treatment. The truth of the matter is that no patient can or should be coerced into treatment. Ultimately, both the family and physician must respect the patient's wishes.

Generally, the effort expended by a physician in attempting to change the mind of a patient who has refused treatment is directly related to the potential benefit of treatment. Whenever therapy offers the possibility of cure, the physician exerts every effort (e.g., enlisting the family's help) to convince the patient to choose treatment. The majority of these patients do, in fact, reverse their decisions. When treatment promises to improve but not cure the patient's condition, the physician still typically tries to persuade the patient to try therapy. However, when improvement with treatment appears unlikely, most physicians readily accept the patient's decision not to be treated. Physicians advocate no therapy as a treatment approach only when they consider it medically reasonable.

Some cancer patients, like R.R., agree to some treatments and refuse others:

R.R. is a 72-year-old retired architect who was diagnosed with inoperable lung cancer. He completed a series of radiation treatments without experiencing side effects. Six months later, however, R.R. began to have shortness of breath. On readmission, testing showed advancing lung cancer. R.R.'s next treatment option was chemotherapy. R.R. was advised that chemotherapy would offer him a 33% chance of improving his breathing but would not be curative. R.R. responded with conviction, "I'm 72 years old and I've had a good life . . . I'm not going to spend the rest of my days on chemotherapy . . . I think that I have been through enough."

Although his family strongly disagreed with his decision, R.R. emphatically refused further treatment. Four months later, R.R. died of the lung cancer.

Although R.R. could have physically tolerated chemotherapy, he did not believe that the odds of improvement were high enough to justify further treatment. R.R.'s family experienced the wrenching conflict that frequently occurs when a patient with advanced cancer chooses to stop treatment. Out of misguided love, family members often insist that they know what is best for the patient. In R.R.'s case, the decision not to pursue therapy was medically reasonable, a legitimate exercise of the patient's right to no therapy. Ultimately, the treatment choices of a terminally ill patient must be respected by both physician and family.

Perhaps the overriding emotional response to the alternative of no therapy is an intense ambivalence. Actually, ambivalence is a natural response to a situation surrounded with so many conflicting ideas and feelings. This ambivalence is an unconscious expression of our cultural biases in favor of active treatment. Patients equate the choice of no therapy with "giving up" and subconsciously regard the decision not to be treated as inherently wrong.

Unlike traditional medical interventions in which the patient is told how to get better, no therapy offers the patient a certain untested autonomy or independence. This role reversal, in itself, can cause tremendous stress and anxiety in the patient who fears assuming responsibility for a decision of such magnitude.

When these fears of giving up or autonomy abound, the patient needs to be reassured about the nature of the patient–doctor relationship. Only when no therapy is medically reasonable does a physician recommend such a course and, as the patient's knowledgeable ally, the physician bears ultimate medical responsibility for the decision. In the arena of confusing treatment choices, the patient considering no therapy must trust the physician's judgment.

19

Cancer Quackery

with John Schlicht, Pharm. D.

Cancer quackery, the treatment of a cancer with unproven methods, has been practiced in America since colonial times. Although most medical authorities dismiss the practitioners of quackery as charlatans and their patients as uninformed victims, such a view is too simplistic, serving only to propagate stereotypes. Actually, cancer quackery is a complex problem stemming from cultural expectations and values, the state of modern cancer therapy and, of course, human nature. Ironically, unproven cancer therapies appear to be gaining in popularity today even as biomedical breakthroughs pervade the field of cancer treatment.

The terms *cancer quackery* and *unproven therapy* are used interchangeably in this discussion to refer to those treatments not scientifically proven to be safe and effective. It is also essential to differentiate quackery from *investigational therapy*. An investigational therapy is a treatment that the U.S. Food and Drug Administration (FDA) is currently in the process of evaluating for both safety and efficacy. (See Chapter 17, Investigational Therapy.)

The Roots of Quackery

As evidenced by the Bill of Rights, Americans consider the rights of the individual to be sacred. Balancing the individual's right to choose is the need to protect consumers from dangerous or useless therapies. In the early 20th century, tragedies resulting from drug therapies prompted the U.S. government to create the FDA, an agency assigned the task of assuring that medications are both safe and effective. Many proponents of unproven therapies regard the FDA's mandate to review and approve cancer treatments as a violation of the patient's fundamental right to choose therapy. These proponents view the highly regulated FDA process of review as unnecessary governmental intervention in patients' lives. However, without a process of review and regulation, cancer patients would be left on their own to evaluate the promises of unconventional therapy.

Americans also tend to distrust monolithic organizations and industries. Not surprisingly, such distrust is at times directed toward organized medicine and the drug industry, particularly in the area of cancer research. Some Americans even suspect that this powerful medical establishment deliberately withholds cancer cures in order to reap continued profits from treatment. In any case, a nagging distrust of the medical establishment does serve to foster the growth of unproven therapies.

As patients become more knowledgeable about medical care, expectations quite naturally rise, as does their dissatisfaction with conventional methods of care. For example, because of chemotherapy's well-known toxic side effects, some patients consider this standard treatment unacceptable. Patients are also frustrated by what they perceive as a lack of new and dramatically improved cancer treatments.

Also contributing to the growing use of unorthodox cancer therapies is the strong consumer movement. As a result of this movement, the patient no longer wholly depends on the physician for medical information but can now consult a variety of books, videos, and health groups for information on illnesses and therapies, both orthodox and unorthodox. The cancer patient frequently turns to health periodicals such as *Prevention* magazine for a discussion of "alternative" cancer remedies.

Expectedly, patients rarely resort to unproven therapy for diseases, such as pneumonia and diabetes, that can be effectively controlled by orthodox therapy. However, when the effectiveness of conventional treatment is questionable, patients are apt to find the prospect of unproven therapy compelling. The tragic fact is that all too many cancer patients, regardless of the method of treatment, succumb to their diseases. In a desperate attempt to beat the odds, many cancer patients choose to experiment with unproven therapies. Clearly, the failure of medical science to find cures for many cancers is the dominant reason that patients hazard the risks of unorthodox therapies.

A patient is especially prone to turn to unconventional therapy when faced with a poor prognosis. Then, an overwhelming sense of helplessness and despair can induce the patient to "do something" in order to improve the chances of recovery. In such an instance, seeking an alternative treatment can constitute an understandable attempt to sustain or restore hope.

Perhaps hope can be defined as the difference between what is and what should be. Every human being, and surely every cancer patient, thrives on an appreciation of this precious difference. Cancer quackery exists, in part, because orthodox medical approaches so often fail to provide the cancer patient with a measure of hope. In other words, physicians and other members of the health care team often abdicate one of their primary responsibilities, that is, to preserve hope in the cancer patient—even when the benefits of therapy are marginal. After all, to live is to hope.

Indeed, the patient whose cancer is judged untreatable may well perceive the scientific process as lacking in humanity. Moreover, medical experts cannot identify the causes of most cancers, much less offer guarantees of cure. The suffering cancer patient quite understandably turns elsewhere when informed, "I do not know the cause of your cancer. I can offer you no cure." An incontestable fact is that cancer quackery will continue to exist until cures are found for all cancers.

Unproven Therapy: Patients and Practitioners

The use of unproven cancer therapies has steadily escalated, reaching rather astounding proportions today. In 1984, a U.S. Senate Select Subcommittee on Quackery estimated that cancer patients spent more than $10 billion annually for unorthodox therapies. It has been further estimated that between 15 and 50% of cancer patients utilize unproven therapy at some time during the course of illness.

Cancer patients who choose to pursue alternative therapy have a rather distinct profile. They tend to be affluent, fairly well educated, and white. Quite typically, they trace the cause of their disease to poor nutrition and stress. Moreover, they believe that the standard cancer therapies of chemotherapy and radiation therapy are more harmful than helpful.

Dr. Barrie Cassileth, a noted medical researcher at the University of Pennsylvania, has provided additional data on this class of cancer patients. In a study conducted in 1984, Dr. Cassileth found that 39% of patients choosing unproven therapy were initially attracted by its "natural and nontoxic" qualities. Six percent of alternative therapy patients reported that a terminal diagnosis had prompted their choice. Whereas only 8% of alternative therapy patients flatly refused conventional therapy, the vast majority did receive some form of standard treatment. In fact, fully 60% chose to receive alternative and conventional therapies simultaneously. A particularly telling statistic in this study is that more than half of all cancer patients, regardless of their therapy orientation, believed that both the medical establishment and government attempt to deny freedom of choice concerning cancer treatment.

Dangers of Cancer Quackery

Unproven therapy poses a number of potential dangers for its recipients. The most serious consequences usually occur in that minority of patients who completely forego conventional therapy.

Currently, standard therapy that is curative is available for many malignancies including testicular cancer, Hodgkin's disease, leukemia, and breast cancer. Patients with highly treatable cancers who avoid such therapy risk tragic outcomes.

In addition to the dangers of foregoing conventional therapy, some unproven therapies are directly injurious to the patient. Laetrile, which is perhaps the most widely known unproven cancer drug, contains cyanide, a poison that has proved fatal to some patients. Certain anticancer diet regimens can create disturbances in the levels of essential proteins in the blood. One popular alternative therapy, megadoses of vitamins, can produce a toxic level of calcium in the blood. Coffee enemas, an element of several popular alternative therapies, can cause ruptures in the user's colon.

Yet another inherent danger of such therapy is its cost. Literally billions of dollars are wasted each year on treatments that are wholly ineffective. Although the per-patient cost of different therapy modes varies considerably, the cost of a typical course of treatment at freestanding clinics located in the United States, Mexico, and the Bahamas ranges from $5,000 to $40,000.

In most cases, the patient must assume full responsibility for the cost of such therapy. Because government programs like Medicare and Medicaid agree to compensate only for "reasonable and necessary care," which generally includes FDA-approved drugs, patients using alternative therapy must often shoulder the entire medical bill. Private insurance companies like Blue Cross follow similar guidelines, specifically excluding therapies such as laetrile from coverage.

Types of Cancer Quackery

The types of unproven cancer therapies change constantly, often paralleling popular societal beliefs. Dr. Cassileth has found that whereas in the past, unproven therapies were applied to a specific disease, today's alternative cancer therapies are often applied to chronic illnesses as well. Within the context of an increasingly holistic orientation to health care, alternative cancer therapies are now being employed to treat such diseases as arthritis and chronic fatigue syndrome.

One of the most widely used unproven cancer treatments is immuno-augmentative therapy (IAT). IAT involves the daily injection of blood products extracted from the blood of donors, including cured cancer patients. These blood products allegedly contain substances that improve the body's ability to destroy cancer cells.

In 1986, the FDA banned this therapy in the United States "due to the direct hazards that have been associated with IAT agents." Of course, the primary danger involves the recipient's risk of infection, including acquired immunodeficiency syndrome (AIDS), from the use of blood products. The American Cancer Society, the National Cancer Institute, and the Centers for Disease Control have also issued similar warnings.

For more than 25 years, an unproven cancer treatment that has sparked considerable publicity and controversy has been the drug laetrile. Produced from the pulverized pits of apricots and peaches, this drug bears the chemical name *amygdalin*. In the 1970s, the National Cancer Institute conducted research trials on laetrile, finding no evidence of anticancer activity. Although laetrile is not approved for use in the United States, it is still extensively used in Mexico, often in combination with other alternative regimens. As previously noted, the cyanide present in laetrile can induce serious and possibly life-threatening side effects.

An increasingly popular type of alternative treatment involves dietary therapies. These methods seek to eliminate all meats and dairy products from the patient's diet and to introduce only "natural" foods such as uncooked vegetables and fruits. Often these regimens require a "cleansing" procedure, typically involving some type of enema. Examples of dietary treatments include macrobiotic diets and the Gerson treatment.

Proponents of macrobiotic diets claim that the careful selection, preparation, and consumption of proper foods not only promotes general health and well-being but also functions to relieve illnesses such as cancer and AIDS. Macrobiotic diets typically consist of whole grains, organically grown fruits and vegetables, bean products, and sea vegetables. Generally excluded from the diet are meats, poultry, eggs, dairy products, and all refined or processed foods. A nutritional risk associated with some macrobiotic diets is malnutrition or a deficiency in vitamin B_{12}, an essential vitamin found in meats.

The Gerson treatment is based on the theory that cancer results from an "impaired metabolism," that is, the body's flawed processing of fats, proteins, carbohydrates, vitamins, and minerals. In order to create an environment unfavorable to cancer, the Gerson treatment seeks to eliminate toxins from the body with the use of frequent coffee enemas. Other cleansing measures in this regimen include ozone or hydrogen peroxide treatments, which are given orally or rectally, potassium supplements, vaccines, and laetrile. The dietary portion of the program involves the consumption of large quantities of raw fruits and vegetables.

Like many other centers of alternative treatment, the Gerson Clinic, which is located in Tijuana, Mexico, specializes in the treatment of multiple diseases. In addition to cancer patients, this clinic accepts patients with heart disease, diabetes, arthritis, and multiple sclerosis. According to a Gerson Clinic brochure, the clinic welcomes "people with no apparent serious disease, who come to the Center simply to detoxify themselves . . . to prevent disease."*

Another type of alternative treatment is herbal therapy, a treatment that generally utilizes plant parts or extracts to treat cancer. Although many important drugs, such as penicillin, were originally isolated from plants, these drugs differ from herbal therapy remedies in that the drugs have been scientifically purified and tested. For example, in 1993 the FDA approved taxol, a derivative of the bark of yew trees, for the treatment of breast and ovarian cancer.

The unproven treatments mentioned here typify most alterna-

* Gerson Institute. *Gerson Therapy Center Open. When Cancer Becomes Incurable by Orthodox Methods, Perhaps Gerson Therapy Is the Answer.* Brochure, undated.

tive therapies. Represented as "harmless" and "natural" methods to rid the body of disease, such therapies can attempt to dissuade patients from continuing conventional therapy by stressing the right of individual choice. Not infrequently, alternative clinics are located outside the United States.

Psychological Therapy of Cancer

The precise role and benefits of psychological therapy as a cancer treatment remain quite controversial. Some scientific studies conclude that mental attitude can affect the outcome of orthodox cancer therapy, but most indicate no such correlation. Without conclusive proof that psychological techniques applied independent of standard therapy are curative for cancer, medical authorities such as the American Cancer Society continue to regard psychological therapy as an unproven cancer treatment. This position, however, in no way denigrates the crucial role of a patient's mental attitude during illness or the possible benefits of adjunct psychological therapy. To do so would be a disservice to this needed aspect of cancer support.

In fact, psychological interventions are used quite regularly today in orthodox cancer therapy. In attempting to control cancer pain, medical staffs frequently employ the techniques of hypnosis, distraction, and relaxation training. (See Chapter 23, Control of Cancer Pain.) When chemotherapy patients experience persistent nausea, they are often similarly instructed in methods of relaxation and meditation. Moreover, cancer patients are routinely encouraged to maintain emotional and mental health by participating in local support groups such as The National Coalition for Survivorship and the Wellness Community.

Two of the most widely known psychological "treatments" of cancer are the Simonton and LeShan methods. Dr. O. Carl Simonton graduated from medical school in 1967 and founded a cancer center in Fort Worth, Texas that specializes in the study and treatment of the emotional aspects of cancer. Dr. Simonton theorizes that each person actively contributes to the development of cancer and must assume a correspondingly active role in its cure. Cancer researchers investigating the Simonton method have noted the following benefits.

1. The technique has no adverse side effects.
2. As Dr. Simonton does not advocate the cessation of standard therapy, both types of therapy may be used simultaneously.
3. The technique promotes relaxation; it also counteracts the patient's sense of hopelessness by encouraging active participation in treatment.
4. With its emphasis on positive attitude, the technique may help the patient to adapt more effectively to the situation at hand.

Cancer researchers note these negative aspects of the Simonton method.

1. There is no scientific basis for its theories or claims.
2. There is no evidence that the use of imagery or stress reduction alters the course of the disease.

Another popular mind–body cancer treatment is the LeShan method. Dr. Lawrence LeShan, a psychologist, believes that psychological stresses contribute to the development of cancer. He describes his approach as one-on-one psychological treatment aimed at analyzing the "blocks that keep the patient from being able to live out his or her true nature."* Despite the lack of scientific proof, LeShan claims that such psychotherapy has caused tumor regression in some patients.

Given the still dubious status of psychological therapy, this particular mode of treatment should be used as an adjunct to orthodox therapy rather than as a substitute for it. Unlike other unproven treatments, therapeutic methods that address the mental and emotional needs of the cancer patient undoubtedly serve to enhance the patient's quality of life during therapy. Understanda-

---

* LeShan LL. *Cancer as a Turning Point.* New York: E. P. Dutton, 1989.

bly, most cancer patients need to know that they are doing everything in their power to mitigate illness.

Short of cure, what patients ultimately seek is hope—and psychological therapy, with its positive approach, can sometimes most adequately instill this sense in those most needful of it. In the future, perhaps the scientific explanation and benefit of psychological therapy may be established. However, until that day arrives, the cancer patient is best served by selecting proven treatments for the body while seeking to maintain the health of the mind and spirit through methods that aid rather than undermine primary standard therapy.

III

Common Problems Encountered by the Cancer Patient

20

Getting a Second Opinion

After an initial diagnosis, a patient has the option of seeking a *second opinion*, that is, consulting an independent physician about the validity of the diagnosis and recommended treatment. Although the process of seeking a second opinion may, at times, be difficult, the cancer patient who entertains any doubts about the diagnosis or proposed treatment is well advised to seek another opinion. Through this very process, the cancer patient often claims greater peace of mind, a powerful therapy in itself.

The seeking of a second opinion is an increasingly common practice today. In fact, many insurance companies require that participating members obtain a second opinion before elective surgery. Cancer patients, in particular, tend to seek a second opinion. For example, 25% of patients in the oncology department of Sewickley Valley Hospital seek a second opinion at some time during their illnesses. The increasing tendency of cancer patients to seek a second opinion is attributable to a number of factors.

First, the increase in second opinions quite naturally results from the consumer movement, the grass roots effort that emphasizes patient education and advocacy. A valid tenet of this movement is that patients are capable of assuming a greater share of responsibility for their own health care. By seeking a second opinion, patients are better able to control their own destinies in that they exercise a certain freedom of choice regarding such pivotal issues as therapy and personal physician. Younger patients, in particular, appreciate the legitimacy and importance of obtaining a second opinion.

Second, patients with cancer desire optimal treatment for diseases that they generally regard as life threatening. Whereas patients suffering from heart attack and pneumonia routinely seek treatment at local hospitals, patients with cancer often seek treatment from prominent research centers where they can benefit from the latest technological breakthroughs. Such patients are well served by referral to these regional centers. However, faith in "high-tech" treatment does need to be tempered by the reality that limitations are inherent in all therapies.

Third, given the nature of the disease, cancer patients typically have the latitude to seek a second opinion. Unlike critical diseases such as acute appendicitis and heart attack that require emergency treatment, most cancer therapies can be delayed, allowing patients ample time to seek two or even three opinions about the diagnosis and proposed treatment.

Because of values and trends in our society, second opinions in cancer treatment will continue to become increasingly common. As one would expect, requests for second opinions are already a frequent fact of life in small community hospitals.

Sewickley Valley Hospital, a 200-bed facility in suburban Pittsburgh, is one such example of a community-based hospital fostering the collaborative approach to cancer care. The oncology staff there attempts to facilitate the process of obtaining second opinions in the following ways: an independent oncologist affiliated with a local research hospital visits the Oncology Clinic weekly for consultations; a system exists for gathering and transferring a patient's complete medical records promptly to designated physicians or cancer centers; the staff makes a conscious effort to assure the patient that this process is an entirely reasonable and beneficial one for all concerned.

Obviously, knowing when and how to obtain a second opinion are crucial issues for the cancer patient. The following discussion offers practical suggestions for resolving these issues.

Reasons for a Second Opinion

Perhaps the most common reason for obtaining a second opinion is to verify the proposed treatment plan. Quite simply, most patients want to know that they are receiving appropriate care. Often, too, close relatives wish to confirm that a loved one is "getting good medical care." The second opinion frequently confers this much-needed peace of mind.

Another valid reason for the cancer patient to seek a second opinion is dissatisfaction with the initial attending physician. Perhaps personality differences interfere with the patient–doctor relationship, or serious problems in communication arise. Because it is of paramount importance that the patient both trust and feel at ease with the attending physician, the patient who experiences problems in this relationship is well advised to seek a second opinion. The experience of G.W. illustrates this point:

G.W. is a 60-year-old businesswoman who was receiving chemotherapy for a non-Hodgkin's lymphoma. She relates:

I awoke the morning after the second treatment looking like a monster from outer space—a deep purple rash covered every part of my body, including my face, and I had a fever. When informed of this, my physician's reaction was, "Oh, yes. You are experiencing a reaction to the chemotherapy drug, procarbazine." He suggested no remedy. When I complained, his comment was, "You're just not strong enough." I was furious about this remark; he had known me for 2 weeks! As a businesswoman, I could not function in that condition. I saw my own dermatologist who told me a certain medication could clear up the rash within 3 days. Dissatisfied with the first physician's handling of my case, I asked for a different oncologist.

The patient and physician have to work together as a team; therefore, they must have a good rapport. If the patient is dissatisfied, he or she should change physicians—after all, the patient's life is at stake.

As exemplified by the case of G.W., cancer treatment is most effective when the patient and physician trust and understand each other.

A third precipitating cause for the cancer patient to seek a second opinion is an unfavorable diagnosis. Quite expectedly, many patients experience denial in accepting a serious diagnosis and request a second opinion in the hope that a particularly grave prognosis may be amended. Obtaining a second opinion is often a first step in the patient's coming to terms with serious illness.

Other reasons for the cancer patient to seek a second opinion include an extremely slow recovery and unexpected medical complications. When patient recovery does not proceed "on schedule," frustration naturally builds, prompting the patient to request a second opinion. Moreover, cancer therapy can cause many potential side effects. When a particularly serious side effect occurs, a patient may request a second opinion to ascertain if treatment is being managed appropriately.

Depending on individual circumstances, any of these reasons might justify the cancer patient's quest for a second opinion. At the same time, no patient benefits by second-guessing or questioning every decision of the attending physician. However, that leaves a wide range of potential problems that are neither trivial nor life threatening. The decision to seek a second opinion is ultimately a matter of the patient's judgment.

Types of Second Opinions

Two kinds of second opinions exist for the cancer patient: pathological and clinical. A pathological second opinion confirms the presence and type of cancer. An expert pathologist, a specialist trained in interpreting slides of cancerous tissue with the aid of a microscope, provides this review. The importance of pathological review in the second-opinion process cannot be overemphasized. The patient is not actually examined by the pathologist, but prepared slides of the patient's tissue biopsy are delivered by courier to the appropriate laboratory for a second analysis. Once the diagnosis is firmly established, the appropriate therapy can be planned.

Whenever the exact type of a cancer cannot be determined, further testing must be performed. In this setting, the slides are stained with special diagnostic markers that may elucidate the cancer type. Should a diagnosis still not be reached, the slides are then sent to a second expert pathologist for further review.

The differences between cancer types are frequently so subtle that definitive diagnoses can only be made by such expert pathologists. For example, one of the most difficult cancers to classify precisely is lymphoma, a cancer originating in the lymph nodes (that is, infection-fighting glands throughout the body). The pathological diagnosis of lymphoma must be made from among approximately 11 subclassifications. Therefore, an expert pathological opinion is often routinely sought for lymphoma slides.

In the case study previously cited, such pathological uncertainty existed regarding G.W.'s diagnosis.

> Four local pathologists were evenly divided on my diagnosis—Hodgkin's or non-Hodgkin's lymphoma. Routinely, they sent a set of specimen slides to an expert in Pittsburgh. However, my husband and I asked that specimen slides also be sent to an expert in Rochester who had been recommended to us. These two experts concurred that I had non-Hodgkin's lymphoma. . . . Patients should seek a second, or even a third opinion, because treatment plans will differ according to the diagnosis.

The other type of second opinion is the clinical opinion, given by a physician who treats patients with cancer. Unlike pathologists and radiologists who objectively interpret the results of testing, clinicians directly provide patient care. Depending on the circumstances, the physician rendering this clinical opinion may be a surgeon, a radiation oncologist (a specialist who treats cancer with x rays), or a medical oncologist (a specialist who treats cancer with chemotherapy). The patient seeks a clinical second opinion for the sole purpose of determining the optimal treatment for a given disease.

In the "best case" scenario, the first and second clinical opinions concur on the patient's course of treatment. The patient, having thus gained a fuller understanding of both the disease and proposed treatment during this opinion process, is then generally able to commence therapy with greater confidence.

However, clinical opinions differ in as many as one out of three cancer patients. Such disagreements commonly result from the physicians' own biases or preferences. For example, research has verified that surgery and radiation therapy are equally effective in the treatment of early-stage prostate cancer. Consequently, when presented with this particular cancer, a surgeon often recommends surgery, whereas a radiation oncologist opts for radiation therapy. In such cases, the patient is forced to assume a greater measure of responsibility for his own welfare by choosing between treatment options. Admittedly, the patient may find this position of choice quite stressful.

At times, the disagreement in clinical opinions is profound and additional clinical opinions may be needed to clarify the situation. As opinions abound, the treatment decision can become an exceedingly heavy burden on the patient, family members, and physicians alike. Ultimately, though, this difficult choice is the patient's to make, as exemplified by the case, M.Z.

> M.Z. is an 81-year-old man who, on consulting a lung specialist, was found to have a malignant tumor of the lung. A chest scan further revealed mildly enlarged lymph nodes. Due to M.Z.'s advanced age, his emphysema, and the possibility that the tumor might not be surgically removable, the lung specialist advised M.Z. to undergo radiation therapy instead of surgery.
>
> However, as M.Z. was extremely interested in having the cancer "cut out," he sought supporting opinions from a medical oncologist as well as a chest surgeon. On reviewing M.Z.'s situation, the oncologist concluded that the tumor might, indeed, be surgically removable but that the risks of surgery were unreasonably high for an elderly man in his condition. The physician recommended radiation therapy.
>
> The following week, M.Z. was examined by the chest surgeon, who believed that the surgical removal of the tumor was a viable option. Fully aware of the risks inherent in this procedure, M.Z. chose to proceed with it. At the time of surgery, the tumor was successfully removed, and the enlarged lymph nodes were determined to be benign. He made a slow but otherwise uneventful recovery from the surgery. Five months later, M.Z. experiences slight shortness of breath but continues to do extremely well.

M.Z.'s case illustrates two important points. First, as clinical opinions involve judgment calls about complex medical issues, doctors are bound to err. In this case, both the lung specialist and the oncologist calculated that the risks of lung surgery were too high, yet the outcome proved both of them wrong! Second, when-ever clinical opinions conflict, the treatment decision must ulti-mately be made by the patient.

The "Nuts and Bolts" of Seeking a Second Opinion

Once the decision is made to obtain a second opinion, a num-ber of practical issues need to be considered. First, the patient must arrange for all pertinent medical records to be forwarded to the consulting physician. Such records include x-ray films and reports, pathology reports, and the records of the diagnosing physician.

As this information is typically stored in three different areas, the patient must personally visit each department or office to au-thorize the transfer. X-ray films and reports should be "signed out" in the hospital's radiology department. Pathology reports and, if necessary, a set of specimen slides may be obtained in the pathol-ogy department. The records of the diagnosing physician may be procured either in the hospital's medical records department or in the physician's private office.

In order to render a meaningful second opinion, the physician requires a complete set of medical records. To ensure that these records arrive safely and promptly at the office of the consulting physician, the patient should hand-deliver them at the time of the scheduled appointment.

The patient who decides to seek a second opinion should, as a matter of courtesy, inform the diagnosing physician of this deci-sion. In all likelihood, the office staff can then help to facilitate the process of securing the needed records. This disclosure may also lead to fuller communication between patient and doctor and quite possibly a "clearing of the air" between them. As the patient who intends to seek a second opinion frequently needs assistance in locating a qualified consultant, such a conversation also provides an opportunity for the patient to ask for recommendations.

The act of choosing a qualified consultant can be one of the most difficult steps in the second-opinion process. Many patients understandably desire an independent opinion, that is, one given by a consultant who has not been recommended by the attending physician.

A primary way of locating a qualified consultant is to tap into the "medical grapevine." Requesting a referral from a friend or an associate who is involved in the medical field, such as a nurse, lab technician, respiratory therapist, or hospital administrator, is likely to yield positive results. As such personnel know the local reputations of physicians, these insiders are often able to provide excellent recommendations. Another source of referral information can be found in the cancer support groups that are commonly affiliated with hospitals. Perhaps no better referral source exists, however, than other cancer patients who personally recommend their physicians.

Another way of locating a qualified consultant is to identify the "doctor's doctor." By dint of association, physicians are able to appraise one another's expertise with a fair degree of accuracy—and for their own relatives as well as for themselves, they tend to choose "good" doctors. Ferreting out such information may require some discreet inquiries; the effort is guaranteed to result in the names of qualified consultants.

Another obvious approach is to evaluate the training of physicians under consideration. To be licensed to practice medicine, a student must graduate from an accredited medical school and complete a year-long hospital internship. After the internship, a physician chooses to study a particular area of medicine, serving a residency ranging from 2 to 6 years in such specialties as surgery, family practice, radiology, or obstetrics. On successfully completing this residency, a physician is regarded as *board eligible*. Only after passing a certifying exam in the chosen specialty does the physician become *board certified*.

When attempting to locate a qualified consultant, the patient would be wise to check whether the physician has completed specialty training in an accredited residency program. Unfortunately, a number of physicians advertise as specialists without having served the required residency.

Formal networks also exist to assist patients in the search for second opinions. In addition to offering support services throughout the course of illness, The American Cancer Society can provide the names of board-certified physicians.

Another excellent resource is the National Cancer Institute (NCI), the cancer agency funded by the U.S. government. Included among the NCI's many programs aimed at the detection, prevention, and treatment of cancer is a toll-free hotline known as the Cancer Information Service (1-800-4-CANCER). By contacting this hotline, patients can receive valuable information about their individual diseases as well as second-opinion referrals.

Moreover, the NCI has developed a program to foster standards of excellence in cancer therapy nationwide. The Institute's own facility for research and treatment is located in Bethesda, Maryland, but certainly not all cancer patients can expect to be treated there. Consequently, the NCI has awarded the title, National Cancer Institute–Designated Cancer Center, to approximately 25 medical centers throughout the United States that have demonstrated superior achievement in the areas of research, detection, treatment, and the training of medical personnel. These particular medical centers are then eligible to receive federal funding to support their cancer programs. Obviously, the patient seeking a qualified consultant can be fairly certain of finding one at such a reputable center.

Another fine source of second-opinion physicians is the staff of any hospital affiliated with the Community Clinical Oncology Program (CCOP). In this program, the NCI collaborates with community hospitals to make the latest cancer therapies available on a local basis. Funded by the NCI, CCOPs are located throughout the United States. For example, the aforementioned Sewickley Valley Hospital is a member of the Allegheny Singer CCOP, an affiliation of five local hospitals in or near Pittsburgh, Pennsylvania. For a complete listing of National Cancer Institute–Designated Comprehensive Cancer Centers and CCOPs, consult Appendix A: Resources.

21

Day-to-Day Symptoms

with Marmee Maylone, R.N., M.S.N., O.C.N.

Regardless of the specific type of the disease, cancer tends to cause certain common symptoms in patients. If anticipated and appreciated as essentially disease related, such symptoms can be better recognized by the cancer patient and family, thus reducing anxiety and enabling them to seek appropriate help whenever necessary. Although cancer patients often quite naturally fear that every physical problem encountered after diagnosis is directly due to the cancer, many such symptoms are entirely unrelated. To attain peace of mind as well as a conclusive evaluation, the cancer patient needs to report troubling symptoms promptly to the attending physician.

Bone Pain

Bone pain may be caused by a number of noncancerous conditions, including arthritis, the flu, and trauma. Certainly, any bone pain that is new, persistent, or escalating needs to be evaluated thoroughly. All types of cancer can spread (metastasize) to the bone, with the most common being cancers of the breast, lung, prostate, and rectum. Fully 30 to 70% of patients who develop metastasis have bone involvement, the classic symptom of which is bone pain. X rays and a bone scan can reliably establish the presence of a bone metastasis. Bone metastasis can also be detected by such laboratory abnormalities as low blood counts and elevated calcium levels, because metastasis can impede the production of blood cells in the bone marrow and cause calcium to leak from the bones into the bloodstream.

Initial therapy of a bone metastasis is aimed at eliminating pain and preventing fractures. Typically, treatment consists of radiation therapy and pain medication, often narcotics. (See Chapter 23, The Control of Cancer Pain.) Because radiation therapy successfully controls pain in about 75% of patients, pain medication can often be reduced or stopped. On completion of radiation therapy, subsequent treatment is determined by the specific type of cancer that caused the recurrence.

The patient with a bone metastasis is advised to take precautions to avoid falling, as the affected bones may be particularly brittle. Unfortunately, 10% of such patients do suffer fractures of the arms, legs, and hips, generally requiring orthopedic surgery. The goal of this surgery is to preserve the patient's ambulation by inserting a metal pin into the bone in order to strengthen and stabilize it.

Confusion

Confusion is a change or reduction in a patient's mental function. In cancer patients, confusion is often caused by medications, particularly narcotics. However, if medication is excluded as the cause, the patient must undergo further testing, generally bloodwork and a computed tomography (CT) scan of the head. The former commonly reveals abnormalities in the body's level of sodium or calcium, the correction of which resolves confusion in more than 80% of patients.

Should the cause of confusion be a brain tumor, a CT scan of the head generally proves diagnostic. Actually, brain metastases are somewhat common, developing in 13% of cancer patients, only 14% of whom survive longer than 1 year. The types of cancer most inclined to spread to the brain include melanomas and cancers of the lung, breast, and kidney. Approximately 50% of these patients experience headaches, although seizures, dizziness, weakness, and walking disturbances are also common.

Treatment of a brain metastasis may involve radiation therapy to the site as well as the administration of dexamethasone (Decadron), a medication that reduces swelling in the brain. In a minority of patients, those who are in good physical condition with a single spot of brain metastasis, neurosurgical removal of the cancer is a possibility.

Diarrhea

Diarrhea is a disturbing symptom that can cause considerable discomfort and eventually lead to dehydration. As diarrhea typically results from intestinal "bugs," either bacterial or viral, most patients are instructed to take antidiarrheal medication and increase fluid intake. Any cancer patient who experiences this symptom for more than a day or two, however, should be weighed, because rapid weight loss often signifies dehydration, a condition that may require the administration of intravenous fluids in a hospital.

Patients receiving antibiotics can also develop diarrhea. This type of diarrhea is caused by intestinal bacteria (*Clostridium difficile*) that proliferate as the balance of benign bacteria is disrupted by the antibiotic. *C. difficile* diarrhea is treated with antidiarrheal medication, yogurt, and the antibiotic vancomycin.

Diarrhea can also be induced by chemotherapy drugs, especially methotrexate, 5-FU, leucovorin, and adriamycin. Usually developing 10 days after the drugs are initiated, such diarrhea is frequently accompanied by mouth sores. Treatment includes the temporary cessation of chemotherapy, an increased intake of fluids, an antidiarrheal medication, and a topical application for mouth sores.

Depression, Loss of Appetite, and Weight Loss

More than 50% of cancer patients experience depression at some point in the course of illness. Such manifestations as crying, loss of appetite, and social withdrawal are often associated with depression, but an underappreciated symptom of depression is the inability to sleep. Many cancer patients are quite reluctant to admit to depression, believing as they do that the condition is a sign of personal weakness. They must often be helped to understand that depression is an entirely normal and appropriate reaction to a life-threatening diagnosis.

Should symptoms persist longer than a few weeks, an antidepressant is usually prescribed to alleviate the patient's distress. As anti-depressants have proven especially effective in treating this type of depression, the patient is advised to allow the medication sufficient time to take effect, generally a period of several weeks.

Two related symptoms that the cancer patient and family find disturbing are reduced appetite and weight loss. It is often assumed, especially in the case of weight loss, that growth of the cancer is the cause. Weight loss among cancer patients is extremely common, however, and the reasons for it are varied. One highly treatable cause that must be considered is depression, particularly when x rays and laboratory tests indicate a good response to treatment. Drugs, too, can contribute to loss of appetite, principally chemotherapy drugs. Narcotic pain medications can also induce nausea and resultant weight loss, thus necessitating a change in drug.

Even when such symptoms are attributable to the cancer, several techniques can be employed to promote weight gain. First, the patient should mimic the eating pattern of a premature infant, that is, eat frequent snacks rather than whole meals and drink a high-calorie supplement like Ensure daily. Moreover, caregivers are encouraged to make favorite foods available and to coach the patient gently to sample them. Medications may also be employed to stimulate appetite. A highly effective stimulant is the female hormone progesterone, known by the brand name *Megace;* it is prescribed in 40-mg doses to be taken every 6–8 hours. The steroid prednisone is another widely prescribed stimulant, taken in daily doses of 10 to 60 mg.

When coping with cancer-induced weight loss, families often ask about the possibility of intravenous feeding. In that the patient's nutritional status is such an important determinant of outcome, this request is quite reasonable. Indeed, in some instances, intravenous feeding is standard practice, particularly for patients who have undergone major surgery or bone marrow transplantation. However, in cancer patients whose weight loss clearly results from the progression of the disease, studies indicate that intravenous feeding does not improve survival rates. Consequently, most oncologists attempt to treat this problem with medication and altered menu. Should the patient become dehydrated, fluids rather than nutritional supplements are generally administered in order to maintain hydration and comfort.

Fever

Fever in cancer patients has varied causes. Both chemotherapy and radiation therapy can precipitate a reduction in the white blood cell (WBC) count, thus predisposing the patient to infection. If a patient undergoing such therapy runs a fever, a blood test is given; if the WBC count proves low, the patient is generally hospitalized in order to receive antibiotics by vein. As soon as the WBC count returns to normal, the antibiotics are then stopped, and the patient is discharged. (See Chapter 14, Common Side Effects of Chemotherapy.)

Even in cancer patients whose WBC counts are normal, fevers sometimes arise, usually as the result of infection. Whenever a cancer patient registers a temperature above 101°F, the patient should contact the physician. Depending on the overall condition of the patient, such infections can ordinarily be treated with oral antibiotics on an outpatient basis.

Another related cause of fever in cancer patients is medication, often the most recently prescribed one. Because cancer patients frequently take a variety of drugs to control bothersome symptoms, these patients run an elevated risk of developing a drug-induced fever. The hallmark of this drug reaction is a fever accompanied by a diffuse skin rash, a phenomenon that resolves when the offending medication is stopped.

However, a cancer patient's fever may also emanate from the cancer itself, particularly in kidney cancers, lymphomas, and liver metastases. After the possibility of serious infection has been excluded for such patients, acetaminophen or aspirin may be prescribed on a regular basis to suppress the fever.

Jaundice

Jaundice does not medically qualify as a rash; this condition manifests itself in a yellowish cast to the skin. Resulting from various forms of liver damage, jaundice requires a thorough evaluation in order to be appropriately treated. When gallstones block the drainage of the liver into the intestine, surgical removal of the stones restores the liver's access, thereby causing the jaundice to resolve. The viral infection, hepatitis, may also cause jaundice that resolves over time in more than 90% of patients.

Whereas cancer can induce jaundice by either impeding liver drainage with tumors or disrupting normal function through invasion of the organ, successful treatment of the cancer results in resolution of the problem. A CT scan or sonogram of the liver can generally determine whether a patient's jaundice is cancer induced.

So common is metastasis to the liver that it accounts for approximately 35% of metastases in general. As the liver performs a variety of crucial body functions—including the synthesis of needed proteins, regulation of sugars, elimination of toxins, and recycling of red blood cells—the symptoms of a liver metastasis vary according to the specific processes that are impaired. Common symptoms other than jaundice include right upper abdominal pain, abnormalities in laboratory tests, and bleeding.

Treatment of a liver metastasis typically involves chemotherapy. When the metastasis is confined to the liver, chemotherapy can be directly infused into the liver through a surgically implanted pump and a catheter. This procedure is performed by a surgeon, who places the pump under the skin of the abdominal wall and inserts the catheter into the main artery of the liver. Low doses of chemotherapy drugs can then be infused continuously at a determined rate for weeks at a time.

In a minority of patients, the surgical removal of an isolated spot of metastasis in the liver may be possible. Not only must the patient be able to withstand the rigors of invasive surgery but also the metastasis must be located in a surgically accessible area of the liver. This aggressive surgery has been proven especially effective in patients with a single liver metastasis of colorectal cancer. A promising alternative treatment that is currently under investigation is cryosurgery, a method of surgically freezing and removing tumors.

Shortness of Breath

Although shortness of breath can arise from a variety of medical conditions, any increase in this symptom merits prompt medical attention. In many cancer patients, shortness of breath is due to a coexisting medical condition like heart failure or emphysema. However, the stress of cancer therapy often exacerbates the condition, the timely treatment of which generally yields successful results. For example, when shortness of breath is caused by heart failure, treatment is aimed at improving the heart's ability to pump. Should the breathing difficulty be caused by emphysema, inhalers and medications like prednisone and theophylline are prescribed.

Shortness of breath that is accompanied by cough or fever may be caused by pneumonia, an infection requiring prompt medical attention. Cancer patients, particularly those receiving chemo-therapy, are predisposed to pneumonia because of lowered immunity. In most cases, a chest x ray is needed to establish this diagnosis, with the condition typically resolving after a course of antibiotics.

In the event that shortness of breath fails to subside, the use of oxygen in the patient's home can be prescribed. Of course, strict regulations exist concerning the patient's demonstrated need for oxygen, including diagnosis and overall medical condition, as well as the allowable level of oxygen in the blood. Home oxygen, avail-able in both stationary and portable units, is given continuously through a small, low-flow tube that is attached to the nose.

Skin Rashes

An ailment commonly affecting cancer patients is skin rashes. Found in all body locations, drug-induced rashes generally appear as diffuse, raised, reddened, itchy areas of skin. Although such rashes can occur at any time after a medication is initiated, they typically develop within the first 3 weeks, frequently in association with fevers. Treatment involves stopping the suspected drug and controlling the itchiness with medications such as diphenhydra-mine (*Benadryl*) and steroids.

Another cause of rashes in cancer patients is skin infections. A bacterial skin infection generally appears as an extremely tender and localized rash, often developing at intravenous sites. Treat-ment consists of warm compresses and antibiotics. A common viral skin infection in cancer patients is shingles. A reactivation of the chicken pox virus, this rash causes pain and blisters along major nerve routes, frequently involving the back, face, and chest. Treat-ment involves pain medication and the drug acyclovir.

Swallowing Difficulty

Unlike many symptoms with causes unrelated to the patient's primary cancer, difficulty in swallowing is most often attributable to either the cancer or its therapy. Difficulty in swallowing usually originates in the esophagus, the tube that connects the mouth to the stomach. The two standard tests used to evaluate the esophagus are (1) the *barium swallow*, in which an x ray reveals the passage of swallowed barium through the esophagus, and (2) *endoscopy*, in which a visual examination of the esophagus is performed with the aid of a flexible lighted tube called an endoscope.

Difficulty in swallowing emanates from any narrowing of the esophagus, such as that which develops in cancers affecting the chest, like lung cancer and Hodgkin's disease. Treatment of the cancer generally alleviates this symptom. When unsuccessful, however, a *gastrostomy tube* can be inserted directly into the stomach through the abdominal wall for feeding.

Treatments such as chemotherapy or chest radiation can also cause esophageal inflammation, a condition that generally resolves after suspension of treatment. To provide temporary relief, the liquid anesthetic, viscous lidocaine (Xylocaine), is often prescribed. Another irritation occurs when the esophagus becomes coated with *Candida*, the yeast also responsible for many vaginal infections. Such an infection of the esophagus is easily treated with a lozenge medication clotrimazole (*Mycelex troche*). Moreover, cancer patients with lowered immunity may develop a herpes infection or cold sore virus in the esophagus, a condition treatable with the antiviral medication acyclovir.

Swelling

An easily recognizable symptom, swelling results from the abnormal accumulation of fluid in body tissue. Swelling can be caused by a variety of noncancerous conditions such as

1. *Heart failure*, in which the pumping of the heart is weak. This results in pressure building up in the veins of the body with resultant accumulation of fluid;
2. *Kidney abnormalities* that prevent the elimination of fluids;

3. *Phlebitis,* in which clots in the leg veins impede the blood's return to the heart;
4. *Malnutrition,* in which the cells, lacking proteins, leak fluid into body tissues; and
5. *Steroid medications* that alter the distribution of body fat, inducing a distinctive facial puffiness that is often referred to as a "moon face."

In general, the therapies used to treat swelling are directed at the primary cause. For example, phlebitis is controlled with the administration of a blood thinner; heart failure is treated with medications that increase the heart's ability to pump. In the interim, the patient may also be advised to limit the intake of fluids, take a diuretic (water pill) to increase the discharge of urine, wear support stockings, and elevate the legs as much as possible.

Most body cavities normally contain small amounts of lubricating fluid. However, a build-up of fluid in the abdominal cavity, known as *ascites,* causes uncomfortable bloating, loss of appetite, and swelling of the abdomen. The diagnosis of ascites usually requires a *paracentesis,* the insertion of a needle into the abdominal cavity in order to remove a sample of fluid. If cancer cells are detected by paracentesis, the condition is known as malignant ascites. Treatment initially involves a restriction of fluid intake and the administration of a water pill. If these measures prove unsuccessful, repeated paracentesis, chemotherapy, or the insertion of drugs directly into the abdominal cavity may be recommended.

Fluid can also collect in the sac that encases the lung; this swelling is known as an *effusion.* Triggered by pneumonia, heart failure, or malignancy, an effusion causes breathing difficulty, usually shortness of breath. The diagnosis of an effusion is made through a physical examination and a chest x ray. Initial treatment involves *thoracentesis,* the removal of fluid via a needle that is inserted into the chest cavity. Only laboratory analysis of the extracted fluid can establish malignancy, a condition known as *malignant effusion.* Should thoracentesis prove ineffective in alleviating this malignant effusion, a chest tube can then be inserted to drain the lung sac, a procedure that usually requires a short hospitalization. If necessary, chemotherapy drugs can also be instilled through the tube to destroy malignant cells.

22

Cancer and the Elderly

The media have given extensive attention to many aspects of the aging process, but both the lay and medical press have essentially ignored the problem of cancer in elderly Americans. Given the prevailing "health and youth" focus of our society, this omission is understandable. In truth, Americans apply broad taboos to the subjects of cancer and aging; polite society discusses neither subject. However, such an attitude ignores what will become an increasingly common American phenomenon in the 21st century—elderly citizens having cancer.

Age as a Cancer Risk Factor

Age is considered cancer's predominant risk factor. In the United States, 50% of all cancers develop in people older than 65 years, an age group now constituting 12% of the population. An increased risk with age accompanies the following common cancers: breast, colon, prostate, bladder, skin, and cervical cancers. A person's risk of developing cancer actually escalates during the fourth decade of life, climbing steeply with each successive decade. Moreover, men are more susceptible to this risk than are woman.

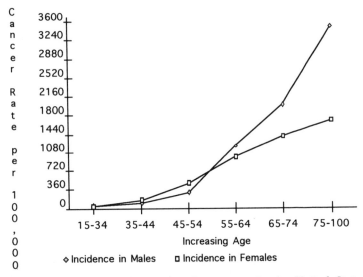

Figure 22-1. Cancer incidence according to age in the United States. Adapted from *Surveillance Epidemiology and End Results Program, 1977–1982.* Bethesda, MD: National Institutes of Health, 1984.

Figure 22-1 clearly illustrates the increase in cancer incidence with advancing age.

The cause of the elderly's increased risk of cancer is rather poorly understood. Some researchers postulate that changes in the elderly's immune system can account for a heightened susceptibility to the disease. This view holds that the elderly's immune system, weakened in its capacity to fight infections, is also diminished in its capacity to ward off cancer. Another possibility is that cancer in the elderly is the cumulative result of lifelong exposure to carcinogenic substances. Promoters of this theory point to such causal relationships as the long-term exposure to sunlight and skin cancer.

The demography of this particular population, however, is well defined. Today, 12% of the American population is 65 years or older, a statistic in contrast to that of 1900 when only 4% of the population reached this age bracket. Moreover, today's "baby boomers" will become the "aging boomers" of tomorrow; it is estimated that fully 22% of the population, or 65 million Americans, will be 65 years or older by 2030. Furthermore, the elderly are continuing to live longer. In 1900, a 65-year-old woman could expect to live, on average, to age 77. Today, a 65-year-old woman is expected to live to age 83. By 2030, the number of Americans who are 85 years of age or older is expected to quadruple from 2.2 million to 8.6 million. This rapid "graying of America" means that most families will soon have at least one elderly relative who is coping with cancer.

Who Are the Aged?

People older than 65 are generally referred to as *the elderly.* In the field of geriatrics, which is the study of aging, the elderly are classified into three groups: the *young old* are aged 65 to 74; the *older old* are aged 75 to 84; and the *frail old* are aged 85 and older. Such a system of classification allows all concerned to appreciate the differences that exist among elderly patients.

In an evaluation of the elderly cancer patient, a factor equal in importance to chronological age is the patient's overall medical condition. Although some 65-year old patients, due to preexisting medical conditions, can best be described as frail elderly, some 83-year-old patients may be in fine physical condition and aptly described as young old. Obviously, elderly cancer patients are unique individuals whose therapy must be tailored to their specific conditions and needs.

To fully appreciate the problems encountered by elderly cancer patients, the behavioral and biological changes associated with aging must be understood. It is, in fact, such changes that so often impede the early detection of cancer in these patients.

Behaviors of the Elderly

Elderly patients do not typically report significant health problems to their physicians. International studies confirm that elderly patients frequently fail to report symptoms of serious disease such as blackouts, passing blood in the urine or stool, and even pain. When questioned about this injurious behavior, the elderly generally believed that illness was an expected and entirely normal function of the aging process. In other words, they were fully prepared to suffer in silence.

Another behavior that is quite common among the elderly, although it is certainly not limited to this age group, is procrastination in seeking medical attention out of a sense of fear. The elderly fear knowing the "true" nature of troublesome symptoms; they especially fear receiving the diagnosis of cancer. Not surprisingly, the cancer phobia that plagues our society appears to intensify among the elderly, who dread the pitfalls of a life-threatening illness. Frequently, the elderly view any type of therapy with pessimism, thoroughly skeptical that therapy can be either helpful or successful. The elderly also quite reasonably fear the high cost of medical care, Medicare notwithstanding.

These common behaviors and fears result in the elderly seeking medical attention for serious symptoms much too late, as illustrated in the case of I.B.

> I.B. is an 88-year-old widower, living independently, who developed intermittent rectal bleeding over at least 3 months. After blacking out during a Sunday church service, he was taken by ambulance to the emergency room of a local hospital where he was found to have severe anemia due to blood loss.

> Following a blood transfusion, I.B.'s condition stabilized. However, routine diagnostic tests revealed that I.B. had colon cancer. Although rectal bleeding is a common symptom of this disease, I.B. had mistakenly assumed that his bleeding was caused by hemorrhoids. Due to his otherwise fine medical condition, I.B. qualified as a candidate for surgery.

> In the course of surgery, the colon cancer was determined to be early stage and the tumor was successfully removed. As no further therapy was needed,

I.B. was simply advised to have routine check-ups. Recently, I.B. celebrated his 90th birthday, duly noted in the local newspaper.

I.B. is representative of many elderly patients who choose not to seek medical attention for obviously serious symptoms. As I.B. tellingly commented, "I just figured that the bleeding would either go away or I would bleed to death." Unfortunately, all too many elderly Americans share this view.

The behavior of most diseases is quite different in elderly patients from that in younger patients. A prime example of this difference is the common heart attack, which typically causes a loss of consciousness or shortness of breath in elderly patients as opposed to "classic" chest pain in younger patients. Similarly, cancers in elderly patients can induce nonspecific symptoms such as confusion, weight loss, or changes in personality. As these symptoms are atypical and subtle, it is often extremely difficult to diagnose cancers promptly in the elderly.

Physical Changes Associated with Aging

Coexisting medical problems increase dramatically with age, especially problems such as diabetes, high blood pressure, heart disease, arthritis, and strokes. Research has proven that individuals older than 70 years who live in the community average three and a half significant diseases per person. Among the hospitalized elderly, this number increases to six diseases per person! Obviously, the presence of one or more serious medical conditions in the elderly cancer patient strongly influences, and often limits, the choice of cancer treatments.

The loss of mental function due to age, often called senility, is a major cause of disability in the elderly. Studies have found that approximately 3% of the 65+ population suffer from severe senility, whereas as many as 10% of this population suffer from a milder but still measurable form of senility. Furthermore, it is estimated that 50 to 70% of the senile elderly have Alzheimer's disease, a chronic and progressive loss of mental function that is essentially untreatable at present. Of course, the patient's mental function is a significant factor in the choice of appropriate treatment options: Which therapy, if any, can improve the quality of the elderly cancer patient's life?

Another physical change occurring with age is a decrease in the capability of certain organs, including the kidneys and lungs. This characteristic decrease in capacity accounts for the elderly's extreme vulnerability to sudden ailments like pneumonia. Because of a condition commonly referred to as *hardening of the arteries*, elderly patients with high cholesterol also are especially prone to strokes and heart attacks.

Cancer Screening in the Elderly

Regrettably, little research has been performed on the benefits of cancer screening for the elderly population. Rarely have the elderly been targeted for widespread screening and, moreover, they are usually excluded from most early-detection studies. Nevertheless, cancer experts do recommend that elderly persons engage in the cancer-screening practices already prescribed for younger age groups. Such cancer-screening practices include, yearly stool and rectal exams, routine Pap smears, and biyearly mammograms.

Just as elderly patients often fail to seek medical attention for serious medical conditions, many elderly are likewise uninterested in utilizing cancer screening programs. Given the increased risk of cancer with age, such passive behavior is especially harmful. Most geriatric authorities maintain that the majority of elderly patients cannot be relied on to initiate appropriate health care, including cancer screening procedures, for themselves.

The statistics of cancer diagnosis in the elderly appear to support such a thesis. When compared to younger cancer patients, elderly patients have advanced-stage cancers at the time of diagnosis. A prime example of this contrast is cervical cancer, a disease that can be detected in its early stages through Pap smears and cured. Although early cervical cancer (stages I and II) is highly curable, detection at these stages decreases significantly with age. In contrast, detection of cervical cancer at an advanced stage (stages III and IV) increases dramatically with age, largely because elderly women neglect to have routine Pap smears.

Clearly, the need for conscientious cancer screening intensifies rather than diminishes with age. The elderly, as well as all concerned with their welfare, must become aware of this critical fact.

Dealing with Elderly Cancer Patients

The care of elderly cancer patients typically differs in a number of ways from that of younger cancer patients. First, older patients often delegate major decisions regarding their treatment to either their families or physicians. Unlike younger patients who tend to "take charge" of their health care, the elderly frequently want to be told what to do. Such passivity can often result in a somewhat paternalistic relationship between family and patient or even the doctor and patient.

In such situations, family members may quite understandably resort to making decisions by "committee." The doctor–patient relationship becomes more a doctor–family relationship. When disagreement exists among family members regarding therapy, the decision-making process can become quite complicated.

Second, inasmuch as elderly patients often fail to report symptoms or problems accurately to their physicians, an intermediary is generally relied on to provide additional information about the elderly patient. For example, pain is a serious symptom that elderly patients often downplay. Consequently, the physician must assume the role of a detective, questioning the patient as well as concerned "witnesses," that is, family members or caregivers, about the sleeping habits, appetite, and disposition of the patient. By consulting several reliable sources, the physician is best able to assess the elderly patient's level of pain.

Third, the expectations of the elderly cancer patient regarding prognosis and therapy are much lower than are those of the younger cancer patient. Whereas younger patients press for the most aggressive therapies available, elderly patients primarily seek comfort. On a practical level, elderly cancer patients rarely request second opinions or pursue experimental treatment at cancer centers. In essence, they accept their diagnosed condition and its consequences as a natural part of the life cycle; they generally regard the doctor–patient relationship as one of trust.

Of course, each elderly cancer patient must be treated on an individual basis. What appears to be a reasonable treatment approach for one 85-year-old patient may be totally inappropriate for another. For the elderly patient, a nonaggressive approach is certainly always an option. If the patient does not desire treatment, this decision must be respected. (See Chapter 18, No Therapy, for more extensive discussion of this subject.)

Treatment of Elderly Cancer Patients

The therapies used to treat elderly cancer patients are identical to those used to treat young cancer patients. They include surgery, chemotherapy, and radiation therapy. As investigational or experimental therapy is rarely used to treat the elderly population, such therapies will not be considered here. (For further discussion of these therapies, see Chapter 17, Investigational Therapy.)

Surgery

Most studies have found that young old cancer patients, aged 65 to 74, fare as well with surgery as do younger patients, but the success of surgery on those aged 75 years and older is dependent on the patient's general medical condition. To ascertain this condition, a medical evaluation is routinely performed on each patient for whom surgery may be a viable treatment option. Such an evaluation includes heart, lung, and kidney tests as well as a complete physical examination.

This scrutiny of the elderly patient's general condition is crucial in light of the characteristic reluctance to report symptoms and the likelihood of coexisting medical conditions associated with age. In one study focusing on the presurgical evaluations of cancer patients older than 70 years, results indicated that 13% of patients had normal medical conditions, 63% had correctable medical problems, and 24% had serious medical problems prohibiting surgery. As shown in the case of K.K., however, elderly patients with serious medical problems can be treated successfully for cancer.

> K.K. is an 87-year-old man with chronic heart failure. After suffering a heart attack 7 years ago, he has been hospitalized regularly for treatment of this condition. When he recently experienced shortness of breath, he was again admitted to the hospital and found to have anemia.
>
> On questioning, K.K. admitted to having noted red clots in his stool for the previous 2 weeks. This bleeding had caused his blood count to drop, thus stressing his heart and inducing shortness of breath. After receiving a blood transfusion, K.K. improved markedly. Testing subsequently revealed that his rectal bleeding had been caused by a small cancer of the colon.
>
> With surgical removal of the cancer an appropriate treatment option, K.K.'s family doctor requested that a cardiologist evaluate K.K. Granting that K.K.'s heart condition increased his surgical risks, the cardiologist concluded that K.K. could, indeed, undergo surgery with close cardiac monitoring. After a discussion with the physicians, K.K. and his family decided to proceed with surgery.
>
> A special monitor was inserted in the heart, a measure that enabled the cardiologist to treat K.K.'s heart problem during both surgery and recovery. After the successful removal of the colon cancer, K.K. spent 2 extra days in intensive care and recovered steadily. He was discharged 10 days after surgery. Recently, he celebrated his 89th birthday!

K.K.'s case serves to emphasize a number of important points. First, elderly patients with significant medical problems can safely undergo surgery. Second, elderly patients such as K.K. often wait until they are quite ill before seeking medical attention. Third, caring for the elderly cancer patient typically requires a team approach. In K.K.'s case, this team included the family doctor, surgeon, cardiologist, intensive care staff, and, of course, K.K. and his family. Any decision regarding the most appropriate treatment for the elderly cancer patient is best made in conjunction with all members of this team.

Chemotherapy

Chemotherapy refers to treatment with a class of cancer-fighting drugs that travel throughout the bloodstream to destroy cancer cells in the body. With rare exceptions, these drugs possess potential side effects. The aim of the oncologist is to balance the benefit of chemotherapeutic drugs against the threat of their side effects. Younger patients tend to be in strong enough medical condition to withstand such side effects, but the condition of elderly patients is often questionable.

Scant research has been done on the side effects of chemotherapy in the elderly. Psychologically, the elderly appear to cope even better than their younger counterparts do with these side effects, experiencing a lower level of emotional distress and less disruption in their daily routines during the course of therapy. Because of their reduced reserves of bone marrow, however, the elderly are prone to develop markedly low blood counts during therapy.

Two factors essentially govern the choice of chemotherapy for the elderly cancer patient. The first critical factor is the overall condition of the patient. As the patient should be able to report any serious problems experienced during chemotherapy, the extremely senile patient is not considered reliable enough to engage in this mode of therapy. Bedridden patients also are generally considered inappropriate candidates for chemotherapy because they often are not strong enough to tolerate the chemotherapy. Frequently, quality-of-life considerations determine chemotherapy decisions. In such instances, the oncologist should clearly explain to the family what the anticipated results of the patient's treatment will be in terms of both the quality and duration of life. It is difficult to generalize, but it should be noted that any treatment decision regarding the elderly patient should be based on the patient's medical condition and not age.

The second critical factor influencing the choice of chemotherapy for the elderly cancer patient is the specific cancer's degree of responsiveness to therapy. Because every type of cancer possesses a predictable response to chemotherapy, a cancer's responsiveness is obviously a pivotal factor in planning treatment. For example, small-cell lung cancer is so responsive to chemotherapy that such treatment is typically recommended in lieu of surgery for the treatment of this disease. In contrast, prostate cancer is only slightly responsive to chemotherapy and, as a result, either radiation or surgery is the preferred treatment for this disease.

When the type of cancer is responsive to chemotherapy, the chemotherapy is often given cautiously. In administering drugs to the elderly patient, dosage is typically decreased. For example, one standard combination of chemotherapy drugs includes adriamycin, a medication that can impair the function of the heart. Because cardiac conditions are quite common in the elderly, adriamycin is often excluded or reduced from the drug combinations that are administered to elderly patients.

In fact, choosing the proper combination of drugs for the elderly cancer patient involves considerable judgment on the part of the physician. Often, an unorthodox choice of drugs appears to be most appropriate for the patient, as illustrated in the case of C.N.

C.N. was an 88-year-old man who had a history of diabetes with related heart and kidney failure. Nearly bedridden, C.N. consulted his family doctor, complaining of continued weight loss and severe bone pain. On admission to the hospital, C.N. was found to have a small-cell lung cancer that had spread to the bones and liver.

An oncologist advised C.N. and his family that although the lung cancer, itself, was highly treatable, C.N.'s poor medical condition intensified the risks of treatment. After much discussion, the decision was made to initiate chemotherapy in an attempt to control the pain.

In order to accommodate the patient, the choice of chemotherapy drug was quite unusual. Because of C.N.'s heart and kidney conditions, the drugs most effective in the treatment of small-cell lung cancer could not be given to him.

Moreover, C.N. desired to be at home with his family. Consequently, the oncologist decided to treat C.N. with VP-16. This drug can be taken orally at home and has few side effects. This medication improved C.N.'s appetite and effectively reduced his pain for nearly 7 months. By the following month, however, the cancer had become wholly resistant to the drug's effects, and C.N. died in his sleep.

The unorthodox chemotherapy given to C.N. illustrates the type of individualized treatment that the elderly cancer patient both requires and deserves. The standard treatment for small-cell lung cancer is a combination of chemotherapy drugs, given intravenously, but C.N. could not physically tolerate such therapy. The oral therapy was well tolerated by C.N., controlled his pain, and enabled his family to keep him at home.

Radiation Therapy

Radiation therapy (RT) utilizes x rays to destroy cancer cells in the body. It is administered by specialists known as radiation oncologists. RT is widely used in the treatment of elderly cancer patients because it is viewed as easier on the patient than either chemotherapy or surgery.

RT generally induces fewer side effects than does chemotherapy. Unlike chemotherapy, which acts systemically throughout the body, RT acts on specific sites, affecting only those tissues that are directly exposed to the x-ray beam. Given the more limited side effects of RT, elderly cancer patients with coexisting medical conditions tend to tolerate this method of treatment well.

RT involves less risk to the elderly patient than does extensive cancer surgery. Although RT may not necessarily be the treatment of choice in curing or controlling a given cancer, RT is frequently selected for the elderly patient because it is considered the safest form of therapy. Two cancers for which elderly and younger patients often receive such different treatment are prostate and non–small-cell lung. (See Chapters 4, Prostate Cancer, and 2, Lung Cancer.) The case of B.B. is representative of many elderly patients with non–small-cell lung cancer.

B.B. is an 84-year-old matriarch of a large family who had smoked heavily since the age of 16. After coughing up blood, she was admitted to the hospital. Tests confirmed the presence of emphysema as well as a non–small-cell cancer in the right lung.

As the cancer had not spread outside the lung, treatment choices included surgery and RT. The family doctor asked a surgeon to review B.B.'s situation. The surgeon believed that surgery would probably entail complete removal of the right lung, an option likely to result in cure of the cancer. In view of B.B.'s emphysema, however, the doctors estimated that she had a 35% chance of becoming oxygen dependent after such surgery. In contrast, RT would offer a less effective treatment for the lung cancer but would pose no risk to B.B.'s breathing capability.

After discussing the situation thoroughly with both physicians, B.B. and her family decided in favor of RT; they chose not to risk having B.B. become incapacitated as a result of surgery. Six months after therapy, there is no evidence of the cancer, and B.B. is enjoying an independent life.

B.B.'s treatment decision was a complicated one. Because RT offered a moderately effective treatment without the risks of surgery, B.B.'s decision to "play it safe" was quite appropriate for her situation. A relatively safe treatment, RT is often used this way with elderly patients.

Many generalizations accurately describe the problems and behavior of the elderly. The elderly are at high risk for developing a cancer, do not participate in cancer screening, underreport symptoms, and usually have preexisting medical conditions. Like any group in America, they are easy to stereotype. Ultimately, the best cancer treatment for the elderly cancer patient is individualized therapy.

23

Control of Cancer Pain

"Doctor, do not let me suffer . . . ."

Pain is the single most dreaded complication of cancer. It is also the least understood. During the past 20 years, a revolution has occurred in pain control. Although breakthroughs in open-heart surgery or cholesterol reduction make the news daily, dramatic improvements in pain control remain largely ignored by the media.

Cancer patients and their families fear the onset of pain and doubt that it can be controlled. So taboo is the entire subject of pain that patients rarely voice their deep-seated fear of pain before its development. Like all taboo topics, pain is surrounded by a number of myths. These myths must be dispelled before a practical and successful approach to pain control can be developed for each patient.

Myth #1: Cancer pain cannot be controlled. The hospice movement of the 1960s generated a great deal of research into pain and its control. As a result, doctors more fully understand the physiological basis for pain and can successfully control it. In the 1990s, inadequate pain control is due to poor application of current knowledge rather than a failure to understand the problem.

For most cancer patients, the best method of pain control is treatment of the cancer. Conventional cancer treatment consists of radiation, chemotherapy, or both (discussed in Part II). Radiation

279

to painful bone sites is successful in 80% of patients. Such patients typically experience pain relief within a week of initiating treatments. Chemotherapy works to control pain by shrinking the cancer. Studies show that when the cause of cancer pain is appropriately treated, patients can stop taking narcotics.

Myth #2: Pain is inevitable. Surprisingly, most cancer patients never experience pain. Studies report that only one third of all cancer patients experience significant pain. This, however, rises to 60% in patients with advanced cancer. For these patients, pain is a serious problem.

Myth #3: I will become addicted. Narcotics are frequently used to control cancer pain. Families, patients, and even physicians are understandably concerned about the possibility of drug addiction. Addiction is defined as dependency on a narcotic and is associated with drug-craving or drug-seeking behavior. The vast majority of cancer patients do not become addicted. When addiction does occur, the patient usually has a history of alcohol or drug abuse.

A narcotic is always prescribed for a specific purpose. Cancer patients require their narcotics just as patients with heart failure require their heart medications. If the heart medication is stopped, the patient develops heart failure. Similarly, abrupt cessation of narcotic medication results in the return of cancer pain.

Myth #4: I will become immune to the pain killer and will need more and more of it. This fear is shared by patients and many physicians. It refers to the development of *tolerance.* Tolerance is seen in street addicts who require increasingly higher doses of drugs for comfort. However, it rarely develops in cancer patients taking narcotics. The majority of cancer patients simply do not become immune to their pain medications. Patients become *comfortable* on a given dose of narcotic and can be maintained on that dose for prolonged periods. In those cases in which tolerance develops, a different narcotic can be given.

The Nature of Pain

Pain is a subjective phenomenon. An x ray can detect a broken bone, but no test can determine the degree of pain felt by the person who has broken the bone. The truth is that no person can experience another's pain. As a matter of principle, the presence of pain in a patient with advanced cancer is not questioned by the physician.

Pain presents itself in varied ways. It can be constant or fleeting, dull or sharp, localized or diffuse, mild or severe. The source of pain usually determines its nature. For example, abdominal pain is frequently dull, intermittent, and diffuse. Bone pain is characteristically sharp, constant, and localized. Determining the specific cause of pain enables the doctor to provide appropriate treatment.

The physical cause is one of pain's two key determinants; the patient is the other. The patient brings to the situation certain attitudes, beliefs, and expectations that determine the threshold of pain. Studies verify that age, sex, religion, cultural background, and level of anxiety all contribute to the reported intensity and severity of pain. Given such diversity, it is understandable that nearly identical medical conditions can result in widely different pain perceptions.

Because pain is subjective and variable, it needs to be accurately measured in some way. Many physicians use a *pain scale* to facilitate measurement. Such a scale is a 10-unit imaginary line where 0 is equal to the absence of pain and 10 is "the worst pain of your life." All patients, regardless of background, are able to indicate where their pain registers on this scale. They are also able to indicate where they desire their pain to be. The scale allows the subjective sensation of pain to be measured in a useful fashion.

The scale is one of the major tools used in a system of pain management. Patients are instructed to evaluate their pain continually. If pain increases, then the medication is changed. For example, when a patient who has rated pain last month as a 4, now reports that the pain is a 9, medication must be changed immediately. This point cannot be overemphasized: For the patient with advanced cancer, pain control requires accurate measurement (on a scale of 1 to 10) followed by appropriate action. When the patient and family understand how to use this simple system of pain measurement, the treatment team can begin to individualize medication both at home and in the hospital. This team consists of clinic nurses, ward nurses, home hospice nurses, pharmacists, and doctors.

Analgesic Drugs

Analgesic drugs are medications prescribed to control pain. They are used extensively in the management of cancer pain. Although they can be used temporarily during cancer treatment, they are often employed for prolonged periods in patients with advanced cancer.

Pharmacology is the study of drugs; it provides essential information about their composition, effects, and uses. The pharmacology of analgesic drugs must be considered to understand how they are best used.

Basic Pharmacology of Analgesics

Therapeutic Window

One of the most fundamental characteristics of a drug is the *dose–response relationship.* Simply stated, this means that the amount of drug given to a patient must be enough to be helpful, yet not enough to become harmful.

Figure 23-1 illustrates the typical dose–response relationship for a hypothetical analgesic drug. The horizontal axis measures the dose of the drug in milligrams and the vertical axis measures its analgesic effect. At lower doses (1–3 mg), the patient has no noticeable benefit. When the dose is increased to 4 mg, the patient first reports a decrease in pain (Point A). As the dose is increased to 5 mg, pain disappears (Point B). At a dose of 7 mg, the patient begins to experience sleepiness as a side effect of the drug (Point C). The amount of drug must be sufficient to cause benefit. Increasing the dose, however, can lead to side effects.

The distance between the desired effect (analgesia, Point A)

INTENSITY OF
ANALGESIC EFFECT

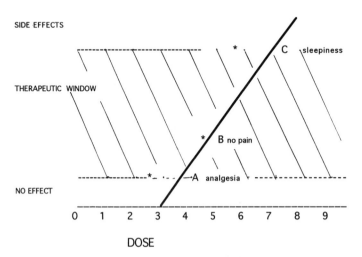

Figure 23-1. Dose–response relationship of a hypothetical drug. Doses are in milligrams. See text for explanation.

and the undesired effect (sleepiness, Point C) is termed the margin of safety or the *therapeutic window* (shaded area). This window refers to the amount a drug can be increased without causing side effects. Drugs with a wide therapeutic window can be safely increased without creating side effects. Medically, the aim is to keep drug levels within the therapeutic window where patients experience comfort without side effects.

Half-Life

The time that a drug remains in the therapeutic window is determined by its rate of elimination by the body. Doctors use the

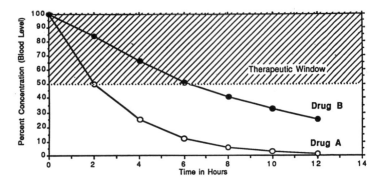

Figure 23-2. Effect of half-life on drug concentration.

term *half-life* to describe drug elimination. A half-life is the amount of time it takes a drug to decrease its concentration by 50% in the bloodstream. The slower the rate of elimination is, the longer the half-life.

Figure 23-2 illustrates the half-life of two hypothetical drugs, A and B. These drugs are identical except for differences in half-life. The graph measures drug concentration over time. The horizontal axis represents time in hours, and the vertical axis measures drug concentration in percentages. The drugs are injected at time zero at 100% dosage and initially reach identical concentrations in the blood. Drug A decreases its concentration by 50% in 2 hours; its half-life is thus 2 hours. In contrast, drug B decreases its concentration by 50% in 6 hours; its half-life is 6 hours.

Which drug, A or B, will best control a patient's pain? Because drug B maintains its concentration in the therapeutic window for a longer period, it is the drug of choice. Drug B needs to be taken only every 6 hours to provide pain relief, whereas drug A needs to be taken every 2 hours. Half-life thus determines how frequently a drug must be taken to achieve results.

Most analgesics used to treat cancer pain are taken on a fixed schedule or "round the clock." The goal here is to keep a drug's concentration constantly in the therapeutic window of comfort. A drug reaches its fixed concentration in the blood after four half-lives. Drug B, with its half-life of 6 hours, takes 24 hours (4 × 6 = 24) to reach its fixed concentration. Similarly, drugs with long half-lives (12 to 18 hours) can require several days to reach their fixed concentrations.

Practically speaking, drugs with short half-lives need to be taken frequently but reach their fixed concentrations rapidly. Any dose adjustment can usually be made a day or two after the drug has been introduced. In contrast, drugs with longer half-lives can be taken less frequently, but their full effects may not be reached for days. A patient who is taking a drug with a long half-life is always cautioned to wait for the drug to "kick in."

Drug Exchange Rate

When comparing or changing analgesics, potency of a drug needs to be considered. The process is analogous to calculating the exchange rate for a foreign currency. We readily know that $1 equals a given number of yen in the marketplace. A similar phenomenon occurs with analgesics. When taken orally, 30 mg of morphine equals 200 mg of codeine. One simply needs to know the proper exchange rates for the drugs in question.

Another factor that determines this drug exchange rate is the method of administration. Whether the drug is given orally or by injection (a shot) is important. Whereas injected analgesics go directly from the muscle into the bloodstream, oral drugs are absorbed by the intestine and pass through the liver before entering the bloodstream. During the digestive process, the liver degrades a portion of the analgesic, thus delivering less to the bloodstream than an injection would. Consequently, larger doses of oral drugs are required to equal the potency of an injection. For example, a 30-mg pill of morphine produces the same analgesia as a 10-mg injection of morphine. These doses are equivalent in controlling pain and are termed *equianalgesic* doses.

A exciting and new method of administering analgesics is skin patches. The patch delivers the analgesic continuously through the skin and into the bloodstream. The patches deliver a fixed amount of a potent drug known as fentanyl each hour for 72 hours. The patch is generally changed every 3 days. Calculating the drug exchange rate between skin patches and oral analgesics involves measuring the amount of drug given per a 24-hour period. It is believed that 360 mg of oral morphine per 24 hours is equal to the 100-mg per hour of fentanyl delivered by the skin patch.

It is commonly assumed that analgesics given by injection are superior to both oral analgesics and skin patches. This is not true! *When given in appropriate doses, the pain control achieved by oral drugs and skin patches equals that of injected drugs.*

In summary, three drug characteristics are important in the control of pain.

1. Therapeutic window is the optimal dose of the drug with which the patient experiences analgesia without side effects.
2. Half-life controls how frequently the drug needs to be given and when results can be expected.
3. Drug exchange rate enables the doctor to calculate a comparable dose of a new analgesic. The potency of the drug and its route of administration determine the equivalent dose.

Three general classes of analgesics are used to treat cancer pain: nonnarcotics, narcotics, and adjuvants.

Nonnarcotic Analgesics

Nonnarcotic drugs possess two characteristics that distinguish them from narcotic drugs. First, nonnarcotics do not cause tolerance or physical dependence. Second, nonnarcotics possess a *ceiling effect,* which refers to their unique dose–response relationship. After a certain amount of drug, the patient reaches an analgesic ceiling where increasing the dose does not increase the amount of analgesia. In contrast, escalating doses of narcotic drugs can result in increasing analgesia even to the point of coma.

An important fact needs to be emphasized: *NONNARCOTIC ANALGESICS WORK.* Patients frequently believe that over-the-counter drugs cannot work. Nothing can be further from the truth. These drugs are frequently as effective as prescription drugs and are usually much cheaper.

Aspirin and Acetaminophen

Aspirin has been in use for more than 100 years and continues to be a mainstay for treatment of mild pain. Aspirin appears to work in the body by interfering with the production of substances known as prostaglandins. Prostaglandins are important messengers of pain and inflammation in the bones. Aspirin interferes with prostaglandin production and thus reduces inflammation and pain.

Aspirin is an extremely effective drug; two regular aspirin (650 mg) are the equivalent of 30 mg of codeine. However, because of side effects (i.e., ringing in ears, nausea, stomach irritation, and bleeding), aspirin is poorly tolerated in cancer patients. Consequently, most physicians rarely prescribe it for cancer pain.

As effective as aspirin is the nonprescription drug, *acetaminophen* (Tylenol). It is unclear exactly how acetaminophen controls pain. Its major side effects appear limited to kidney and liver damage only after years of use. As a rule, most cancer patients tolerate acetaminophen better than aspirin.

For mild pain, aspirin and acetaminophen are appropriate analgesics. They are frequently the first drugs prescribed in treating cancer pain.

Nonsteroidal Antiinflammatory Drugs (NSAIDs)

These drugs were developed to treat arthritis and have been on the market for approximately 25 years. Like aspirin, they interfere with prostaglandin function. Because prostaglandins work to transmit bone pain, it is only natural that aspirin and the NSAIDs are especially effective in the treatment of bone cancer pain. With severe bone pain, these drugs may even increase the analgesia of narcotic drugs. They possess side effects similar to

Table 23-1
Selected Nonnarcotic Analgesics

Drug[a]	Oral dose[b]	Comments
Aspirin	650 mg every 4–6 hours	"Gold standard" nonnarcotic. Can cause ulcers and bleeding
Acetaminophen *Tylenol*	650 mg every 4–6 hours	Safer than aspirin in most cancer patients. Can rarely cause liver problems
NSAIDS Ibuprofen *Motrin*	400 mg every 4–6 hours	NSAIDs are similar to aspirin in their side effects. Considered to be especially useful in bone pain
Naproxen *Naprosyn*	375 mg every 8–12 hours	
Diflunisal *Dolobid*	500 mg every 8–12 hours	

[a] Drug names are generic with brand names in italics.
[b] Doses are approximately *Equianalgesic*. For reference, 650 mg of aspirin is equal to 30 mg of codeine.
SOURCE: *Principles of Analgesic Use in the Treatment of Acute Pain and Chronic Cancer Pain*, 2nd ed. Skokie, Ill: American Pain Society, 1989.

those of aspirin: stomach irritation and bleeding. Recently, ibuprofen has become an over-the-counter drug.

Table 23-1 shows representative nonnarcotic drugs used to control mild or moderate pain. These drugs are taken orally.

Narcotic Drugs

The human brain has specialized structures that control pain perception. These are *opiate receptors*. The brain also manufactures substances called *endorphins* that reduce pain by attaching to the opiate receptors. The entire process is similar to lighting a string of Christmas lights. Opiate receptors are like the sockets into which light bulbs or endorphins are fitted. Just as light bulbs fit into sockets and produce light, endorphins bind to opiate receptors and produce analgesia.

Narcotic drugs, like endorphins, attach to opiate receptors in the brain and produce analgesia. Physicians believe that narcotics can markedly increase a patient's tolerance of pain without affecting the ability to perceive it. Patients who take narcotics report that, although they still experience pain, the pain no longer bothers them. In essence, narcotics control the patient's symptoms but do not alter the process of the disease.

Narcotics, however, produce a number of side effects that the physician must anticipate and seek to minimize. Unwanted symptoms vary from patient to patient and from drug to drug. Frequently, changing the narcotic can eliminate a particular side effect. Finding the best narcotic drug for a cancer patient is often a process of trial and error. Several common side effects of narcotic drugs include sedation, nausea, and constipation.

Sedation is a feeling of sleepiness produced by narcotics. Sedation is dose dependent in that, when dosage is increased, sedation develops. Extreme sedation can lead to unconsciousness or respiratory depression (shallow breathing). Of course, the best way to treat respiratory depression is to avoid it! It is important to note that sedation develops *before* respiratory depression. For this reason, a physician must use extreme caution in increasing the dose of the narcotic. The physician typically waits an appropriate period before evaluating the response, allowing the drug to reach a new fixed concentration. (Remember, it takes four half-lives to reach a fixed concentration.) Should sedation develop, a switch to another narcotic or a slight dose reduction can lessen the sedation. Some doctors use amphetamine to combat sedation, but its use remains controversial.

Mild to moderate nausea develops in as many as 30% of the cancer patients receiving narcotics. It is believed that narcotics stimulate brain receptors that trigger nausea. Such nausea often resolves after a few days. However, when it persists, medication can be prescribed to reduce it. Should medication fail to control nausea, a change in narcotic is required.

Constipation develops in *all* patients who take narcotics on a regular basis. The older the patient, the more severe the problem is likely to be. Although it is natural to be concerned with the functioning of the bowels, the concern of some patients becomes obsessive.

As a medical student on the wards for the first time, I became aware of this phenomenon when making rounds early one morning with other students, interns and our professor:

> The three patients we examined were elderly and very ill. The first had pneumonia, the second had severe heart failure, and the third had cancer. All three patients were using oxygen.
>
> I had never seen a patient before, and each of them looked dreadful to my untrained eye. All three complained bitterly about constipation. When the third patient, who could not even get out of bed, requested an enema, I smirked and thought to myself: this man has more problems than his bowels.
>
> The professor knew what I found amusing. He said, "You learned an important practical lesson today. . . . You see, a man's life can be divided into thirds. In the first third, all he thinks about is sex. In the middle third, all he thinks about is making money and, in the last third of his life, all he thinks about is moving his bowels!"

At the time, I did not fully appreciate how true this is. Narcotics make senior citizens of us all.

In order to combat this problem of constipation, patients should be placed on a bowel program at the onset of their narcotic treatment. Unfortunately, simple dietary modifications and bulk laxatives are rarely successful. With the initiation of a narcotic, the patient should be placed on a stool softener and mild laxative. The patient needs to have specific instructions and expectations. Table 23-2 illustrates a representative approach to the problem of constipation. A common goal of a bowel program is that each patient have a bowel movement every 2 to 3 days. If the patient does not, medication should be added to stimulate a bowel movement within the next few days. A patient who requires a daily enema is not meeting the program's goal and needs some adjustment in the program.

The side effects of narcotics are so frequent that they actually determine which narcotic is prescribed. Narcotics are most often switched to eliminate a particular side effect. A physician makes

Table 23-2
A Bowel Program

---

1. With the initiation of routine narcotic medication, take one of the following stool softeners or laxatives:
   Peri-Colace 1 capsule 2–3 times a day, or
   Doxidan 1 capsule 2–3 times a day, or
   Senokot 1 capsule 2–3 times a day
2. If constipation worsens or causes problems add one of the following:
   Dulcolax 10 mg 1–2 times a day, or
   Milk of Magnesia 1 teaspoon 1–4 times a day, or
   Haley's M-O 1 teaspoon 1–4 times
3. If you have no bowel movement in 48 hours, call the nurse or the doctor for advice. You may be asked to try one of the following:
   Dulcolax suppository 10 mg, or
   Magnesium citrate, 6 oz. orally, or
   Fleet enema
   Please contact the doctor before trying the directions given in no. 3. If you have severe abdominal pain, contact the doctor or go to the emergency department.

---

every attempt to tailor the analgesic program to a patient's need, choosing the narcotic in accordance with that need. *There is no best analgesic; there is only the analgesic that works best for an individual patient.* Morphine is the most commonly used narcotic, and no drug listed in Table 23-3 is more effective than morphine when given in equivalent (equianalgesic) doses. However, for patients who cannot tolerate morphine, Table 23-3 contains many useful alternative narcotic drugs.

In branches of medicine other than cancer treatment, pain medication is taken on an *as-needed* basis. The direction on a prescription bottle will read: "Take one tablet every 4 hours as needed for pain." Because this method of administration results in peaks and valleys in drug concentration, the drug cannot reach a fixed concentration in the blood. Predictably, the patient will experience pain. Such a schedule is inappropriate for cancer pain, because most cancer pain is constant. The cancer patient needs a fixed concentration of the analgesic. To achieve this, most cancer specialists use a fixed schedule or round-the-clock dosing interval.

Table 23-3
Selected Narcotic Analgesics

Drug[a]	Oral	Injection	Comments
Shorter acting			
Morphine	30 mg	10 mg	"Gold standard" of narcotics
Codeine	200 mg	130 mg	Often first narcotic used. Frequently causes nausea
Oxycodone	30 mg	Not available	With acetaminophen, known as *Percocet*
Meperidine	300 mg	75 mg	Infrequently used for long term. Brand name is *Demerol*
Hydromorphone	7.5 mg	1.5 mg	Very potent. Available in suppository form. Widely used. Brand name is *Dilaudid*
Longer acting			
Methadone	20 mg	10 mg	Potent. Inexpensive. Long half-life requires caution. Brand name is *Dolophine*
Slow-release morphine	60 mg	Not available	Potent. Expensive. Brand names are *MS Contin* and *Roxanol-SR*

Skin patch
The patch is changed every 3 days. For comparison purposes, 360 mg of oral morphine taken over 24 hours is equal to 100 μg (microgram) of fentanyl delivered through the skin by the patch. Brand name is *Duragesic Patch*.

[a] Drug names are generic with brand names in italics. Doses are approximately equianalgesic.
SOURCE: Adapted from *Drug Information 93*. Bethesda, MD: American Society of Hospital Pharmacists, 1993.

The medical objective is to eliminate the peaks and valleys of the drug level and to maintain the narcotic in the therapeutic window. Only when the drug reaches its fixed concentration can the degree of pain control be fully evaluated. As previously discussed, a drug's half-life determines when the drug reaches its fixed concentration. This may take as long as 3 days for some of the longer-acting drugs, such as methadone.

Whenever possible, physicians prefer to use narcotics with longer half-lives to control severe cancer pain. Because these drugs need not be taken as often as the shorter-acting narcotics, they are more convenient. They also produce a more even sense of pain control. Initially, the patient is instructed to take a short-acting drug on an as-needed basis simultaneously with the longer-acting drug on a round-the-clock basis. As the round-the-clock medication is increased and takes effect, the as-needed drug can be eliminated.

Patients are often confused by the two pain medications. A simple analogy can clarify the need for more than one drug. Controlling pain is like cooking on a grill, and pain relief is analogous to the heat of the fire. Shorter-acting drugs are like the lighter fluid required to start the grill. These drugs take effect quickly and soon dissipate as do the flames produced by lighter fluid. Once the coals become whitened and hot, though, they give off a constant heat similar to the even pain control eventually achieved by the longer-acting narcotics. The "moral of the grill" is that shorter-acting drugs are needed to control pain until longer-acting narcotics take effect.

At times, neither oral nor injectable narcotics are successful in controlling severe cancer pain. In such instances, morphine can be given directly into the vein on a continuous basis. Such *continuous infusion* aims to break the cycle of pain by maximizing comfort while minimizing the side effects. Once pain is controlled, the patient can be switched back to an oral or injectable regimen. Because a real risk of overdose exists with this method, infusion is initiated only in a hospital.

Perhaps the following case studies can serve to further clarify the process of pain control.

Mr. O. is a 60-year-old man who was hospitalized for back pain originating from a form of bone cancer known as multiple myeloma. Before admission, Mr. O. had been receiving as-needed oxycodone (*Percocet*).

On examination, the doctor found that Mr. O.'s pain was incapacitating, with Mr. O. grading it "10." He was immediately place on an oral round-the-clock regimen of ibuprofen 400 mg every 6 hours and slow-release morphine 60 mg every 12 hours. Oxycodone was prescribed every 4 hours as needed. Two days later Mr. O. still experienced pain, but he now graded it "6." In an attempt to further reduce his pain, the morphine was increased to 60 mg every 8 hours. Although this dose of morphine curbed his pain, it also induced nausea and vomiting that could not be controlled by antinausea medication. Consequently, he was switched to a comparable dose of methadone, and the nausea resolved.

Once Mr. O. resumed eating, however, he developed severe constipation. When docusate sodium casanthranol (*Peri-Colace*) and bisacody (*Dulcolax*) proved unsuccessful, his bowel program was escalated. He became comfortable on *Peri-Colace* three times a day, *Dulcolax* two times a day and magnesium citrate 3 oz, once a day.

As an essential part of his hospital regimen, Mr. O. received radiation to his back as well as chemotherapy. At the time of discharge, he was pain free while taking the following medications: methadone 10 mg every 6 hours, ibuprofen 400 mg every 6 hours, oxycodone as needed every 4 hours, and his bowel program.

Over the next 10 months, Mr. O. received further chemotherapy, and the cancer went into remission. As the multiple myeloma shrunk, his pain lessened. Gradually, his methadone and bowel program were decreased. At present, Mr. O. takes only ibuprofen 400 mg every 8 hours and is quite pleased with his pain control.

Mr. O.'s case illustrates how the side effects of the narcotics dictate the choice of drugs and that successful pain control is a process of trial and error. The first side effect, nausea, required that methadone be substituted for morphine. When the second side effect of constipation developed, still another adjustment in medication was needed. Moreover, the intense pain that patients experience sometimes masks the discomfort of constipation.

Mr. O.'s case illustrates another important point regarding pain control. Once the cancer is successfully treated, the patient is often able to stop taking pain medication. Unfortunately, not all cancer patients can be weaned from their medications, as seen in the case of Mrs. M.

Mrs. M. is a 36-year-old woman whose breast cancer had spread exclusively to her bones. Four years ago, she was admitted to the hospital with a broken hip, and she required a hip replacement.

When initially examined, she graded her pain before the fracture as "10" despite receiving 100 mg of morphine by injection each day. Although this dose did not cause many side effects, it also did not effectively control her pain. After the operation, she received injections of 25 mg of morphine every 4 hours as needed. However, her pain was so severe that it limited her progress in physical therapy.

Clearly, Mrs. M. required higher doses of round-the-clock medication. She was started on a regimen of 40 mg of methadone every 6 hours and morphine injections every 4 hours as needed. A few days later, she graded her pain "8" and continued to take the morphine injections. At this point, ibuprofen was added to the regimen, and her methadone was increased to 50 mg every 6 hours. With these medications, her pain was controlled. Once pain free, she began to make steady progress in physical therapy.

Over the past 4 years, Mrs. M.'s breast cancer has been intermittently treated. With each flare-up of the cancer, her pain has increased. At the time of her most recent examination, she was pain free while taking both 90 mg of methadone and 300 mg of ibuprofen every 6 hours. She rarely took oxycodone every 4 hours as needed. Mrs. M. was comfortable enough to carry on a relatively normal life to the point of engaging in light housework without difficulty.

Mrs. M.'s case illustrates the importance of accurate dose adjustments according to the *drug exchange rate*. When hospitalized, she was initially given large doses of oral methadone because it is equivalent to the injectable morphine that she had previously received at home. Mrs. M.'s case also exemplifies how narcotics can be safely given, in large doses, over many years. It is most unlikely that Mrs. M. will ever be weaned from the narcotics, but these drugs have enabled her to "live" with breast cancer.

Adjuvant Analgesics

Adjuvant analgesics are a group of unrelated drugs sharing one distinctive feature: they are useful in controlling pain. These drugs are used in addition to the previously mentioned analgesics and can be viewed as additional or adjuvant analgesics. Although approved for medical purposes other than analgesia, they are widely used by oncologists to control pain. The manner in which they act to control pain is poorly understood.

Corticosteroids (steroids) are extremely potent inhibitors of inflammation and swelling. They are commonly used to treat pain caused by swelling in the brain or nerves. Corticosteroids have *serious side effects*, which include ulcers, diabetes, suppression of the immune system, and osteoporosis. Because of their numerous side effects, physicians prescribe them with caution and attempt to decrease dosages as quickly as possible.

Antidepressants are used in combination with other analgesics. They seem most effective in patients with bone or nerve-compression pain, although how these medications work remains a mystery. Their primary side effects are dryness of the mouth, sedation, and constipation. When used to treat depression, antidepressants usually require 4 to 6 weeks to take effect. However, cancer patients typically respond in a matter of days to very low doses. They also experience fewer and shorter-lived side effects.

Anticonvulsants are used with success in the treatment of intermittent, stabbing pains commonly known as tics. Ticlike pains are intense, sporadic, and believed to involve an irritation of the nervous system. Although this type of pain is generally not well controlled by narcotics, anticonvulsants often prove successful.

The precise role of adjuvant analgesic drugs remains controversial in pain management. It is a medical reality, though, that they are widely and effectively used. Many oncologists consider them extremely beneficial under certain conditions. In all honesty, however, the appropriate use of adjuvant analgesics tends to be much more an art than a science. Table 23-4 lists several of the most commonly used adjuvant analgesics.

Following is a case study that illustrates the untraditional but effective use of adjuvant analgesics in the control of cancer pain.

Mr. A. is a 70-year-old man who visited the doctor for the first time in his life after experiencing severe pain in his left shoulder for 6 weeks. A chest x ray revealed a mass in the upper portion of the lung.

On admission to the hospital, he was found to have a lung cancer that pressed on the nerve roots of the left shoulder and could not be surgically removed. In an attempt to control his pain, an array of narcotics was tried,

Table 23-4
Adjuvant Analgesics

Drug[a]	Dose[b]	Comments
Steroids		
Dexamethasone (*Decadron*)	2–8 mg every 8 hours	Many side effects. Usually given with medication to prevent stomach ulcers
Prednisone	10–20 mg every 8–12 hours	
Antidepressants		
Amitriptyline (*Elavil*)	25–75 mg at night	Dry mouth, sedation, and sexual dysfunction are common
Imipramine (*Tofranil*)	50–100 mg at night	
Anticonvulsants		
Carbamazepine (*Tegretol*)	200–600 mg a day	Drug levels must be checked to avoid toxicity
Phenytoin (*Dilantin*)	100 mg three times a day	

[a] Drug names are generic with brand names in italics.
[b] All doses are oral. The doses are representative but *not* equianalgesic.
SOURCE: *Principles of Analgesic Use in the Treatment of Acute Pain and Chronic Cancer Pain,* 2nd ed. Skokie, IL: American Pain Society, 1989.

including codeine, oxycodone, hydromorphone, and morphine. Each narcotic caused severe nausea and vomiting.

When first seen by the oncologist, Mr. A. reported that his pain was "10." The narcotics were stopped and NSAIDs and adjuvant analgesics were introduced. Mr. A. was started on naproxen 375 mg every 8 hours, prednisone 20 mg every 12 hours, and amitriptyline 50 mg at bedtime. Over the next 2 days, both the nausea and the pain completely resolved. Mr. A. has since completed a course of radiation and, when last seen, was doing quite well.

Mr. A. was a prime candidate for adjuvant analgesics because his pain appeared to stem from irritation of the nerve roots, a problem commonly alleviated by adjuvant analgesics. Although adjuvant analgesics are rarely substituted for narcotic drugs, Mr. A.'s sweeping intolerance of narcotics made the adjuvant analgesics worth trying. The rather unorthodox use of NSAIDs and adjuvants for this patient emphasizes again the trial-and-error nature of pain control.

The Patient's Personal Contribution to Pain Control

More than any other aspect of cancer therapy, the psychological dimension determines successful pain control. Although pain is caused by physical circumstances, pain is essentially a psychological experience, and the patient's psychological make-up is the single most important variable in pain control. Pain control is most effective in cooperative, motivated patients; it is least effective in angry, self-pitying ones. In the management of pain, a positive attitude is an absolute prerequisite for success.

Psychological factors can curb pain by causing a release of endorphins. Research into hypnosis and acupuncture indicates that both therapies rely, to some degree, on increasing the body's level of endorphins. Doctors now believe a patient can experience self-induced analgesia by stimulating the production of endorphins. Although the complex functions of the brain are minimally understood, the vital importance of psychology in pain control is unquestioned.

Traditional medical intervention is passive in that the patient takes a prescribed medicine, and the medicine makes him better. *In contrast, the process of pain control is interactive.* This means that the patient owns his pain and must participate actively in the process of controlling it. On a continual basis, pain must be monitored and analgesics adjusted. Pain control is a process requiring an intense commitment not only from the patient, but from the family and health care team as well. One of the most common reasons for ineffective pain control is the failure to view the process as fully interactive.

In an interactive approach to pain control, psychosocial elements play an extremely important role. Family support, religious convictions, the desire to get well, faith in the doctor, and a strong circle of friends all positively contribute to successful pain control. The more positive elements present in the patient's outlook and situation, the more likely he or she is to experience effective pain control.

Psychological Techniques of Pain Control

Distraction is one of the easiest methods to master and also the most successful. Everyone employs this method, almost reflexively, when in pain. Opportunities for distraction are numerous, but the aim is to use as many senses as possible. Suggestions include rocking back and forth, singing, reading, listening to music, playing video games, and watching television. Working puzzles is my personal favorite. In our waiting room, there is always a large puzzle in progress for just this purpose.

Skin stimulation is a form of distraction that includes a number of interventions that reduce pain. *Massage,* performed by either a family member or professional, can be of particular benefit. It requires a gentle circular motion with light pressure and can be given with a lotion. Another type of skin stimulation is the application of *cold* or *heat* several times a day, 15 to 20 minutes per session. Strategies include ice pack, cold running water, hotwater bottle, heat lamp, sunlight, and tub bath. In order to avoid burns, the patient must be alert, and the heat applied should always be lukewarm.

A *TENS unit* (transcutaneous electrical stimulation unit) is a battery-operated device that gently stimulates the skin with an electrical current. Electrodes are placed on the skin near the site of pain, and the patient, who can wear the device continuously, controls the intensity of the electrical current. Finding the best position is often a process of trial and error. TENS units function best in patients with localized pain.

Hypnosis enables the patient to control the severity of pain through the power of concentration. By focusing intently on a pleasant experience or object, the patient is able to block the perception of pain. This is similar to the technique taught by proponents of natural childbirth. Hypnosis requires a motivated patient and an experienced instructor. At home, the patient uses an audio-cassette provided by the instructor.

Relaxation training is a related technique that reduces muscle tension. Its purpose is to break the cycle of pain–anxiety–tension through breathing exercises and biofeedback, thereby enabling the patient to gain a greater sense of self-control. Such a sense is crucial for those patients who have come to consider their disease and pain "out of control."

24

Getting One's Affairs in Order

with Edward Kabala, J.D.

For both patient and family, the emotional stress accompanying the diagnosis of cancer is enormous. Quite understandably, the patient may feel that life is suddenly spinning out of control. With normal routines interrupted, life seems to revolve around hospital tests and doctors' appointments. As the focus of life becomes day-to-day, planning for the future appears to be either an insignificant or an impossible task.

The situation is an extremely delicate one. Emotionally and often spiritually burdened by the diagnosis, the patient and family may find themselves unable to discuss feelings, let alone their concerns about finances and the future. Loved ones do not want to be insensitive. In order to avoid inflicting further pain, the subject is simply not addressed at all.

However, the hard truth of the matter for the cancer patient is that the results of treatment may not be positive; the patient may be facing prolonged disability, incompetence, or even death. It takes a great deal of courage to acknowledge this fact, and there may be no greater act of love than to discuss the future with the patient.

Once the issue is raised, there is still the matter of how and what to do. Decisions need to be made, and it is difficult to prioritize them in such an emotionally charged setting. One practical way to organize this process is to separate the planning into medical and financial areas. As will soon be seen, both of these areas are full of choices, most of which are governed by state laws. Planning usually requires the assistance of a professional advisor, either attorney, banker, or financial planner.

Medical Planning

Profound changes in America have altered health care for seriously ill individuals. New technology provides the capability of extending patients' lives. An obvious and rather commonplace example is the respirator, a machine that actually breathes for the patient.

As individuals live longer, a greater percentage of the seriously ill population succumbs to mental incapacity of several common types. The first is a preexisting mental incapacity, common in elderly patients, that results from a prior illness such as Alzheimer's disease. Another is the sudden onset of mental incapacity during the course of serious illness as in the case of the elderly cancer patient who suffers a stroke and resultant loss of mental functioning. Sometimes seriously ill patients simply deteriorate as disease progresses. Tragically, these patients are incapable of deciding on medical treatments when they are needed; patients must plan in advance.

When asked, most patients voice strong opinions about *life support* and the use of machines to prolong life. However, human nature being what it is, most individuals postpone making this decision regarding treatment. Unfortunately, when the medical crisis arrives, families often find themselves divided over the issue of life support. If a patient's wishes are unknown, or the family is unable to reach a consensus, the legal and medical reality is that the physician must assume that the patient desires all possible measures be taken even if the result is life in a coma. In those situations where the family is of one mind, the Cruzan case makes it clear that more direction is often required.

In order to avoid such a dilemma, patients are strongly advised to specify their wishes in a formal written fashion while both competent and out of grave risk. Such a declaration can spare the family and physician the burden of making difficult treatment decisions, and it most importantly ensures that the patient's wishes are respected at all times. Such a declaration is known as an advance medical directive. As of 1991, the federal government has required that all persons, on hospital admission, be informed in writing of their right to dictate decisions in the form of an advance medical directive.

An advance medical directive is a written document stipulating the medical care that the patient either wishes or does not wish to receive in the event of mental incapacity or terminal illness. Two types of advance medical directives are currently in common use: the *living will* and the *durable power of attorney for health care.*

Living wills describe the type of life-sustaining treatments that may be withheld or withdrawn from a patient in case of terminal illness. Whereas the living will does not include instructions regarding all types of treatment, it does relate to situations in which medical therapy would only serve to prolong the process of dying or to maintain the patient in a permanent state of unconsciousness.

Living wills are legally recognized throughout the United States, but the forms and filing process may differ in various states. Generally, the patient is required to sign the will in the presence of two adult witnesses. It also should be noted that this document may be revoked simply by making a verbal request in the presence of witnesses. Of course, the patient should inform family members or a trusted friend of both the existence and location of the living will, a copy of which should be given to the attending physician and other health care providers.

A power of attorney for health care is a legal document that allows the patient to name another person to make medical decisions. The designated person can authorize the patient's admission to a medical facility, enter into agreements for care, and sanction medical/surgical treatments. A power of attorney for health care generally allows authorization of treatment but rarely authorizes withholding of treatment.

In the past, a power of attorney was revoked when the patient became incompetent. Now legislation permits a durable power of attorney that remains valid in the case of incompetence. Such a power of attorney for health care may be applicable immediately or may become operative at specified times such as when the patient becomes unconscious or incapacitated. The latter type is known as a *springing* power of attorney.

In many cases, health care provisions are found in a durable general power of attorney, although many people think of general powers of attorney as financial documents. Many forms of living wills also contain health care durable power of attorney provisions.

Some living will forms include a designation of a health care proxy who is empowered to make any of the life-or-death decisions that are not clearly stated in the living will. The proxy is usually much more limited that the durable power of attorney for health care in terms of the authority it gives to the named person.

The choice of an advance medical directive, either a living will or a durable power of attorney for health care, is a matter of personal choice and state law. Patients are well advised, though, to consult an attorney in order to determine accuracy under the laws of the specific state. Such an important decision also merits discussion with family and close friends. Table 24-1 compares in general terms the two types of advance medical directives.

In 1991 the federal government required hospitals to inform patients on admission to the hospital of their right to sign a written advance medical directive. Obviously, the patient should not wait for the day of admission to read, understand, and sign such an important document.

The following is an example of a living will written by a female patient with advanced lung cancer. After thoroughly discussing her situation with all members of her large and very close family, she wrote and signed this document some months before her death:

Table 24-1

Comparison of Advanced Medical Directives

Living will (with or without proxy)	Durable power of attorney for health care
Takes effect when the patient is in a terminally ill state or a state of permanent unconsciousness	May be effective immediately or will take effect in the case of incapacity or, in some states, incompetence
Spells out what kind of life-sustaining therapy the patient wishes to receive or not receive	Names someone to make health-care decisions with or without describing the decisions. It rarely spells out therapy to be withheld
Narrow in scope of empowerment	Can be narrow or broad in scope of empowerment depending on its terms
Recognized in all states	Recognized in all states

I look upon death as a part of my life. . . . I want everyone to understand my wishes. . . . Where there is no reasonable expectation that I can survive and if I am unable to decide for myself, let it now be known that I do not want to be kept alive by artificial means, either medication or therapy or machinery. . . .

I want it made abundantly clear that I do not fear death as much as I fear the indignity of deterioration, dependence, and hopeless pain. I ask that no heroic measures be undertaken in regard to life support . . . It is my intent to remove any feelings of guilt on the part of anyone.   M.F. 2-8-91

Financial Planning

Regardless of the prognosis, any person who is diagnosed with cancer should take stock of his or her financial affairs. For most patients, such a financial analysis is best accomplished by a planning team that includes family members and trusted friends as well as professional advisors.

Finding a trustworthy professional advisor may initially pose a problem; it is important to select a financial advisor who is experienced in planning. Capable advisors can take many forms: an attorney who specializes in estate planning, an accountant who has performed similar services for a friend, a relative who is successful in business, or a trusted family insurance agent or financial planner.

Although word-of-mouth references often lead to credible advisors, other avenues that can be explored include the local bar association and legal referral services. A professional organization that often proves helpful in supplying local names is The National Academy of Elder Law Attorneys, Inc., 135 S.W. Ash Street, Suite 500, Portland, OR 97204. Another source of many relevant publications is the American Association of Retired Persons (AARP).

The fee arrangements for financial planning services vary. Whereas accountants, attorneys, and many financial planners charge hourly fees, brokers, insurance salespersons, and some financial planners receive compensation on the basis of commissions. The fee arrangement should be thoroughly discussed early in the selection process.

Certainly, a key aspect of the planning process is the personal involvement of the patient. Because each patient must ultimately define personal goals and priorities, thus making estate wishes known, the individual's prognosis must at some point be acknowledged. Such an acknowledgement may involve a candid and sometimes painful discussion of undesirable outcomes, but it is the prognosis that establishes the time frame for planning.

Financial planning is essentially a two-step process. The first step involves the assembly of a complete list of assets, and the second requires a financial analysis of the situation.

Step 1: Inventory

A complete and accurate inventory of the patient's financial assets and liabilities is fundamental to the planning process. It is important to establish the form of ownership of each asset, because this may determine who controls or receives the given asset. Once completed, the inventory file should be placed in an accessible and safe location. This file should contain the following.

Personal Records

1. All names used in one's life.
2. Social Security number.
3. Names and addresses of spouse, children, next-of-kin, and others who will be considered as heirs (e.g., stepchildren not legally adopted). The exact legal connection of each designee should be noted.
4. Location of all original legal documents such as certificates of birth, marriage, adoption, and relevant deaths; copies of wills, trusts, divorce and separation agreements; documents of power of attorney and living wills.
5. A list of personal advisors such as attorneys, accountants, insurance agents, and stockbrokers.
6. Records of education, employment, and military service.
7. Statements concerning medical and funeral requests/preferences.

Financial Records

1. Tax returns of at least the previous 3 years.
2. A list of actual and potential sources of income such as salaries, contracts, pensions, dividends, and inheritances.
3. A list of assets including deeds, bonds, stocks, certificates of deposit, automobiles, mutual funds, jewelry, objects of art, and bank accounts. The approximate value of each should be listed as of a specific date.
4. All insurance policies such as life, disability, health (including Medigap), long-term care, homeowners, and special purpose (e.g., liability umbrella policy.) All policies held through clubs, unions, or employers.
5. Location of safe-deposit boxes.
6. A list of all liabilities including specific amounts and other relevant details.

Step II: Analysis and Planning

Once the inventory has been completed and the advisors selected, the actual planning process can begin. Ideally, all members of the planning team should attend a meeting during which an individual is chosen to serve as the coordinator and responsibilities of each member are clearly identified. At this time, both short-term and long-term goals are determined. A strategy for each asset also must be decided in terms of lifetime planning and for estate purposes.

The first item of business is the establishment of a budget. To accomplish this, all potential income and expenses should be listed and categorized.

If the patient is or was employed, the employer's personnel policies also need to be reviewed. What is the duration of salary, medical insurance, and other benefits? Should the patient take a leave of absence or apply for disability? Is retirement a viable option?

Disability insurance is an important source of income for seriously ill patients. In the course of denying the serious nature of their illness, however, many patients need to be persuaded to file a disability claim. Crucial to filing such a claim is its correct completion. As this task often proves somewhat intimidating for the patient, he or she should receive some line-by-line coaching when first attempting to complete any claim form for social security or other insurance benefits. An experienced insurance agent can help avoid problems by discussing the client's pertinent medical information with the attending physician. Some insurance advisors conclude that the decisions of claim reviewers are sometimes influenced by the language and tone of the medical report that is submitted.

A disability policy must be carefully examined in order to determine the definition of disability, potential of partial disability, likelihood of a waiting period, scope of benefits, and duration of benefit payments.

Rehabilitation benefits should also be reviewed. Disability

policies that cover rehabilitation should be evaluated to ascertain whether claims are to be made through the disability policy or the patient's medical coverage. Whereas some medical expenses are fully covered by medical insurance, others are covered under the rehabilitation provision of the disability policy.

The complexity of disability regulations is well illustrated by the contrasting cases of A.G. and Z.Z., office managers for the same Fortune 500 corporation.

A.G. was diagnosed with lung cancer at the age of 62. As the entire right lung was to be surgically removed, A.G. was disabled by the need to have continuous oxygen after discharge. A.G. immediately applied for his pension as well as disability insurance benefits. A.G.'s employer granted him an "early" retirement and pension.

Because the disability insurance policy replaced only the amount of reduced total income, A.G. was given a reduced disability payment. These payments constituted only a partial disability insurance benefit equal to the difference between his salary and his pension.

Z.Z. was also 62 years of age when he became disabled with non-Hodgkin's lymphoma. Before deciding his course of action, however, Z.Z. consulted with both his insurance agent and accountant. His advisors instructed Z.Z. to apply initially for disability and thus receive 36 months of full disability benefits. Three years hence, Z.Z. will then apply for a pension benefit that, because of its later starting date, will be significantly higher than that granted to A.G.

The cases of A.G. and Z.Z. illustrate the importance of seeking professional advice when faced with serious illness or disability. Both patients were intelligent and successful managers in a company, but only one had the foresight to seek professional advice concerning a complex financial matter.

In planning a patient's affairs, relevant governmental agencies should also be contacted in order to investigate the possibility of benefits. The two most obvious sources of such benefits are the Veterans Administration and the Social Security Administration. For some patients, Medicaid can provide needed benefits, especially medical and nursing home expenses. When a patient's limited resources are nonetheless above Medicaid's eligibility standards, legitimate planning that might involve simple asset transfers to spouse and family members may prove helpful.

Life insurance policies may contain disability waivers that relieve the patient of the obligation to pay premiums. Certainly, the possibility of increasing life insurance should not be overlooked. Some policies guarantee the holder the right to increase coverage at specific times without providing evidence of insurability. Although normal insurance channels may be closed to the patient as a result of the current illness, some guaranteed issue programs base coverage on salary classification, employee contributions, or membership in a club or fraternal organization. T.S. is one such cancer patient who increased his life insurance coverage in this way:

> T.S. is a 34-year-old father of three who was diagnosed with Hodgkin's disease. Although his prognosis was favorable, T.S. desired to increase the amount of his life insurance coverage, believing that he was underinsured. After two private insurers refused this request, T.S. consulted the human services department at his place of work. T.S. was relieved to learn that he could add to his life insurance without submitting a health report through the employees' group plan. T.S. applied for and received the increased life insurance. Two years following his diagnosis, T.S. works full-time and shows no evidence of Hodgkin's disease.

Although T.S. was fortunate that he was able to increase his insurance, too many patients remain unaware of such opportunities. T.S.'s case emphasizes the need to obtain qualified professional advice concerning these issues.

Estate Planning

The main goals of estate planning are to ensure that the patient's wishes are carried out, to minimize problems for the survivors, and to reduce estate taxes. The legal documents used to accomplish these goals include a durable power of attorney, a will, and, for some patients, a trust. Estate planning usually requires the services of an experienced attorney.

A durable power of attorney is a financial document that allows a named person, the attorney-in-fact, to handle the patient's assets in certain specified ways. This document is called durable because it remains in effect even in the event that the patient becomes incapacitated.

The previously discussed durable power of attorney for health care is a special power of attorney encompassing only medical decisions. In many cases, the durable power of attorney for health care is included in a durable general power of attorney. As seriously ill patients find that they require a legal document that addresses financial concerns, a durable general power of attorney typically fulfills this purpose.

A will is a legal document that specifies how a person's property is to be passed to survivors at the time of his or her death. A will stipulates one or more beneficiaries who will benefit from the estate. It also names an *executor* whose duties include paying residual bills and guaranteeing that the intentions of the deceased are carried out.

Probate refers to the legal process whereby the property is inventoried, expenses are paid, and remaining assets are passed on to the appropriate beneficiaries. The local probate court oversees this process, the administration of which commonly requires a year to complete.

It should be noted that the probate process is sometimes unnecessary in the settlement of an estate. Some types of property, referred to as *nonprobate property*, may legally pass to the designated persons without the authorization of probate court. Such nonprobate properties include annuities, proceeds from life insurance, pensions, and jointly owned assets like bank accounts or houses.

Because joint ownership yields the double benefit of avoiding probate and enabling property to pass quickly to the survivors, this strategy is widely relied on in estate planning. The following cases of the Joneses and Smiths serve to illustrate the advantages of consulting professionals and planning ahead.

Bill and Susan Jones were married for 40 years during which time Bill handled the family finances. Although their wills gave everything to each other, the bank accounts were registered in only Bill's name.

When Bill became seriously ill, he added his son, David, as a co-owner of the bank accounts, reasoning that his wife would be spared the aggravation of writing checks. When Bill died 9 months later, David and not his wife became the legal owner of the bank balances. Because the money became David's, there will almost certainly be some death taxes on the bank account "inherited" by David. There also will be gift tax considerations when David attempts to give the money to his mother.

Tom and Barb Smith were married for 25 years during which time Tom completely handled the family finances. Like the Joneses, their wills gave everything to each other, and all bank accounts were registered solely in the husband's name. However, when Tom became seriously ill, the family sought professional advice.

The financial counselor recommended that Barb be placed on the accounts as a co-owner and that their daughter, Mary, be placed on the accounts as an agent. In this capacity, Mary could write checks and thus continue to spare Barb financial aggravation. When Tom died 13 months later, Barb was the legal owner of the balances in the bank accounts without gift tax consequences and, in many states, would not have to pay any death taxes on the assets.

The examples of the Smiths and the Joneses illustrate the importance of sound advice when faced with serious illness. Although the situations of the two families were strikingly similar, the Smiths were able to avoid some financial problems with a simple planning measure.

Another estate-planning technique that circumvents the probate process is the *living trust*. The living trust, like a will, is a legal document that enables a person to transfer property to designated survivors.

When faced with life-threatening illness, patients with sizable assets can consider making cash gifts to children or grandchildren. In so doing, estate taxes may later be reduced. Gifts of up to $10,000 per person per year are exempt from federal gift taxes. These gifts are usually subject to estate taxes if dispersed after one's death.

In summary, an estate plan may involve a host of strategies

including a will, power of attorney, joint ownership, or a living trust. The process of estate planning involves a thorough analysis of the patient's financial situation, followed by an implementation of the proper legal steps to activate the plan. As this process is admittedly complex, the patient facing serious illness is well advised to seek the expertise of professionals in formulating such a plan. The advantages for the patient can prove significant, both financially and emotionally.

25

The Next Step: Being a Survivor

*with Sandra J. Labuda, A.C.S.W., L.S.W., and
Marmee Maylone, R.N., M.S.N., O.C.N.*

From the moment that a person receives the diagnosis of cancer until the final moment of life, this person is quite literally a survivor. The concept of *survivorship* is rooted in a broad-based movement dedicated to helping cancer patients cope with problems that are unique to their disease. As will soon be evident, the challenges of survivorship are often as monumental as those posed by the disease itself.

In the United States, continual advances in cancer therapy have significantly prolonged the lives of cancer patients. Whereas in the 1930s, fewer than 20% of cancer patients could be expected to survive 5 years after diagnosis, today nearly 50% of all cancer patients are cured. Currently, the U.S. population includes more than 7 million cancer survivors, or fully 2% of the general population, with the number expected to grow to 10 million by the year 2000.

Cancer survivors share myriad experiences that transcend the more predictable rigors of treatment. For example, cancer survivors encounter changes in their private lives as relationships are significantly altered by the diagnosis of cancer. The purpose of the survivorship movement is to empower the survivor to anticipate and cope with these changes.

The survivorship movement also aims to prepare the cancer survivor to deal with society at large. Unfortunately, Americans harbor many misconceptions and stereotypes that originated in an earlier time when the diagnosis of cancer was tantamount to a death sentence. Such misconceptions often lead to discrimination against cancer survivors, a reality that the survivorship movement seeks to combat by advocating survivors' rights and accurately informing the public about cancer.

Personal Aspects of Survivorship

Typically, a patient's initial response to the diagnosis of cancer is utter shock. As the disbelief abates, the patient begins to wonder, "What may I expect now?" and "How should I feel?" At this point, it is crucial for the patient to realize that no "right" or "normal" way of coping with the aftermath of powerful emotions exists; whatever works for the individual is best for that individual. Many survivors find that ventilating their feelings is helpful, whether this be with relatives, friends, other survivors, members of the health care team, psychotherapists, or clergy. However, other survivors discover that they can cope best by not talking about their diagnosis. In any case, learning how to manage feelings is one of the fundamental skills required of all cancer survivors.

Newly diagnosed cancer patients often find that everyday relationships become particularly strained. Although the patient's friends and family genuinely desire to be helpful, they may simply be at a loss as to what to do or say. Given the uncertainty of the situation, these same close relatives and friends may distance themselves emotionally from the patient, eventually causing the relationships to become dysfunctional. Often the patient needs to establish the "ground rules" for these relationships by informing family and friends if he or she wishes to discuss the diagnoses and exactly how he or she wishes to be treated by them. As unnecessarily obvious as these directives might seem, the truth is that few relatives or friends know precisely how to interact with a newly diagnosed cancer patient. As a result, the cancer patient often endures what could well be avoidable hurt and misunderstanding.

The experience of M.M., a head nurse at a community hospital, illustrates how one survivor learned to cope with her peers.

> While at home recuperating from surgery for Hodgkin's disease, I remember wondering exactly who at work may have learned about my diagnosis. It was actually foolish to wonder at all because everyone in such a small place knows everybody else's business! At that point, I had personally told only my closest friends.
>
> My first week back at work, a few people came up to me and inquired about my diagnosis. Just knowing that they cared about me was a comfort. However, the majority of people, even some with whom I was really close, ignored the topic altogether. I felt extremely hurt. . . . Did they, in fact, know? Were they respecting my privacy? Were they just unsure of what to say?
>
> Then it dawned on me that talking about the Hodgkin's disease made the situation better. I started to discuss my problem openly and no longer felt hostile about the silence. It occurred to me that if my friends couldn't break the ice, I had to. After all, I was the one with cancer!

M.M.'s solution to her problem evolved over time. She was honest with herself and eventually discovered how best to meet her own basic need for friendship and communication. The pursuit of such health-preserving behaviors enables the cancer patient to become a survivor.

Another crucial aspect of survivorship requires that the patient attempt to maintain as normal a routine as possible. Survivors quite typically desire "business as usual." As sickness is not a part of everyday life, focusing on such illness detracts from normalcy. In contrast, performing routine activities often boosts the patient's morale, as illustrated by the case of G.W., a middle-aged woman diagnosed with non-Hodgkin's lymphoma.

> I refused to consider myself "sick" nor did I permit others to treat me as a "sick" person. I told our friends that I planned to live as normal a life as possible and wanted to be included in all planned events—if I wasn't up to attending, I'd beg off.

> With the help of my staff, I continued to run my business. (Sometimes I
> conducted business from a hospital room telephone!) To this day, none of
> the clients whom I service regularly knows of my past illness.

Four years after diagnosis, both G.W. and her business are thriving. G.W.'s decision to remain active reflects the life-affirming attitude of most survivors.

Perhaps the hallmark of the cancer survivor is adaptability, particularly in the area of relationships. The diagnosis of cancer is certain to alter, at least to some degree, the various roles of each cancer patient, whether that of parent, spouse, daughter/son, employee, or friend. The extent of such change is a function of both the cancer's prognosis and the intensity of therapy, but the adaptive capability of the survivor ultimately determines the impact of role changes in his or her own life.

The survivor is best able to prepare for role changes by obtaining accurate medical information. It is imperative that the survivor candidly discuss the details of all recommended therapy with the physician so that possible side effects may be anticipated and appropriate strategies planned. For example, an employer can mistakenly assume that a given cancer will diminish the survivor's competence on the job; the informed survivor, however, can clarify his or her own medical condition for that employer, accurately describing the schedule and possible limitations caused by treatment.

Medical realities often do require temporary role changes. A number of practical concerns arise that necessitate these changes: hospitalization, provision for childcare, leave of absence from work, or financial considerations. Frequently, the survivor who is undergoing therapy must rely on family and friends to assume novel roles of intervention. Whenever roles are changed, the survivor is well advised to attempt to define the parameters of the helper's role clearly. The experience of K.H. illustrates just how traumatic and complex such role changes may become for the cancer survivor.

> K.H. is a 39-year-old divorced mother of twin girls, 5 years of age. After
> experiencing progressive weakness, she consulted her family doctor, who

detected an elevated white count in K.H.'s blood sample. On admission to the hospital, K.H. was diagnosed with leukemia.

Her oncologist advised 4 to 6 weeks of intense chemotherapy, requiring hospitalization, followed by 6 months of outpatient therapy. K.H.'s chance of cure was estimated to be 40%.

At the prospect of extended treatment, K.H. became distraught. The sole support of the family, she felt as though her life were suddenly spinning out of control. After discussing the situation with her family and friends, she decided to make a number of initially painful changes: K.H. took a leave of absence from work; K.H.'s parents moved into her home to care for the children; K.H. contacted her former husband to ask that he assume a somewhat active parental role in his daughters' lives. To K.H.'s amazement, her husband responded with both emotional and financial support.

Six weeks after diagnosis, K.H.'s leukemia went into remission, and she returned home. After completing 6 months of outpatient therapy, K.H.'s stamina gradually improved, enabling her to resume responsibilities both at home and work. Two years later, K.H. is in excellent health.

K.H.'s experience illustrates the radical role changes faced by some survivors during the course of treatment. Most survivors must, in fact, modify their roles to some degree, though some changes may be as moderate as a shortening of the work day or as temporary as an occasional vacation day for "mental health" reasons.

One particularly challenging role change for the survivor can be, surprisingly enough, the transition from sickness to health. As much as the cancer patient yearns for the completion of therapy, he or she sometimes experiences an emotional void after discharge when the attention and support of the medical team is withdrawn. Fortunately, this fairly common "letdown" does resolve over time. Other cancer survivors find that the anger and depression engendered by the original diagnosis surfaces only after therapy is ended, that is, at the point of cure. Such survivors sometimes need psychological counseling in order to complete the healing process.

Another posttherapy response of survivors is the tendency to overreact to mild illness out of a general fear of cancer recurrence. Unlike other posttherapy reactions, however, this tendency to exaggerate illness never totally resolves in the cancer survivor. The survivor is inclined to wonder, "The doctor says that I'm cured but what if?" Survivors learn to live with this abiding fear and, in doing so, often cultivate a renewed appreciation of life—in all its tentative preciousness. Having walked through the "fire" of their illness, they also often claim a heightened sense of optimism and hopefulness.

After completion of therapy, all survivors are expected to participate in periodic medical examinations. The aim of routine follow-up care is to ensure the best possible outcome for each patient. It typically includes a physical exam, x rays, and appropriate blood tests.

In the course of a follow-up exam, the patient is also evaluated for delayed complications from therapy. For example, a patient whose neck has been radiated runs an increased risk of hypothyroidism (underactive thyroid), whereas a breast cancer patient may develop swelling in the arms as a result of breast surgery. Such complications can occur months or even years after treatment has ended.

Public Policy Aspects of the Survivorship Movement

Any person whose medical history includes cancer is likely to experience some type of discrimination as a result of the disease, particularly in the areas of employment and insurance. Recent studies verify that approximately 25% of survivors face a job-related difficulty ranging from outright dismissal to a reduction in wages.

Like all prejudices, cancer-based prejudice is rooted in misconception and myth. Three of the most prevalent myths about cancer are the following.

1. No one survives cancer. In reality, nearly 50% of cancer patients are cured.
2. Cancer is contagious. In a 1985 survey, 6% of Americans be-

lieved this myth. Yet medical experts unanimously concur that the disease is not contagious.
3. Cancer survivors are too weak to work. Whereas cancer survivors are often presumed to be physically or emotionally incapable of holding a job, fully 80% of cancer patients return to work after diagnosis. Within the workplace, research data have verified that cancer survivors equal their "healthy" co-workers in both attendance and productivity. Literally millions of cancer survivors have excelled in their chosen fields; a few of the more famous survivors include politician Ronald Reagan, sports figures Jeff Blatnick and Mario Lemieux, and entertainer Steve Allen.

Like other people with chronic diseases, some cancer survivors will, indeed, become disabled. However, myth overtakes fact when any diagnosis of cancer is presumed to be cause for imminent disability. Each cancer survivor deserves to be considered individually.

Although cancer survivors, as a class, face the prospect of job discrimination, particular groups of survivors tend to face increased discrimination. For example, blue-collar survivors experience more discrimination in the workplace than do white-collar survivors, primarily because of the physically rigorous nature of their work and the ill-founded assumption that survivors are not able to meet such demands. Another group targeted for job discrimination is that of childhood cancer survivors. After reaching an appropriate age to enter the work force, these survivors face two significant hurdles: a history of cancer and no experience. Many prospective employers, including the U.S. military service and many police departments, deny employment to applicants with cancer histories.

Nonetheless, in a number of recent court decisions, job discrimination due to a history of cancer has been found illegal. To expand this protection under law, Congress passed The Americans with Disabilities Act of 1990 that explicitly protects survivors against on-the-job discrimination.

Such evidence of social justice does not appear to extend into the area of affordable health insurance for cancer survivors, however. The unfortunate truth is that nearly 25% of cancer survivors fail to obtain any health insurance whatsoever. Because the insurance industry regards survivors as high-risk applicants, companies commonly double the premiums for such clients. Other discriminatory practices include the outright rejection of new applications, major reductions in benefits, and exclusions in coverage for preexisting conditions.

Most adult Americans obtain health benefits through their employers. Because a job change might well result in the total loss of health coverage for the survivor, many survivors are advised to remain in their current jobs permanently. This predicament, referred to as "job lock," is a source of major concern for the advocates of survivorship.

The fundamental units of the survivorship movement are peer support networks, that is, groups of concerned survivors who are determined to mitigate the isolating effects of the disease. Even survivors with extremely supportive families and friends have much to gain by interacting with other survivors who, to paraphrase the words of William Faulkner, "have not only endured but prevailed."

Peer support groups are organized in several different ways. Some groups are small units associated with local hospitals, whereas others are large nonprofit organizations. Regardless of size, each peer support group is owned and operated by its members, who seek to meet the needs of a specific cancer community.

During the past decade, the survivorship movement has gained considerable momentum. Whereas prior to 1986 no formal organization existed to coordinate various survivor groups or to promote educational and political activities, today the National Coalition for Cancer Survivorship (NCCS) functions to fulfill four key objectives.

1. To serve as a clearinghouse for information and materials for survivors.

2. To provide a voice for the many common and recurring issues addressed by these organizations that reflect the spirit, skills, and needs of the survivorship community.
3. To advocate the interests of survivors and to secure the rights of survivors.
4. To promote the study of survivorship.

Currently, NCCS serves as the umbrella organization for more than 400 peer support groups nationwide. Based in Albuquerque, New Mexico, NCCS has published a helpful guide for survivors entitled *Cancer Survivors Almanac of Resources* (Consumer Reports Books: 1990). The interested reader can obtain a copy by contacting: NCCS, 323 Eight Street, S.W., Albuquerque, NM 87102, (505) 764-9956.

Helpful Hints

The challenges faced by the cancer survivor begin at the time of diagnosis and continue for the duration of life. Although no blueprint exists to guide the survivor through the trauma of cancer, the journey and the choices belong uniquely to the individual. Perhaps the voices of those who have lived through this experience may prove helpful. Following is a distillation of many discussions with survivors, a collective wisdom, if you will, addressing concerns that they, in retrospect, wish that they might have known or better understood at the time of diagnosis.

• Prepare for each meeting with your oncologist. It is extremely beneficial to write down thoughts and questions beforehand, because important issues are often forgotten at the time of the session. Because the medical information discussed may be technical and somewhat confusing the first time that it is heard, bring along a tape recorder or, better yet, a family member or close friend. The sheer presence of a loved one in the examining room provides you with support and another listening ear to sift through exactly what is said.

- Attempt to understand as fully as possible the diagnosis, the treatment options, the chance of success for each option and the possible side effects of therapy. (See Chapter 17, Investigational Therapy, for suggested questions to ask at this juncture.) It is most important that you understand the diagnosis in terms of your particular cancer with its own grade, stage, and subtype and your individual medical condition. As much as is humanly possible, try to avoid comparing your own unique situation with that of other cancer patients.
- Find a physician who listens and responds to you. Establishing levels of trust and ease with one another is critical because you and the physician will be managing your illness together. Your perceptions are bound to differ, but you must be able to listen attentively to each other. Certainly, your physician should be available to you, especially during initial diagnosis, changes in the treatment plan, and emergencies. Fortunately, most physicians who have chosen this specialty are willing to give this time when needed.
- Communicate openly with the health care team. The sole job of the doctors and nurses who are involved in planning and administering your treatment is to guide you through the cancer experience. When problems and fears arise, as they most assuredly will, discuss your concerns honestly with team members.
- Acknowledge that the cancer has made an impact on your identity, and begin to accept the changes that have occurred. After all, few problems in life are remedied without effort.
- Be positive. The implementation of a positive attitude varies with the patient, but positive cancer survivors are grounded in hope, and reasonably so. Today, more than 50% of cancer patients are cured! Although scientific evidence does not confirm that a patient's positive attitude guarantees survival, such an attitude undoubtedly enhances the quality of a survivor's life. Sometimes, the cancer patient and family believe that any acknowledgement of uncertainty about the future may diminish the hard-won feelings of hope and positivity; however, the opposite is generally true. By verbalizing fears and uncertainties, the patient may gain

control of life; by discussing unpleasant possibilities, both the patient and family may be able to cope more competently with the disease. In some instances, a family may need professional counseling to facilitate such an open discussion.

- Don't be afraid to consider *quality-of-life* concerns. Although modern cancer therapies have eradicated many previously incurable malignancies, in still far too many cases, the chance of medical improvement must be weighed carefully against the risks of treatment. For many patients, quality of life is the predominant issue of life. Such a concern must be openly discussed with the physician and family members in order to arrive at the best possible decisions throughout the course of disease. (See Chapter 18, No Therapy, and Chapter 24, Getting Your Affairs in Order.)
- Expect fatigue. At some point, most patients experience some degree of fatigue, aptly described as "a tiredness that sleep can't fix." Whether this problem surfaces at the time of initial diagnosis, during periods of treatment, after the completion of treatment, or in the final stages of the disease, daily routines must be altered to allow for adequate rest. Although this problem eventually resolves over time, sometimes only after several months, such fatigue is a source of considerable frustration for the survivor.
- Avoid the pain phobia. The most common concern voiced by cancer patients is the fear of pain. Admittedly, unrelenting pain can influence every aspect of a person's existence. No longer, however, does the cancer patient have to be a victim of pain and simply "learn to live with it." In 1994, pain can be effectively controlled in every stage of the disease. (See Chapter 23, The Control of Cancer Pain.)
- Be aware that you may have long-term side effects from therapy. As more patients live longer after cancer therapy, medical researchers are increasingly learning about delayed side effects. Initially, most of these results surfaced in follow-up studies involving pediatric cancer survivors; however, recent studies are focusing on the adult population as well. As these residual effects

are varied, cancer survivors should not hesitate to broach health concerns long after the completion of successful therapy. Moreover, distinguishing between serious and simple medical problems can be extremely difficult for the cancer survivor. Consequently, when concerns arise, they should be promptly evaluated by a physician.

On the long road to recovery, another stumbling block for the cancer survivor may prove to be psychosocial problems, including depression, stress, and anxiety about possible recurrences. Initially, the major challenge is simply to survive the disease, but later, the challenge is to survive the aftermath of the crisis.

- Ask for help as it is needed. Many family members and friends are actually waiting for a cue from you, a simple request as to how they may be of help to you. State your needs clearly, secure in the knowledge that you do, indeed, know what is best for you. In asking for help, you are allowing yourself to be entirely human, a rather remarkable way to be, after all.

  In dealing with the terminal phases of illness, realize that intensive intervention is generally required. Important comfort issues such as the need for a hospital bed, a home oxygen unit, and a bedside commode should be addressed. Social services, home care support, and hospice services are indispensable.

- Above all, be patient with yourself. You can become an expert in living with cancer only one day at a time. On the day of your diagnosis, you became a survivor with the journey of a lifetime to make. Now make it—one step, one day, one resolve at a time.

Coping with these challenges can actually become a way of life for the survivor, offering possibility in the very midst of difficulty. Appendix A contains a list of resources for the cancer patient and survivor.

Appendixes

Appendix A

Resources

This appendix includes the names of national organizations, a list of the National Cancer Institute's designated Comprehensive Cancer Centers and Community Clinical Oncology Programs. Many additional resources can be found in the bibliography. Two of the best resource books are *Charting the Journey* and *Surviving Cancer*, both listed in the bibliography.

National Organizations

American Cancer Society
1599 Clifton Road, N.E.
Atlanta, GA 30329-4251
(800) ACS-2345

American Geriatric Society
10 Columbus Circle
New York, NY 10019

Center for Medical Consumers
237 Thompson Street
New York, NY 10012
(212) 647-7105

Committee on Pain Therapy and Acupuncture
American Society of Anesthesiologists
1515 Busse Highway
Park Ridge, IL 60068

Hospice Association of America
519 C Street, N.E.
Washington, DC 20002
(202) 546-4759

Leukemia Society of America, Inc.
733 Third Avenue
New York, NY 10017
(212) 573-8484

National Alliance of Breast Cancer Organizations (NABCO)
1180 Avenue of the Americas
New York, NY 10036
(212) 719-0154

National Cancer Institute
Cancer Information Service
Building 31, Room 10A18
Bethesda, MD 20892
(800) 422-6237

National Coalition for Cancer Survivorship
323 Eight Street, S.W.
Albuquerque, NM 87102
(505) 764-9956

National Hospice Organization
1901 North Moore Street, 901
Arlington, VA 22209
(800) 658-8898

National Lymphedema Network
2211 Post Street, Suite 404
San Francisco, CA 94115
(800) 541-3259

Physician Data Query (PDQ)
Cancer Fax (301) 420-5874

Society for the Right to Die
250 West 57th Street
New York, NY 10107
(212) 246-6973

United Ostomy Association, Inc.
1803 North Meridian Street
Irvine, CA 92714
(714) 660-8624

National Cancer Institute–Designated Comprehensive Cancer Centers

These medical centers have passed extensive peer review and have demonstrated excellence in the fields of research, prevention, teaching, diagnosis, and treatment.

Alabama

University of Alabama Cancer Center
1918 University Boulevard
Basic Health Sciences Building
Room 108
Birmingham, AL 35294
(205) 934-6612

California

Kenneth Norris, Jr. Comprehensive Center
University of Southern California
1441 Eastlake Avenue
Los Angeles, CA 90033
(213) 226-2370

Jonsson Cancer Center
10-247 Factor Building
10833 Le Conte Avenue
Los Angeles, CA 90024-1781
(213) 825-8727

Connecticut

Yale University Cancer Center
333 Cedar Street, Rm 205 WWW
New Haven, CT 06510
(203) 785-4095

District of Columbia

Lombardi Cancer Research Center
Georgetown University
Division of Medical Oncology
3800 Reservoir Road, N.W.
Washington, DC 20007
(202) 687-2223

Howard University Cancer Center
Cancer Screening Clinic
2041 Georgia Ave., N.W.
Washington, DC 20060
(202) 636-5665

Florida

Sylvester Comprehensive Cancer Center
1475 N.W. 12th Avenue

P.O. Box 016960 (D8-4)
Miami, FL 33101
(305) 548-4800

Illinois

Illinois Cancer Council (A consortium of nine medical schools
and agencies)
36 South Wabash Avenue, Suite 700
Chicago, IL 60603
(800) 4-CANCER

Maryland

The Johns Hopkins Oncology Center
600 North Wolfe Street
Baltimore, MD 21205
(301) 955-8638

Massachusetts

Dana-Farber Cancer Institute
44 Binney Street
Boston, MA 02115
(617) 732-3214

North Carolina

Duke University Comprehensive Cancer Center
P.O. Box 3843
Durham, NC 27710
(919) 286-5515

Ohio

Ohio State University Cancer Center
410 West 12th Avenue
Columbus, OH 43210
(614) 293-8610

Pennsylvania

Fox Chase Cancer Center
7701 Burholme Avenue
Philadelphia, PA 19111
(215) 728-2570

University of Pennsylvania Cancer Center
3400 Spruce Street
Philadelphia, PA 19104
(215) 662-6364

The Pittsburgh Cancer Institute
200 Myeran Avenue
Pittsburgh, PA 15213
800-537-4063

Texas

The University of Texas M.D. Anderson Cancer Center
1515 Holcombe Boulevard
Houston, TX 77030
(713) 792-3245

Washington

Fred Hutchinson Cancer Research Center
1124 Columbia Street
Seattle, WA 98104
(206) 467-4675

Wisconsin

Wisconsin Clinical Cancer Center
University of Wisconsin
600 Highland Avenue
Madison, WI 53792
(608) 263-6872

Community Clinical Oncology Program (CCOP)

In 1983, the National Cancer Institute (NCI) initiated a program to provide community-based physicians access to NCI-approved cancer treatment protocols. There are 53 NCI-supported CCOPs in 34 states, involving more than 200 community hospitals. This list includes the name and phone number of each CCOP.

Arizona

Greater Phoenix CCOP (602) 239-2413

California

San Joaquin Valley CCOP (209) 442-3959
Central Los Angeles CCOP (818) 960-5581
Bay Area Tumor Institute CCOP (415) 540-1591
Sacramento CCOP (916) 733-1098
San Diego Kaiser Permanente CCOP (619) 528-5352

Connecticut

North Shore University Hospital CCOP (516) 562-4160.

Delaware

Medical Center of Delaware CCOP (302) 731-8116

Florida

Florida Pediatric CCOP (904) 375-6848
Mt. Sinai CCOP (305) 647-2760

Georgia

Atlanta Regional CCOP (404) 851-6615
University Hospital CCOP (404) 722-4245

Illinois

Illinois Kellog Cancer Center Evanston Hospital CCOP
(312) 492-2000

Illinois Oncology Research Association CCOP (309) 672-5780
Springfield Central Illinois CCOP (217) 788-4959
Carle Cancer Center CCOP (217) 337-3010

Iowa

Iowa Oncology Research Association CCOP (515) 244-7586

Kansas

Wichita CCOP (316) 262-4467

Louisiana

Ochsner CCOP (504) 838-3910

Maine

Eastern Maine Medical Center's Cancer Control Program
(207) 945-7481
Southern Maine CCOP (207) 773-1754

Michigan

Grand Rapids CCOP (616) 774-1230
Kalamazoo CCOP (616) 383-7007

Minnesota

Duluth Clinic, Ltd. CCOP (218) 722-8364
W. Metro–Minneapolis CCOP (612) 927-3491

Mississippi

North Mississippi CCOP (601) 844-9166

Missouri

Ellis Fischel State Cancer Center CCOP (314) 875-2100
Kansas City CCOP (816) 276-7834
Ozarks Regional CCOP (417) 883-7422
St. Louis CCOP (314) 569-6959

Nevada

Southern Nevada Cancer Research Foundation CCOP (702) 384-0013

New Jersey

Bergen-Passaic CCOP (201) 441-2363

New York

Twin Tiers CCOP (717) 888-5858
North Short University Hospital CCOP (516) 562-4160
St. Vincent's CCOP (212) 790-8368
Iroquois CCOP (716) 464-3591
Hematology-Oncology Associates of Central New York CCOP (315) 474-6391

North Carolina

Southeast Cancer Control Consortium CCOP (919) 777-3036

North Dakota

St. Luke's Hospitals CCOP (701) 237-2397

Ohio

Columbus CCOP (614) 253-5255
Dayton CCOP (513) 299-7204
Toledo CCOP (419) 255-5433

Oklahoma

Natalie Warren Bryant CCOP (918) 494-1530

Oregon

Columbia River CCOP (503) 239-7767

Pennsylvania

Geisinger CCOP (717) 271-6413
Allegheny CCOP (412) 359-3630
Mercy Hospital CCOP (717) 342-3675

South Carolina

Southeast Cancer Control Consortium CCOP (919) 777-3036
Spartanburg CCOP (803) 585-8343

South Dakota

Rapid City Regional Oncology Group CCOP (605) 342-3280
Sioux Falls CCOP (605) 331-3160

Tennessee

Southeast Cancer Control Consortium CCOP (919) 777-3036

Vermont

Green Mountain Oncology Group CCOP (802) 775-7111

Virginia

Southeast Cancer Control Consortium CCOP (919) 777-3036
CCOP of Roanoke (703) 982-0237

Washington

Seattle CCOP (206) 223-6942
Northwest CCOP (206) 597-7461

West Virginia

West Virginia CCOP (304) 348-9541

Wisconsin

Marshfield CCOP (715) 387-5134
Milwaukee CCOP (414) 672-1892

Appendix B

Index of Case Studies by Chapter and Related Topics

Appendix C

Suggested Reading

Medical Books

American Joint Committee on Cancer. *Manual for Staging of Cancer,* 2nd ed. Philadelphia: Lippincott, 1983.

American Pain Society. *Principles of Analgesia Use in the Treatment of Acute Pain and Cancer Pain.* Skokie, IL: American Pain Society, 1992.

Devita VT, Hellman S, Rosenberg SA. *Cancer: Principles and Practice of Oncology,* 4th ed. Philadelphia: Lippincott, 1993.

Clark JC, McGee RF, ed. *Core Curriculum for Oncology Nursing,* 2nd ed. Philadelphia: WB Saunders, 1992.

Holleb AI, Fink DJ, Murphy GP. *American Cancer Society Textbook of Clinical Oncology.* Atlanta: The American Cancer Society, 1991.

Stedman's Medical Dictionary. New York: Prentice Hall, 1987.

Medical Data Base

PDQ Information for Health Care Professionals. PDQ: Physician Data Query. Bethesda, MD: National Cancer Institute. (800) 4-CANCER (800-422-6237) This is a data base provided by the Cancer Information Service of the National Cancer Institute.

Medical Articles

Selected Articles Covering a Specific Cancer

Bayar DP, Corle DK. Hormone therapy for prostate cancer. *Journal of the National Cancer Institute* Monograph 7, 165–170, 1988.

Belldegrun A, Abi-Aad AS, Figlin RA, et al. Renal cell carcinoma: basic biology and current approaches to therapy. *Seminars in Oncology* 18(5): 96–101, 1991.

Boring CC, Squires TS, Tong T. Cancer statistics, 1993. *CA Cancer Journal for Clinicians* 43(1):7–26, 1993.

Champlin RE, Gale RP. Acute myelogenous leukemia: recent advances. *Blood* 69:1551–1562, 1987.

Champlin RE, Gale RP. Acute lymphoblastic leukemia: recent advances in biology and therapy. *Blood* 73:2051–2066, 1989.

DeVita VT, Hubbard SM. Hodgkin's disease. *New England Journal of Medicine* 328(8):560–565, 1993.

Fisher B, Costantino J, Redmond C. Lumpectomy compared with lumpectomy and radiation therapy for the treatment of intraductal breast cancer. *New England Journal of Medicine* 328(22):1581–1586, 1993.

Freedman S. An overview of bone marrow transplantation. *Seminars in Oncology Nursing* 4(1):3–8, 1988.

Greco FA, Vaughn WK, Hainsworth JD. Advanced poorly differentiated carcinoma of unknown primary site: recognition of a treatable syndrome. *Annals of Internal Medicine* 104:547–553, 1986.

Harris Jr, Lippman ME, Veronesi U, et al. Breast cancer. *New England Journal of Medicine* 327(5):319, (6):390, (7):473, 1992.

Ihde DC. Chemotherapy of lung cancer. *New England Journal of Medicine* 327(20):1434, 1992.

Moertel CG, Fleming TR, Macdonald JS, et al. Levamisole and fluorouracil for adjuvant therapy of resected colon carcinoma. *New England Journal of Medicine* 322(6):352–358, 1990.

National Institutes of Health Consensus Conference: the management of clinically localized prostate cancer. *Journal of the American Medical Association* 258(19):2727–2730, 1987.

National Institutes of Health Consensus Conference: adjuvant therapy for patients with colon and rectal cancer. *Journal of the American Medical Association* 264(11):1444–1450, 1990.

National Institutes of Health Consensus Conference: diagnosis and treatment of early melanoma. *Journal of the American Medical Association* 268(10):1314–1319, 1992.

Piver MS. Invasive cervical cancer in the 1990's. *Seminars in Surgical Oncology* 6(6):359–363, 1990.

Preston DS, Stern RS. Nonmelanoma cancers of the skin. *New England Journal of Medicine* 327(23):1649–1662, 1992.

Richardson GS, Scully RE, Nikrue N, et al. Common epithelial cancer of the ovary. *New England Journal of Medicine* 312(7):415–424, (8):474–483, 1985.

Rosenberg SA. Autologous bone marrow transplantation in non-Hodgkin's lymphoma. *New England Journal of Medicine* 316(24):1514–1542, 1987.

Sporin JR, Greenberg BR. Empiric chemotherapy in patients with carcinoma of unknown primary site. *American Journal of Medicine* 88:49–55, 1990.

No Therapy, Palliative Therapy, and Unproven Therapy (Quackery)

Ad Hoc Committee on Cancer Pain of the American Society of Clinical Oncology. Cancer pain assessment and treatment curriculum guidelines. *Journal of Clinical Oncology* 10(12):1976–1982, 1992.

American Society of Clinical Oncology Committee on Patient Advocacy. The physician as the patient's advocate. *Journal of Clinical Oncology* 11(6):1011–1013, 1993.

Cassileth BR. Contemporary unorthodox treatments in cancer medicine. *Annals of Internal Medicine* 101(1):105–112, 1984.

Cassileth BR, Lusk FJ, Guerry D, et al. Survival and quality of life among patients receiving unproven as compared to conventional cancer therapy. *New England Journal of Medicine* 324(17):1180–1185, 1991.

Eisenberg DM, Kessler RC, Foster C, et al. Unconventional medicine in the United States. *New England Journal of Medicine* 328(4):246–252, 1993.

Horning SJ, Rosenberg SA. The natural history of initially untreated low-grade non-Hodgkins lymphomas. *New England Journal of Medicine* 311(23):1471–1475, 1984.

Levy MH (guest ed). Palliative care. *Seminars in Oncology* 12(4):355–485, 1985.

U.S. Congress, Office of Technology Assessment. Unconventional cancer treatments. Washington, DC: Government Printing Office, (OTA-H-405), 1990.

Cancer and Aging

American Cancer Society. Cancer and the elderly. Fifth National Conference on Cancer Nursing, 1-19, (88-25M-No. 3480.05PE), 1988.

Ershler WB (guest ed). Cancer in the elderly. *Seminars in Oncology* 16(1):1–84, 1989.

Lipschitz DA, moderator. Cancer in the elderly: basic science and clinical aspects. *Annals of Internal Medicine* 102(2):218–218, 1985.

Rowe JW. Health care of the elderly. *New England Journal of Medicine* 312(13):827–835, 1985.

Rubens RD. Age and the treatment of breast cancer. *Journal of Clinical Oncology* 11(1):3–4, 1993.

Nonmedical Books Dealing with Cancer

Anderson G. *Fifty Essential Things To Do When the Doctor Says It's Cancer.* New York: Plume, 1993.

Bloch R, Bloch A. *Cancer . . . there's hope.* Kansas City: R. A. Bloch Cancer Foundation, 1981.

Bloch R, Bloch A. *Fighting Cancer.* Kansas City: R. A. Bloch Cancer Foundation, 1985.

Benjamin H. *From Victim to Victor.* New York: Dell, 1987.

Bruning N. *Coping with Chemotherapy.* Garden City, NY: The Dial Press, 1985.

Cox B. *Living With Lung Cancer.* Gainesville, FL: Triad Publishing, 1987.

Delong M. *Practical and Legal Concerns of Cancer Patients and Their Families.* Durham, NC: Duke University Medical Center, 1984.

Fishman J, Anrod B. *Something's Got To Taste Good: The Cancer Patient's Cookbook.* New York: Signet Paperback, 1982.

Glassman J. *The Cancer Survivors: And How They Did It.* New York: Doubleday, 1983.

Golden S. *Nursing a Loved One At Home.* Philadelphia: Running Press Books, 1987.

Holleb AI (ed). *The American Cancer Society Cancer Book.* New York: Doubleday, 1986.

Johnson P. *Conquering Cancer.* Grand Rapids, MI: Zondervan, 1991.

Kauffman DG. *Surviving Cancer.* Washington, DC: Acropolis Books, 1989.

Kübler-Ross E. *On Death and Dying.* New York: Macmillan, 1969.

Kushner HS. *When Bad Things Happen to Good People.* New York: Avon, 1981.

Larschan EJ, Larschan RJ. *The Diagnosis Is Cancer.* Palo Alto, CA: Bull Publishing, 1986.

Laszlo J. *Understanding Cancer.* New York: Harper & Row, 1987.

LeShan L. *Cancer as a Turning Point.* New York: Dutton, 1989.

Little M. *Home Care of the Dying.* New York: Dial Press, 1985.

Mohoney JM. *Guide to Ostomy Care.* Boston: Little, Brown, 1976.

Morra M, Potts E. *Choices.* New York: Avon Books, 1987.

Morra M, Potts E. *Triumph: Getting Back to Normal When You Have Cancer.* New York: Avon Books, 1990.

Moyers B. *Healing and the Mind.* New York: Doubleday, 1993.

Mullan F, Hoffman B, (eds). *Charting the Journey, An Almanac of Practical Resources for Cancer Survivors.* Mount Vernon, NY: Consumers Union, 1990.

Mullen BD, McGinn KA. *The Ostomy Book: Living Comfortably With Colostomies.* Palo Alto, CA: Bull Publishing, 1980.

Nessim S, Ellis J. *Cancervive, The Challenge of Life after Cancer.* New York: Houghton Mifflin, 1991.

Patterson JT. *The Dread Disease: Cancer and Modern American Culture.* Cambridge, MA: Harvard University Press, 1987.

Radner G. *It's Always Something.* New York: Simon & Schuster, 1989.

Rosenbaum EH, Rosenbaum IR. *A Comprehensive Guide for Cancer Patients and Their Families.* Palo Alto, CA: Bull Publishing, 1980.

Rous SN. *The Prostate Book.* Mount Vernon, NY: Consumers Union, 1989.

Siegle B. *Love, Medicine, and Miracles.* New York: Harper & Row, 1987.

Shook RL. *Survivors: Living with Cancer.* New York: Harper & Row, 1983.

Smith KS. *Caring for Your Aging Parents.* Lakewood, CO: American Source Books, 1992.

National Cancer Institute Information

PDQ Information for Patients. PDQ: Physician Data Query. Bethesda, MD: National Cancer Institute. (800) 4-CANCER (1-800-422-6237.) This is information provided by the Cancer Information Service of the National Cancer Institute for patients and families.

Nontechnical Pamphlets and Articles Dealing with Cancer

Age bias and cancer treatment. *Harvard Medical School Health Letter* 15 (5): 8, 1993.

Allison M. Cervical cancer: turning back the tide. *Harvard Medical School Health Letter* 18(3):5–8, 1993.

Allison M. Breast cancer: moving toward prevention. *Harvard Medical School Health Letter* 17(10):5–8, 1992.

American Association of Retired Persons Publications:

Guide to medicare and health insurance for older people. Stock No. ML 2654 C38, 1990.

Health care powers of attorney. Stock No. D13895, 1990.

Product report: living trusts and wills. Stock No. D14535, 1991.

Tomorrow's choices: preparing now for future legal, financial, and health care decisions. Stock No. D13479, 1990.

Can your mind heal your body? *Consumer Reports* February 1993, 107–115.

Dunkin AM (ed). The family fortune: can we talk? *Business Week* March 1, 1993, 106–107.

Elmer-Dewitt P. Running against cancer. *Time*, March 9, 1992, 58–59.

Gottschalk EC. Your money matters: financial planning can ease problems for the terminally ill. *Wall Street Journal*, July 2, 1992. C1.

Hospice benefits under Medicare. Social Security Administration, No. HCFA-02154.

National Institutes of Health Publications:

Chemotherapy and you. No. 88-1136, 1987.

Eating hints: recipes and tips for better nutrition during cancer treatment. No. 84-2079, 1984.

Radiation therapy & you. No. 88-2227, 1985.

Facing forward: a guide for cancer survivors. No. 90-2424, 1990.

Understanding the immune system. No. 90-529, 1990.

What are clinical trials all about? No. 88-2706, 1988.

When cancer recurs: meeting the challenge again. No. 85-2709, 1985.

Leukemia Society of America Booklets:

Acute lymphocytic leukemia, Bone marrow transplantation, Chronic lympho-

cytic leukemia, Coping with survival, Leukemia: the nature of the disease, and Understanding chemotherapy.

Schmeck HM. Marrow: a powerful new tool. *New York Times* January 10, 1984.

Second opinions. *Harvard Medical School Health Letter* 14(4):1–3, 1989.

Index

Figures and *Tables* are represented by f and t respectively after the page number

About the Author

Michael M. Sherry, M.D., a practicing medical oncologist in Sewickley, Pennsylvania, is also involved in clinical research with the National Surgical Adjuvant Breast Project and the Southwest Oncology Group. Upon graduation from the University of Pittsburgh's School of Medicine, Dr. Sherry completed his residency in Internal Medicine at Mercy Hospital in Pittsburgh, Pennsylvania, a fellowship in Hematology at Montefiore Hospital in Pittsburgh, and a fellowship in Medical Oncology at Vanderbilt University in Nashville, Tennessee. Dr. Sherry resides in Sewickley, Pennsylvania, with his wife and four children.